"*Just Deserts* is a delight: a sharp and interesting discussion of punishment, morality, choice, and much else. It hits the sweet spot; it's wonderfully clear and accessible – perfect for a newcomer to the free will debates – but also deep and subtle, with plenty to engage experts in the field."

Paul Bloom, Brooks and Suzanne Ragen Professor of Psychology, Yale University, and author of *Against Empathy*

"What it means to make a choice, to deserve praise or blame, to do the right thing – these are all at stake in the debate over free will. Here you will find two different viewpoints, elaborated and defended by true masters. Given the sharpness of both interlocutors, neither has anywhere to hide; a wide spectrum of important points is laid out for careful consideration."

Sean Carroll, author of *The Big Picture: On the Origins of Life, Meaning, and the Universe Itself*

"This is a very lively, engaging, and thoughtful debate between two well-informed and insightful philosophers. It is written in a very accessible style, and students and even scholars in other disciplines or sub-fields of philosophy will learn from it and find themselves drawn in. It does not just re-hash traditional debates, but pushes the frontiers outward. Highly recommended."

John Martin Fischer, Distinguished Professor of Philosophy at UC Riverside

"A philosophical debate in the grand style. Caruso and Dennett play in the philosophical equivalent of a three set tennis championship where the prize is whether free will exists or not and what this means for reward, punishment, and the criminal law. Serve, volley, amazing gets, overheads, long rallies, a few trick shots, several match points. Really smart play from two philosophers at the top of their games."

Owen Flanagan, James B. Duke Distinguished University Professor, Duke University

"*Just Deserts* made me think philosophy should never be done alone, but with a partner of equal strength and opposing views, that the best of it should be made available to the public, and that it should leave readers with an appreciation of the depth and difficulty of the questions but no easy answers. It is a stirring discussion of a difficult issue, that distils the best of what has been said for both sides. I can think of no discussion of free will and desert that gets to the heart of the issues so effectively. It reminds you just how important and difficult and vitally alive philosophical debate can be."

Jenann T. Ismael, Professor of Philosophy at Columbia University, and author of *How Physics Makes Us Free*

"This is a spirited and enlightening debate between an influential defender of compatibilism about freedom, responsibility, and determinism (Dennett) and an astute defender of a hard incompatibilist or free will skeptical position (Caruso). The book breaks new ground on many issues; and it has made clearer to me than anything else I have ever read on the subject how central is the issue of "just deserts" to age-old debates about free will, moral responsibility, and determinism."

Robert Kane, University Distinguished Professor Emeritus of Philosophy and Law, University of Texas at Austin

Daniel C. Dennett is Co-Director of the Center for Cognitive Science and the Austin B. Fletcher Professor of Philosophy at Tufts University. His books include *Content and Consciousness* (1969), *Brainstorms* (1978), *Elbow Room* (1984), *The Intentional Stance* (1987), *Consciousness Explained* (1991), *Darwin's Dangerous Idea* (1995), *Kinds of Minds* (1996), *Freedom Evolves* (2003), *Breaking the Spell* (2006), and *From Bacteria to Bach and Back: The Evolution of Minds* (2017). He is a leading defender of compatibilism, the view that determinism can be reconciled with free will, and is perhaps best known in cognitive science for his concept of intentional systems and his multiple drafts model of human consciousness.

Gregg D. Caruso is Professor of Philosophy at SUNY, Corning, and Honorary Professor of Philosophy at Macquarie University. He is also the Co-Director of the Justice Without Retribution Network at the University of Aberdeen School of Law. His books include *Free Will and Consciousness* (2012), *Rejecting Retributivism: Free Will, Punishment, and Criminal Justice* (2021), *Exploring the Illusion of Free Will and Moral Responsibility* (ed. 2013), *Neuroexistentialism: Meaning, Morals, and Purpose in the Age of Neuroscience* (co-ed. with Owen Flanagan, 2018), and *Free Will Skepticism in Law and Society: Challenging Retributive Justice* (co-ed. with Elizabeth Shaw and Derk Pereboom, 2019). He is a leading proponent of free will skepticism, which maintains that who we are and what we do is ultimately the result of factors beyond our control, and because of this we are never morally responsible for our actions in the basic desert sense – i.e. the sense that would make us truly deserving of blame and praise, punishment and reward.

Just Deserts

Just Deserts

Debating Free Will

Daniel C. Dennett
and
Gregg D. Caruso

polity

Copyright © Daniel C. Dennett and Gregg D. Caruso 2021

The right of Daniel C. Dennett and Gregg D. Caruso to be identified as Authors of this Work has been asserted in accordance with the UK Copyright, Designs and Patents Act 1988.

First published in 2021 by Polity Press

8

Polity Press
65 Bridge Street
Cambridge CB2 1UR, UK

Polity Press
101 Station Landing
Suite 300
Medford, MA 02155, USA

ISBN-13: 978-1-5095-4575-9 (hardback)
ISBN-13: 978-1-5095-4576-6 (paperback)

A catalogue record for this book is available from the British Library.

Library of Congress Cataloging-in-Publication Data

Names: Dennett, D. C. (Daniel Clement) author. | Caruso, Gregg D., author.
Title: Just deserts : debating free will / Daniel C. Dennett and Gregg D. Caruso.
Description: Medford : Polity Press, 2021. | Includes bibliographical references and index.
| Summary: "An eye-opening debate on the philosophy and psychology of free will and what they tell us about our societies"-- Provided by publisher.
Identifiers: LCCN 2020029874 (print) | LCCN 2020029875 (ebook) | ISBN 9781509545759 (hardback) | ISBN 9781509545766 (paperback) | ISBN 9781509545773 (epub)
Subjects: LCSH: Free will and determinism. | Free will and determinism--Psychological aspects. | Civilization, Modern--21st century.
Classification: LCC BJ1461 .D4276 2021 (print) | LCC BJ1461 (ebook) | DDC 123/.5--dc23
LC record available at https://lccn.loc.gov/2020029874
LC ebook record available at https://lccn.loc.gov/2020029875

Typeset in 10.75pt on 14pt Janson by
Servis Filmsetting Limited, Stockport, Cheshire
Printed and bound in Great Britain by TJ Books Limited

For further information on Polity, visit our website: politybooks.com

Contents

Foreword

Derk Pereboom

This exchange between Daniel Dennett and Gregg Caruso on free will, moral responsibility, and punishment is intense and engaging, and will captivate any reader who is interested in the cutting edge of the contemporary free will debate. It has much to offer newcomers and seasoned veterans alike. This exchange serves as an excellent introduction and at the same time provides details about the contested positions not available elsewhere.

Caruso is an incompatibilist about free will and determinism. If determinism is true, then there are factors beyond our control, events in the distant past and natural laws, that causally determine all of our actions, and incompatibilists maintain that this would rule out free will. Incompatibilists divide into those who hold that determinism is false and that we have free will – the libertarians – and those who hold that determinism is true and we lack free will – free will skeptics. Dennett affirms compatibilism about free will and determinism, and he contends that we do have free will. Caruso argues that we would lack free will if our world is deterministic, but also if it were indeterministic, say in the way some interpretations of quantum physics propose. Caruso and Dennett are thus situated on opposite sides of a traditional divide – Dennett is a compatibilist and affirms free will, Caruso is an incompatibilist and a free will skeptic.

There is also a conceptual issue about how "free will" should be defined, which divides Dennett and Caruso. Dennett is well known for recommending that we should use "free will" so that it refers to a kind of free will *worth wanting*.

The kind of free will worth wanting is a capacity for rational response to stimuli in our natural and social environment, which has developed in our species in its evolutionary history and matures in individuals as they become adults. This is clearly a valuable capacity, and I think that Dennett's proposal is defensible.

But a question that arises about Dennett's characterization is whether it works for dividing the sides in the debate. Because few believe that Dennett's notion of free will is incompatible with determinism, his definition results in a challenge for defining compatibilism so that it's controversial. Caruso, by contrast, defines free will as the control in action required for attributions of desert in its *basic* form, as do a number of other participants in the current debate. In the basic form of desert, someone who has acted wrongly deserves to be blamed and perhaps punished just because she has acted for morally bad reasons, and someone who has acted rightly deserves credit or praise and perhaps reward just because she has acted for morally good reasons. Such desert is basic because these desert claims are fundamental in their justification; they are not justified by virtue of further considerations, such as anticipated good consequences of implementing them. According to Caruso, in order to facilitate the free will debate, so that there are substantial numbers of participants on each side, free will should be defined as the control in action required for basically deserved praise and blame, reward and punishment.

Dennett and Caruso disagree about the prevalence of the notion of basic desert. By contrast with Dennett, Caruso believes it is widespread. He supports his view by using a thought experiment that derives from Immanuel Kant, in which there are no good consequences to be achieved by punishing a wrongdoer (1785: Part II). Here is a version of such an example. Imagine that someone on an isolated island brutally murders everyone else on that island, and that he is not capable of moral reform, due to his inner hatred and rage. Add that it is not possible for him to escape the island,

and no one else will ever visit because it's too remote. There is no longer a society on the island whose rules might be determined by a social contract aimed at good consequences, since the society has been disbanded. Do we have the intuition that this murderer still deserves to be punished? If so, then punishment would be basically deserved if the example in fact does eliminate the options for non-basic desert, as it seems to.

But on Dennett's side, do we want to define "free will" so that anyone who rejects basic desert counts as denying free will, or so that anyone who denies that we have the control in action required for attributions of basic desert counts as denying free will? Perhaps enough of the role that the concept "free will" has in our thought and practice would survive the rejection of basic desert and the control in action required for it. We have many concepts that we've retained even though we've revised how they are characterized, say due to scientific advance.

Dennett contends that enough of the role of the concept "free will" would indeed survive the rejection of basic desert because we have a notion of non-basic desert that can do the work we want. Practice-level justifications for blame and punishment invoke considerations of desert, while that desert is not basic because at a higher level the practice is justified by good anticipated consequences, such as deterrence of wrongdoing and moral formation of wrongdoers. On Dennett's account, our practice of holding agents morally responsible in this non-basic desert sense should be retained because doing so would have the best overall consequences relative to alternative practices.

One might object that penalties and rewards justified by anticipated consequences on Dennett's model do not really qualify as genuinely *deserved*, since on such a view they ultimately function as incentives. In reply, citing the type of analogy Dennett provides in the exchange, it seems legitimate to say that someone who commits a foul in a sport deserves the penalty for that foul. But such sports-desert isn't basic – it's instead founded in considerations about how the particular sport works best. Similarly, suppose penalties for criminal behavior are justified on deterrence grounds, by the anticipated good consequence of safety. Imagine that lawyers and judges consider only backward-looking reasons to convict and punish, while their practice is justified on forward-looking grounds that lawyers and judges never consider or invoke. Arguably, it then would make sense for the lawyers and judges to think of the penalties as deserved.

Accordingly, the exchange between Dennett and Caruso involves substantive issues, and some conceptual and verbal issues as well. The conceptual issues are important, and their resolution depends on whether the role of the relevant concepts can be retained. Neither Dennett nor Caruso contends that the role of the concept of "basic desert' in justifying actual practice is worth preserving. But Dennett argues that "desert" and its role should be retained, while Caruso disagrees. Throughout the exchange, separating the verbal and conceptual from the substantive issues is a challenge, as it is generally in philosophy. Caruso and Dennett take it on in the classic way, by regularly prodding each other to clarify terms.

My sense is that Caruso's and Dennett's positions are substantively quite close on the basics of the free will debate, but that they do differ on other matters, such as the value of manipulation arguments for incompatibilism, the discussion of which is especially intense. They also diverge on recommendations for treatment of criminals, despite both agreeing that current American practice requires serious reform. But it is not clear whether they differ on this issue because Dennett endorses justifications in terms of desert, while Caruso rejects them, or for some other reason. The reader will enjoy sorting out these issues in this valuable and timely dialogue.

Preface

The genesis of this book can be traced back to May of 2018, at a rooftop bar in Beirut, Lebanon, where the two of us first met and spent an enjoyable evening eating, drinking, and debating our respective views on free will during a conference on moral psychology at the American University of Beirut. We stayed in touch after that conference and eventually decided to work out our differences in the form of a conversation or debate, which resulted in a published exchange in *Aeon Magazine* on October 4, 2018 under the title: "Just Deserts: Can we be held morally responsible for our actions? Yes, says Daniel Dennett. No, says Gregg Caruso. Reader, you decide." After that exchange was published, Pascal Porcheron from Polity Books approached us about continuing our conversation and expanding it into a book. We both agreed to the project immediately, since we have mutual respect for each other and thought there would be great value in continuing our conversation. The result is this book. It begins with a brief introduction in which Caruso discusses the problem of free will and defines some terminology. This is designed to aid readers unfamiliar with the problem of free will and to provide a brief summary of the various positions on the issue. The introduction is followed by three separate exchanges. The first is an edited and expanded version of our initial *Aeon* exchange, while the second and third are new and appear here for the first time.

D. D. and G. C.

Introduction
Gregg D. Caruso

The problem of free will has real-world implications for our self-understanding, our interpersonal relationships, and our moral and legal practices. The assumption that we have free will lurks behind the justification of many of our everyday attitudes and judgments. For instance, when someone morally wrongs us, not only do we experience resentment and moral anger, we typically feel that we are *justified* in doing so, since we assume that, absent any excusing conditions, people are free and morally responsible for what they do and are therefore appropriate targets for such responses. We also typically assume that when individuals "act of their own free will," they *justly deserve* to be praised and blamed, punished and rewarded for their actions since they are morally responsible for what they do. Similar assumptions are made in the criminal law. The US Supreme Court, for instance, has asserted: "A 'universal and persistent' foundation stone in our system of law, and particularly in our approach to punishment, sentencing, and incarceration, is the 'belief in freedom of the human will and a consequent ability and duty of the normal individual to choose between good and evil'" (United States v. Grayson, 1978). But does free will really exist? What if it turns out that *no one* is ever free and morally responsible in the relevant sense? What would that mean for society, morality, meaning, and the law? Could society properly function without belief in free will? These are just some of the questions to be debated in this book.

To begin, it's important to introduce some key terms and positions. First, we can say that *free will*, as contemporary philosophers tend to understand it, is the control in action required for a particular kind of moral responsibility. More specifically, it's the power or capacity characteristic of agents, in virtue of which they can *justly deserve* to be blamed and praised, punished and rewarded for their actions. Understanding free will as linked to moral responsibility in this way, anchors the philosophical debate in something comparatively concrete and undeniably important to our lives. As Manuel Vargas notes: "This is not a sense of free will whose only implication is whether it fits with a given philosopher's particular speculative metaphysics. It is not a sense of free will that is arbitrarily attached to a particular religious framework. Instead, it is a notion of free will that understands its significance in light of the role or function it plays in widespread and recognized forms of life" (2013: 180).

Contemporary theories of free will can be divided into two general categories: those that endorse and those that are skeptical of the claim that human beings have free will. The former category includes *libertarian* and *compatibilist* accounts of free will, two general views that defend the claim that we have free will but disagree on its nature or its conditions. The latter category consists of a class of *skeptical views* that either doubt or deny the existence of free will. The main dividing line between the two pro-free will positions, libertarianism and compatibilism, is best understood in terms of the traditional problem of free will and determinism. *Determinism*, as it is commonly understood, is the thesis that at any given time only one future is physically possible (van Inwagen 1983: 3). Or put differently, it's the thesis that facts about the remote past in conjunction with the laws of nature entail that there is only one unique future (McKenna and Pereboom 2016: 19). *Indeterminism*, on the other hand, is the denial of this thesis – it's the claim that at some time more than one future is physically possible. The traditional *problem of free will and determinism* therefore comes in trying to reconcile our intuitive sense of free will with the idea that our choices and actions may be causally determined by factors over which we have no ultimate control, that is, the past before we were born and the laws of nature.

Historically, libertarians and compatibilists have reacted to this problem in different ways. *Libertarians* (not to be confused with the political view) acknowledge that if determinism is true, and all of our actions are causally determined by antecedent circumstances, we would lack free will and moral responsibility. Yet they further maintain that at least some of our choices and actions must be free in the sense that they are not causally determined. Libertarians therefore reject determinism and defend an indeterminist conception of free will in order to save what they maintain are necessary conditions for free will – the *ability to do otherwise* in exactly the same set of conditions and/or the idea that we remain, in some important sense, the *ultimate source/originator* of action. *Compatibilists*, on the other hand, set out to defend a conception of free will that can be reconciled with determinism. They hold that what is of utmost importance is not the absence of causal determination, but that our actions are voluntary, free from constraint and compulsion, and caused in the appropriate way. Different compatibilist accounts spell out requirements for free will differently but widely endorsed views single out responsiveness to reasons, self-control, or connection of action to what one would reflectively endorse.

In contrast to these pro-free will positions are those views that either doubt or outright deny the existence of free will and moral responsibility. Such views are often referred to as skeptical views, or simply *free will skepticism*. In the past, the leading form of skepticism was *hard determinism*: the view that determinism is true and incompatible with free will – either because it precludes the ability to do otherwise (*leeway incompatibilism*) or because it is inconsistent with one's being the ultimate source of action (*source incompatibilism*) – hence, no free will. For hard determinists, libertarian free will is an impossibility because human actions are part of a fully deterministic world and compatibilism fails to reconcile determinism with free will. Hard determinism had its classic statement in the time when Newtonian physics reigned supreme and was thought to be deterministic. The development of quantum mechanics, however, diminished confidence in determinism, for the reason that it has indeterministic interpretations. This is not to say that determinism has been refuted or falsified by modern physics, because a number of leading interpretations of quantum mechanics are consistent with determinism. It is also important to keep in mind that even if we allow some indeterminacy to exist at the micro-level of the universe, say the level studied by quantum mechanics, there may still remain *determinism-where-it-matters* – i.e. at the ordinary level of choices and actions, and even the electrochemical activity in our brains. Nonetheless, most contemporary skeptics tend to defend positions that are best seen as distinct from, but as successors to, traditional hard determinism.

Many contemporary free will skeptics, for instance, maintain that while determinism is incompatible with free will and moral responsibility, so too is *indeterminism*, especially if it is limited to the sort posited by certain interpretations of quantum mechanics. Others argue that regardless of the causal structure of the universe, we lack free will and moral responsibility because free will is incompatible with the pervasiveness of *luck*. Others still, argue that free will and ultimate moral responsibility are incoherent concepts, since to be free in the sense required for ultimate moral responsibility, we would have to be *causa sui* (or "cause of oneself") and this is impossible. Here, for example, is Nietzsche on the *causa sui*:

The *causa sui* is the best self-contradiction that has been conceived so far; it is a sort of rape and perversion of logic. But the extravagant pride of man has managed to entangle itself profoundly and frightfully with just this nonsense. The desire for "freedom of the will" in the superlative metaphysical sense, which still holds sway, unfortunately, in the minds of the half-educated; the desire to bear the entire and ultimate responsibility for one's actions oneself, and to absolve God, the world, ancestors, chance, and society involves nothing less than to be precisely this *causa sui* and, with more than Baron Munchhausen's audacity, to pull oneself up into existence by the hair, out of the swamps of nothingness. (1886/1992: 218–219)

The one thing, however, that all these skeptical arguments have in common, and what they share with classical hard determinism, is the belief that our choices, actions, and constitutive characters are ultimately the result of factors beyond our control – whether that be determinism, chance, or luck – and because of this we lack the kind of free will needed to hold agents morally responsible in the relevant sense.

List of Useful Definitions

Determinism: The thesis that facts about the remote past in conjunction with the laws of nature entail that there is only one unique future.

Compatibilism: The thesis that free will can be reconciled with the truth of determinism – i.e. it is possible for determinism to be true and for agents to be free and morally responsible in the relevant sense.

Incompatibilism: The thesis that free will cannot be reconciled with determinism – i.e. if determinism is true, free will is not possible.

Libertarianism: The thesis that incompatibilism is true, that determinism is false, and that some form of indeterminist free will exists.

Free Will Skepticism: The thesis that no one has free will, or at the very least, that we lack sufficient reason for believing that anyone has free will.

Hard Determinism: The thesis that incompatibilism is true, that determinism is true, and therefore no person has free will.

Hard Incompatibilism: The thesis that free will is incompatible with both determinism and indeterminism – i.e. that free will is incompatible with *both* causal determination by factors beyond the agent's control *and* with the kind of indeterminacy in action required by the most plausible versions of libertarianism.

Hard Luck: The thesis that regardless of the causal structure of the universe, we lack free will and moral responsibility because free will is incompatible with the pervasiveness of *luck*.

Basic-Desert Moral Responsibility: For an agent to be morally responsible for an action in this sense is for it to be theirs in such a way that they would deserve to be blamed if they understood that it was morally wrong, and they would deserve to be praised if they understood that it was morally exemplary. The desert at issue here is *basic* in the sense that the agent would deserve to be blamed or praised just because they have performed the action, given an understanding of its moral status, and not, for example, merely by virtue of consequentialist or contractualist considerations (Pereboom 2014: 2).

Consequentialism: The view that normative properties depend only on consequences – i.e. whatever produces the best aggregate set of good outcomes or makes the world best in the future.

Contractualism: The thesis that moral norms and/or political authority derive their normative force from the idea of a contract or mutual agreement.

Deontology: The view that the morality of an action should be based on whether the action itself is right or wrong under a clear set of rules, rather than based on the consequences of the action.

Exchange 1

Debating Free Will and Moral Responsibility

Caruso: Dan, you have famously argued that freedom evolves and that humans, alone among the animals, have evolved minds that give us free will and moral responsibility. I, on the other hand, have argued that what we do and the way we are is ultimately the result of factors beyond our control, and that because of this we are never morally responsible for our actions, in a particular but pervasive sense – the sense that would make us *truly deserving* of blame and praise, punishment and reward. While these two views appear to be at odds with each other, one of the things I would like to explore in this conversation is how far apart we actually are. I suspect that we may have more in common than some think – but I could be wrong. To begin, can you explain what you mean by "free will" and why you think humans alone have it?

Dennett: A key word in understanding our differences is "control." Gregg, you say "the way we are is ultimately the result of factors beyond our control" and that is true of only those unfortunates who have not been able to become autonomous agents during their childhood upbringing. There really are people, with mental disabilities, who are not able to control themselves, but normal people can manage under all but the most extreme circumstances, and this difference is both morally important and obvious, once you divorce the idea of *control* from the idea of *causation*. Your past does not control you; for it to control you, it would have to be able to monitor feedback about your behavior and adjust its interventions – which is nonsense.

In fact, if your past is roughly normal, it contains the causal chains that turned you into an autonomous, self-controlling agent. Lucky you. You weren't responsible for becoming an autonomous agent, but since you are one, it is entirely appropriate for the rest of us to *hold you responsible* for your deeds under all but the most dire circumstances. As the American country singer Ricky Skaggs once put it: "I can't control the wind, but I can adjust the sails." To suppose that some further condition should be met in order for you or anyone else to be "truly deserving" of praise or blame for your actions is to ignore or deny the manifest difference in abilities for self-control that we can observe and measure readily. In other words, the rationale or justification for excusing someone, holding them not deserving of criticism or punishment, is their deficit in this competence. We don't try to reason with bears or babies or lunatics because they aren't able to respond appropriately. Why do we reason with people? Why do we try to convince them of conclusions about free will or science or causation or anything else? Because we think – for good reason – that in general people are reasonable, are moved by reasons, can adjust their behavior and goals in the light of reasons presented to them. There is something indirectly self-refuting in *arguing* that people are not moved by reasons! And that is the key to the kind of self-control which we are justified in treating as our threshold for true desert.

Caruso: I don't disagree with you that there are important differences between agents who have the kind of rational control you highlight and those who lack it. Such a distinction is undeniable. A normal adult who is responsive to reasons differs in significant ways from one who is suffering from psychopathy, Alzheimer's, or severe mental illness. I have no issue, then, with acknowledging various degrees of "control" or "autonomy" – in fact, I think you and other compatibilists have done a great job highlighting these differences. My disagreement has more to do with the conditions required for what I call "basic-desert" moral responsibility. As a free will skeptic, I maintain that the kind of control and reasons-responsiveness you point to, though important, is not enough to ground basic-desert moral responsibility – the kind of responsibility that would make us truly deserving of blame and praise, punishment and reward in a purely backward-looking sense.

Consider, for example, the various justifications one could give for punishing wrongdoers. One justification, the one that dominates our legal system, is to say that they *deserve* it. This *retributive* justification for punishment maintains that punishment of a wrongdoer is justified for the reason that he/she *deserves* something bad to happen to them just because they have knowingly done wrong. Such a justification is purely backward-looking. For the retributivist, it is the basic desert attached to the criminal's immoral action alone that provides the justification for punishment. This means that the retributivist position is not reducible to consequentialist considerations that try to maximize good outcomes in the future, nor in justifying punishment does it appeal to wider goods such as the safety of society or the moral improvement of those being punished. I contend that retributive punishment is never justified since agents lack the kind of free will and basic-desert moral responsibility needed to ground it.

While we may be sensitive to reasons, and this may give us the kind of voluntary control you mention, the particular reasons that move us, along with the psychological predispositions, likes and dislikes, and other constitutive factors that make us who we are, themselves are ultimately the result of factors beyond our control. And this remains true whether those factors include determinism, indeterminism, chance, or luck. This is not to say that there are not other conceptions of responsibility that can be reconciled with determinism, chance or luck. Nor is it to deny that there may be good forward-looking reasons for maintaining certain systems of punishment and reward. For instance, free will skeptics typically point out that the impositions of sanctions serve purposes other than giving criminals what they basically deserve: it can also be justified by its role in incapacitating, rehabilitating and deterring offenders. My question, then, is whether the kind of desert you have in mind is enough to justify retributive punishment? If not, then it becomes harder to understand what, if anything, our disagreement truly amounts to, since forward-looking justifications of punishment are perfectly consistent with the denial of free will and basic-desert moral responsibility. And, if you are willing to reject retributivism, as I think you might be, then I'm curious to know exactly what you mean by "desert"– since it's debatable whether talk of giving agents their *just deserts* makes any sense devoid of its backward-looking, retributive connotations.

Dennett: You grant that the distinction I make between people who are autonomous and those who are not (because of various limits on their abilities to control themselves) is important, but then say that it is not enough for "the kind of desert" that would "justify retributive punishment." I too reject retributivism. It's a hopeless muddle, and so is any doctrine of free will that aspires to justify it. But that doesn't mean there is no "backward-looking" justification of punishment.

It's quite straightforward. On Monday you make me a promise, which I accept in good faith, and rely on when I adjust my own activities. On Friday, I discover you have broken your promise, with no excuse (what counts as an excuse has been well explored, so I will take that on without further notice). I blame you for this. My blaming you is of course backward-looking: "But you *promised me!*"

Autonomous people are justly held responsible for *what they did* because all of us depend on being able to count on them. It is for this reason that among their responsibilities is preserving their status as autonomous agents, guarding against the usurpation or manipulation of their own powers of discernment and decision. So, we can blame them for being duped, for getting drunk, etc. When we blame them, we are not just diagnosing them, or categorizing them; we are holding them *deserving* of negative consequences. If this isn't "basic desert" then so much the worse for basic desert. What is it supposed to add to this kind of desert?

The fact is – and I invite you to consider whether it is a fact – that autonomous people *understand* that they will be held to account and have tacitly accepted this as a condition for their maintaining their freedom in the political sense. I take this to be all the grounds we need for justifying the imposition of negative consequences (under all the usual conditions). The difference between the madman who is physically restrained and removed to quarantine for the sake of public safety, and the deserving culprit who is similarly restrained and then punished, is large, and it is a key feature of any defensible system of government. The culprit has the kind of desert that warrants *punishment* (but not "retributive" punishment, whatever that is).

As I have argued before, we can see this rationale in a simpler domain of human activity: sport. The penalty kicks and red cards of soccer, the penalty box of ice hockey, the ejection of players for flagrant fouls, etc., all make sense; the games they enable would not survive without them. The punishment (consider the etymology of "*penalty*") is relatively mild because "it's only a game," but if the transgression is serious enough, large fines can be assessed, or banishment from the game, and, of course, criminal prosecution for assault or cheating also lurks in the wings. Free will skeptics should consider if they would abolish all these rules because the players don't have real free will. And if they would grant a special exemption for such penalties in sport, what principle would they cite for not extending the same policies to the much more important game of life?

You also say "the particular reasons that move us, along with the psychological predispositions, likes and dislikes, and other constitutive factors that make us who we are, themselves are ultimately the result of factors beyond our control." So what? The point I think you are missing is that autonomy is something one *grows into*, and this is indeed a process that is *initially* entirely beyond one's control, but as one matures, and learns, one begins to be able to control more and more of one's activities, choices, thoughts, attitudes, etc. Yes, a great deal of luck is involved, but then a great deal of luck is involved in just being born, in being alive. We human beings are well designed to take advantage of the luck we encounter, and to overcome or deflect or undo the bad luck we encounter, to the point where we are held responsible for not taking foolish chances (for instance) that might lead to our losing control. There is no incompatibility between determinism and self-control.

Caruso: Well, I'm glad to know that you reject retributivism along with "any doctrine of free will that aspires to justify it." This point of agreement is significant since it entails that major elements of the criminal justice system are unjustified. I'm curious to know, however, with what exactly you would replace retributive legal punishment, and to what extent you reject the status quo. I ask because, though you claim to reject retributivism, you go on to defend a backward-looking conception of blame and punishment grounded in the idea that offenders are "*deserving* of negative consequences." Isn't this just retributivism by another name?

Retributivism is the view that we ought to punish offenders because they *deserve* to be punished. Punishment is justified, for the retributivist, solely by the fact that those receiving it deserve it. And while punishment may deter future crime, incapacitate dangerous criminals, educate citizens, and the like, for a retributivist these are a happy surplus that punishment produces, and form no part of what makes punishment just – i.e. we are justified in punishing deserving offenders even if the punishment produces none of these other surplus good effects. How does your view differ from this? Do you think the forward-looking benefits of punishment are what justified it? If so, then what role does *desert* play? If not, aren't we left with the retributivist claim that backward-looking desert is sufficient to justify blame and punishment?

As for your sports example, I don't see why this would be a problem for free will skeptics. There are good instrumentalist and forward-looking reasons for maintaining penalties even if we reject free will and basic-desert moral responsibility. First and foremost, penalties deter players from breaking the rules. This keeps the game fair, prevents injuries, and serves all kinds of non-punitive purposes. The 24-second clock in basketball, for instance, was introduced to make the game more exciting. Without it, the game was dull, all too often played at a snail's pace with one team opening up a lead and freezing the ball until time ran out. The only thing the trailing team could do was foul, thus games became rough, ragged, boring free throw contests. Penalties for unnecessarily aggressive physical play, on the other hand, protect players, reduce injuries, and deter future bad behavior. All of this can be explained without appeal to free will and *just deserts*.

Lastly, you say that "autonomy is something one *grows into*, and this is indeed a process that is *initially* entirely beyond one's control, but as one matures, and learns, one begins to be able to control more and more of one's activities, choices, thoughts, attitudes, etc." You acknowledge that "a great deal of luck is involved" in this, but I would go further and argue that "luck swallows everything" (to borrow a phrase from Galen Strawson). Consider the significant role luck plays in our lives. First, there is the initial "lottery of life" or "luck of the draw," over which we have no say. Whether we are born into poverty or affluence, war or peace, abusive or loving homes, is simply a matter of luck. It is also a matter of luck what natural gifts, talents, predispositions, and physical traits we are born with. Beyond this initial lottery of life, there is also the luck of what breaks one encounters during one's period of self-formation, and what environmental influences are most salient to us.

Combined, these matters of luck determine what Thomas Nagel famously calls *constitutive luck* – luck in who one is and what character traits and dispositions one has. Since our genes, parents, peers and other environmental influences all contribute to making us who we are, and since we have no control over these, it seems that who we are is at least largely a matter of luck. And since how we act is partly a function of who we are, the existence of constitutive luck entails that what actions we perform depends on luck (Nelkin 2019).

In *Elbow Room* (1984a), your first book on free will, you acknowledge all this, but then go on to say that luck in initial conditions need not "lead to something hideously unfair." You proceed to give the example of a footrace where some are given a head start based on when they were born (an arbitrary fact). You argue that this would be unfair if the race were a 100-yard dash but *not* if it's a marathon. "In a marathon," you write, "such a relatively small initial advantage would count for nothing, since one can reliably expect other fortuitous breaks to have even greater effects." You conclude: "A good runner who starts at the back of the pack, if he is really good enough to deserve winning, will probably have plenty of opportunity to overcome the initial disadvantage." On your analogy, then, since life is more like a marathon than a sprint, "luck averages out in the long run."

While this example has folksy appeal, it is demonstrably false. Luck does *not* average out in the long run. Those who start from a disadvantaged position of genetic abilities or early environment do not always have offsetting luck later in life. The data clearly show that early inequalities in life often compound over time rather than average out, affecting everything from differences in health and incarceration rates to success in school and all other aspects of life. To use another sports example, in his book *Outliers* (2008), the Canadian journalist Malcolm Gladwell documents the rather strange fact that there are more players in the National Hockey League born in January, February, and March than any other months. His explanation is that in Canada, where children start playing hockey at a very young age, the eligibility cutoff for age-class hockey programs is January 1. At the ages of six and seven, being ten or eleven months older gives one a distinct advantage over one's competitors. Since the older players tend to do better, they end up getting more playing time, and as they progress through the ranks they are selected for better teams and more elite programs, receive better coaching, and play more games against better competition. What begins as a small advantage, a mere matter of luck, snowballs and leads to an ever-widening gap of achievement and success.

This kind of phenomenon can be found throughout society. Studies show, for instance, that low socioeconomic status in childhood can affect everything from brain development to life expectancy, education, incarceration rates, and income (see my *Rejecting Retributivism*, ch. 7 for a detailed discussion of the relevant literature). The same is true for educational inequity, exposure to violence, and nutritional disparities. It's a mistake, then, to think that luck averages out in the long run – it does not.

In addition to constitutive luck, there is also *present luck* – luck at or around the moment of a putatively free and morally responsible action or decision. Present luck can include an agent's mood, what reasons happen to come to her, situational features of the environment, how aware she is of the morally significant features of her surroundings, and the like. It is a matter of present luck, for instance, whether our attention wanders at just the right/wrong moment or whether chance features of the environment prime our deliberation. I contend, following my friend and fellow free will skeptic Neil Levy (2011), that the one–two punch of constitutive luck (luck that causes relevant properties of agents, such as their beliefs, desires, and predispositions) and present luck (luck around the time of action) completely undermine basic-desert moral responsibility. Following Levy, we can call this view *hard luck*, since it maintains that the pervasiveness of luck undermines, or is incompatible with, the kind of free will and moral responsibility under debate.

The problem with constitutive luck is that an agent's *endowments* (i.e. traits and dispositions) result from factors beyond the agent's control. Now, I'm sure you will say that as long as an agent *takes responsibility* for her endowments, dispositions, and values, over time she will *become* morally responsible for them (and perhaps even gain some control over them). The problem with this reply, however, is that the series of actions through which agents shape and modify their endowments, dispositions, and values are themselves significantly subject to luck – and, as Levy puts it: "We cannot undo the effects of luck with more luck" (2011: 96). Hence the very actions to which compatibilists point, the actions whereby agents take responsibility for their endowments, either *express* that endowment (when they are explained by constitutive luck) or reflect the agent's present luck, or both. Either way, responsibility is undermined.

Dennett: The sense of "deserve" that I defend is the everyday sense in which, when you win the race fair and square, you deserve the blue ribbon or gold medal; and if you wrote the novel, you deserve the royalties, and if you plagiarized it, you don't; and if you knowingly park in a "No Parking" zone, you deserve a parking ticket; and if you refuse to pay it, you deserve some escalated penalty; and if you committed premeditated murder, you deserve to go to prison for a very long time – provided, in all cases, that you are a responsible agent, a member in the Moral Agents Club, as I have called it. *Of course* it is the "forward-looking benefits" of the *whole system* of desert (praise and blame, reward and punishment) that justifies it, but it justifies the system, while ruling out case-by-case consideration of the specific benefits or lack thereof accruing to any particular instance of blame or punishment – which is not true of therapy, for instance. The system specifically prohibits even raising the issue of whether, in this instance, more good than harm would result from abandoning the verdict and the penalty.

People understand that. They would be incensed by a baseball umpire who took it upon himself to call strikes balls in order to bolster the ego of the depressed batter whose dying mother was watching from the stands, and they would be incensed – and properly so, I claim – by a judge who set aside damning evidence because the defendant had suffered enough already. Jury nullification is, of course, an example of the sort of bending of the rules which we all understand, and we understand it should be reserved for *very* special circumstances in which the laws, as they are written, fail to treat defendants fairly. The reason is that upholding the law and respect for the law is a key "forward-looking" policy. It is the maintenance of the credibility of the law and support for its provisions that governs all adjustments and limits all exemptions, for a straightforward reason: people are not angels, and will be clever (rational) and self-interested enough to explore for loopholes and ways of gaming the system. That is why the burden of proof of moral incompetence must rest on the defendant.

So, is the concept I am defending any kind of desert? It is not "basic desert" – a chimera fantasized by philosophers, apparently. Praise (or royalties, or your paycheck) is not just encouragement or reinforcement, and blame (or fines or incarceration) is not just deterrence or therapy. You are *entitled* to the praise you get for your good deeds and to the paycheck you get for your doing your job; and the criticism, the shame, the blame you get if you offend common decency or violate the laws is quite justly and properly placed at your doorstep. That is not "retributive" punishment, I guess, but it hurts, and so it should.

You think my parallel with rules in sports "can all be explained without appeal to free will and *just deserts*." I disagree. The rules of sports have exclusionary clauses for events outside the control of the players, and also rules obliging players to maintain self-control. (There are cases where a player gets excused if he "could not have done otherwise," and cases where this is no excuse, in exact parallel to the moral cases. No player has ever raised the issue of being exempt from blame because of the truth of determinism!) Players must be capable of *understanding* the rules, and agreeing to play by them, so they are considered to be autonomous, reasoning agents. Rules are composed to make games fair, and as the American political philosopher John Rawls noted long ago, justice is a kind of fairness.

You claim that adopting my non-retributive defense of punishment would require that "major elements of the criminal justice system" would need to be abandoned. I don't see it. What would be jeopardized? I myself have urged all along that we need major *reform* of our penal policies, drastically reducing sentences, eliminating the death penalty, and instituting many programs to help prisoners prepare for the resumption of their full rights of citizenship, but it would still be a system of punishment, not just enforced rehabilitation processes or quarantine. If a magic pill were invented that would turn any convict into a safe honest citizen, it would not obviate the need for punishment, for instance.

Strawson may have said that "luck swallows everything" but, if so, he was wrong. Luck sets the stage, but even you note that – according to Nagel – "who we are is at least largely a matter of luck." Largely, not all. Yes, what actions we perform depend (trivially) on luck, but not entirely on luck. Skill comes into it (and, yes, as I discussed in *Elbow Room*, how good you are at acquiring skill is itself largely – not entirely – a matter of luck). (See the discussion in my *Freedom Evolves* (2003a: 276ff), where I deal with the marathon case and your objection.) When I said that luck averages out in the long run, I was speaking of those of us who (lucky us) *are* competent moral agents. There are manifest differences, of course, between those of us who barely make the grade and those who are fortunate enough to find being moral quite easy, all things considered, and our policies and practices allow for this by setting a "ceiling effect" (2003a: 291). (A test that is so easy that almost everyone gets 100 percent has a ceiling effect; the threshold for passing the moral responsibility test is set low enough to assure that only those who are obviously unable to control themselves are disqualified.) We also take steps to improve the moral competence of all, with practices that amount to compensatory "special ed" instruction and therapy.

In effect, you are stuck on the wrong side of a *sorites* puzzle: if I am born without moral responsibility, utterly dependent on the luck of genes and environment, then how can adding a smidgen of competence ever lead me to be responsible? Two grains of sand are not a pile or heap (*sorites*, in Greek), and adding another does not make a pile. When is there enough sand to make a pile? When does a man lose enough hair to be bald? The gradual accumulation of the grounds for being held responsible, and holding oneself responsible, has no natural moment when "a bell rings" and you acquire free will, but we have devised defensible and adjustable thresholds that measure what matters. Since the benefits of political freedom in a well-governed state are so great, most people aspire to moral competency, and for good reasons. And when they screw up, they would rather be punished than institutionalized as morally incompetent. "Thanks, I needed that!"

Caruso: I don't doubt that the sense of "desert" you defend is the everyday sense. Keep in mind, though, that it is exactly this sense of desert that is used to justify retributivism. And nothing you have said suggests that you reject either of the two main tenets of retributivism – its backward-looking-ness (at least internal to the moral responsibility system) and its appeal to *just deserts*. Quite the opposite, you explicitly state that the premeditated murderer really does "deserve to go to prison for a very long time," irrespective of future consequences in specific instances. I'm confused, then, why you continue to deny that you are a retributivist. It seems to me that your view is indistinguishable from retributivism. Yes, you support sentence reform and eliminating the death penalty, but that doesn't make you a non-retributivist. But rather than get into a debate over your membership in the Retributivist Party, I think it would be more helpful to focus on specifics.

I disagree with you that people deserve to be praised and blamed in the everyday cases you discuss. Consider the case of Albert Einstein. He too was a free will skeptic who believed that his scientific accomplishments were not of his own making. In a 1929 interview in *The Saturday Evening Post*, he said: "I do not believe in free will . . . I believe with Schopenhauer: we can do what we wish, but we can only wish what we must." He goes on to add: "My own career was undoubtedly determined, not by my own will but by various factors over which I have no control." He concludes by rejecting the idea that he deserves praise or credit for his scientific achievements: "I claim credit for nothing. Everything is determined, the beginning as well as the end, by forces over which we have no control." (Side note: my own free will skepticism is agnostic about determinism. I maintain that whether or not the universe is governed by deterministic laws, Einstein's general point remains true, since indeterminate events are no more within our control than determined ones. This is why, following my friend and sometimes-collaborator Derk Pereboom, I call myself a *hard-incompatibilist* rather than a *hard-determinist*.)

Of course, we can *attribute* various accomplishments to Einstein – free will skepticism is perfectly consistent with *attributability*. We can also say that Einstein was extremely intelligent, gifted, and creative. What we cannot say, if we are free will skeptics, is that Einstein *deserves praise* (in the "basic-desert" sense) for his attributes and accomplishments.

I know this sounds counterintuitive, but that's only because *internal to the moral responsibility system*, desert-based praise and blame, punishment and reward come naturally. The problem with appealing to our everyday practices, however, is that it takes for granted the very thing in need of justification. To paraphrase my friend and fellow skeptic Bruce Waller, if we start from the assumption of the moral responsibility system, then the denial of moral responsibility is absurd and self-defeating. But the universal denial of moral responsibility does *not* start from the assumption that under normal circumstances we are morally responsible, and it does *not* proceed from that starting point to enlarge and extend the range of excuses to cover everyone (so that *everyone* is profoundly flawed). That is indeed a path to absurdity. Rather, those who reject moral responsibility reject the basic system which starts from the assumption that all minimally competent persons are morally responsible. For the free will skeptic, it is never fair to treat anyone as morally responsible, no matter how reasonable, competent, self-efficacious, strong-willed and clear-sighted that person may be. Since skeptics like myself, who globally challenge moral responsibility, do not accept the rules of that system, it is question-begging to assume our ordinary moral responsibility practices are justified without refuting the various arguments for global skepticism.

Now, in fairness, you do provide a forward-looking justification for backward-looking blame and punishment. That is, you argue that the *whole moral responsibility system* is justified in terms of its forward-looking benefits, but once we adopt the "system of desert" we need to reject case-by-case judgments of what would produce the best outcomes. *Internal to the system*, you maintain, we need to adopt backward-looking, desert-based practices and policies. But I see at least two problems with this. First, it's an open question whether the moral responsibility system has the forward-looking benefits you maintain. The notion of *just deserts*, for instance, is too often used to justify punitive excess in criminal justice, to encourage treating people in severe and demeaning ways, and to excuse and perpetuate social and economic inequalities. Additionally, resentment, indignation, moral anger, and blame are often counterproductive on the interpersonal level when it comes to the goals of safety, moral formation, and reconciliation.

Rather than argue the point further here, however, I will simply note that it remains an empirical question whether, on balance, we would be better off without a system of desert. I believe we would be. My second concern is that blame and punishment, especially legal punishment, can cause severe harm. If you want to justify the harm caused by blame and punishment on the assumption that agents are free and morally responsible, hence *justly deserve* to suffer for the wrongs they have done, then it would seem you need good epistemic reasons for thinking agents *actually* are free and morally responsible in the sense required. But I don't see how a pragmatic or consequentialist justification of the "whole system of desert" can provide such a justification. Pointing to the *benefits* of adopting a system of desert seems orthogonal to the core question.

Lastly, regarding luck, I go further than Nagel, and maintain that every morally significant act is either constitutively lucky, presently lucky, or both. Your antidote to luck seems to be skill or moral competency. But, as I argued earlier, the series of actions through which agents develop various skills and competencies are themselves either the result of constitutive luck (when they stem from an agent's endowments), present luck, or both.

Dennett: You find my view "indistinguishable from retributivism." This baffles me, since I have all along stressed the "forward-looking" justification I have presented. There are non-retributive, non-deontological, consequentialist justifications of punishment. See, for instance, the excellent entry on punishment in the *Stanford Encyclopedia of Philosophy* by my late friend and colleague Hugo Bedau (2015). The "liberal justification" of punishment he offers there is one with which I, along with many others, concur. As Bedau notes, after making a proper hash of retributivism: "But the basic insights of retributivism cannot be merely brushed aside. There is a role for desert in a liberal theory of punishment, but its scope needs careful restriction."

A key feature of that careful restriction is an appreciation of its role in preserving and enhancing respect for the law. You describe my view as holding that "once we adopt the 'system of desert' we need to reject case-by-case judgments of what would produce the best outcomes." Not quite right; you must add "in the immediate circumstances." The point is that a policy of case-by-case judgments of what would produce the "best outcome" *considered locally* would threaten both the effective administration of justice (by inviting special pleading on behalf of either the perpetrator or the injured party or society as a whole) and respect for the law. That is the point of my examples of the biased umpire and the judge who suppresses evidence. Accepting bad outcomes in specific cases is only justified by the long-run protection of respect for the law, and whenever evidence mounts for adjustments to general policies, laws can be revised, a demonstrably better policy than "taking the law into your own hands."

Bedau usefully lists four requirements for any justification of punishment:

> Accordingly, to justify punishment we must specify, first, what our goals are in establishing (or perpetuating) the practice itself. Second, we must show that when we punish we actually achieve these goals. Third, we must show that we cannot achieve these goals unless we punish (and punish in certain ways and not in others) and that we cannot achieve them with comparable or superior efficiency and fairness by nonpunitive interventions. Fourth, we must show that striving to achieve these goals by way of the imposition of deprivations is itself justified. (2015)

You say "it's an open question whether the moral responsibility system has the forward-looking benefits you maintain" (Bedau's point two) and "it remains an empirical question whether, on balance, we would be better off without a system of desert. I believe we would be" (Bedau's point three). Indeed, these are open empirical questions, but not very open! I cannot see how you can think we would be better off without a system of desert – unless you are granting me *my* kind of desert and merely saying we'd be better off without some as yet undescribed sort of "basic" desert (and I am quite sure we are better off without that). For without my kind of desert, no one would deserve to receive the prize they competed for in good faith and won, no one would deserve to be blamed for breaking solemn promises without excuse, no one would deserve to have their driver's license revoked for drunk-driving, no one would deserve punishment for lying under oath, and so forth. There would be no rights, no recourse to authority to protect against fraud, theft, rape, murder. In short, no morality.

I was astonished by your sentence: "For the free will skeptic, it is never fair to treat anyone as morally responsible, no matter how reasonable, competent, self-efficacious, strong-willed and clear-sighted that person may be." Do you really want to return humanity to the seventeenth-century English philosopher Thomas Hobbes's state of nature, where life is nasty, brutish and short? If you have some other vision of how a stable, secure, and just state can thrive without appeal to moral responsibility, you owe us the details. Waller, in *The Injustice of Punishment* (2018), makes a brave attempt to do that, but even he concedes that you cannot have such a society without punishment, as announced by the title of his Chapter 2: "The Unjust Necessity of Punishment." Well, if punishment is a necessity, it isn't a logical or physical necessity; it's a necessity for a viable state in which as much justice as practically possible might be achieved. In what way would such a necessity be "unjust"? In the same way, it seems to me, that it is "unfair" that everyone can't be above average – in beauty, strength, intelligence, whatever. Life is tough, but not *ipso facto* unjust, and we can use our reason to make life, and its institutions, more and more just, more and more fair, a better world for all.

Caruso: Thank you for clearing some things up for me. You say that my confusion over whether you reject retributivism "baffles" you, since you "have all along stressed the 'forward-looking' justification [you] have presented." I guess my confusion stemmed from the fact that earlier in the conversation you said that rejecting retributivism "doesn't mean there is no 'backward-looking' justification of punishment." You then went on to defend what looked to be a backward-looking justification of blame and punishment grounded in desert. If, instead, you adopt a forward-looking consequentialist account of punishment, then I'm happy to retract my earlier charge that you are a retributivist in all but name. That said, by adopting a forward-looking consequentialist justification, your view comes much closer to that of the skeptic. The main difference, it seems, is that you want to retain the language of desert while the skeptic wants to consign it to the flames – along with libertarian free will, retributivism, and the idea of being self-made men and women (all of which you reject as well).

You go on to say: "I cannot see how you can think we would be better off without a system of desert." Well, for me, the notion of basic desert, which has been my target all along, is a pernicious one that does more harm than good. If that is not the sense of desert you have in mind, then so be it. But my claim is that basic-desert moral responsibility, and with it the notion of *just deserts*, is too often used to justify punitive excess in criminal justice, to encourage treating people in severe and demeaning ways, and to excuse and perpetuate social and economic inequalities. Consider, for example, punitiveness. Researchers have found that stronger belief in free will is correlated with increased punitiveness. They also found that weakening one's belief in free will makes them less retributive in their attitudes about punishment (for details, see Shariff et al. 2013; Clark et al. 2014; Clark et al. 2018; Clark, Winegard, and Sharrif 2019; Nadelhoffer and Tocchetto 2013). These empirical findings concern me.

There are additional concerns as well. As I argue in *Rejecting Retributivism* (2021a), the social determinants of criminal behavior are broadly similar to the social determinants of health. In that work, and elsewhere, I advocate adopting a broad public-health approach for identifying and taking action on these shared social determinants. I focus on how social inequities and systemic injustices affect health outcomes and criminal behavior, how poverty affects brain development, how offenders often have pre-existing medical conditions (especially mental-health issues), how homelessness and education affects health and safety outcomes, how environmental health is important to both public health and safety, how involvement in the criminal justice system itself can lead to or worsen health and cognitive problems, and how a public-health approach can be successfully applied within the criminal justice system. I argue that, just as it is important to identify and take action on the social determinants of health if we want to improve health outcomes, it is equally important to identify and address the social determinants of criminal behavior. My fear is that the system of desert you want to preserve leads us to myopically focus on individual responsibility and ultimately prevents us from addressing the *systemic causes of criminal behavior*.

Consider, for example, the crazed reaction to the then US president Barack Obama's claim that, "if you've got a [successful] business, you didn't build that alone." The Republicans were so incensed by this claim that they dedicated the second day of the 2012 Republican National Convention to the theme "We Built it!" Obama's point, though, was simple, innocuous, and factually correct. To quote him directly: "If you've been successful, you didn't get there on your own." So, what's so threatening about this? The answer, I believe, lies in the notion of *just deserts*. The system of desert keeps alive the belief that if you end up in poverty or prison, this is "just" because you deserve it. Likewise, if you end up succeeding in life, you and you alone are responsible for that success. This way of thinking keeps us locked in the system of blame and shame, and prevents us from *addressing the systemic causes* of poverty, wealth-inequality, racism, sexism, educational inequity and the like. My suggestion is that we move beyond this, and acknowledge that the lottery of life is not always fair, that luck does not average out in the long run, and that who we are and what we do is ultimately the result of factors beyond our control.

Finally, I do not agree that rejecting free will and basic-desert moral responsibility will "return humanity to Hobbes's state of nature where life is nasty, brutish and short." You write: "If you have some other vision of how a stable, secure, and just state can thrive without appeal to moral responsibility, you owe us the details." First, let me reiterate that the kind of moral responsibility I reject is basic-desert moral responsibility. Of course, there are other conceptions of moral responsibility that are perfectly consistent with free will skepticism – such as Waller's notion of *take-charge responsibility*, the *attributability* responsibility I referenced in the Einstein example, and Pereboom's forward-looking notion of responsibility, which focuses on three non-desert-invoking desiderata: future protection, future reconciliation, and future moral formation. Second, I agree that I owe you and others an account of how to maintain a stable, secure, and just society without basic-desert moral responsibility. Fortunately, my good friend Derk Pereboom has already provided most of the details for such an account in his two books *Living Without Free Will* (2001) and *Free Will, Agency, and Meaning in Life* (2014). And I have further developed a detailed account of how to address criminal behavior without basic-desert moral responsibility in *Rejecting Retributivism: Free Will, Punishment, and Criminal Justice* – it's called the *public health–quarantine model*. While I wish we could debate the merits of it here, it unfortunately looks like we have run out of time. The details of my account, however, are readily available for anyone who is interested (see, e.g. Caruso 2016a, 2021; Pereboom and Caruso 2018). [Note to reader: We return to these issues, including a discussion of the public health–quarantine model, in our third exchange.]

Coda: On Determinism

Caruso: I would also like to explore further your thoughts on determinism, since thus far we've said very little about it. *Determinism*, as it's traditionally understood, is the thesis that at any given time only one future is physically possible (van Inwagen 1983: 3). We can say that a world is governed by determinism if and only if, given the way things are at time *t*, the way things go thereafter is fixed as a matter of natural law (Hoefer 2016). Or put differently, it's the thesis that facts about the remote past in conjunction with the laws of nature entail that there is only one unique future (McKenna and Pereboom 2016: 19). As a *compatibilist*, I assume you either accept the thesis of determinism or think it's no threat to the kind of free will and moral responsibility under dispute.

Earlier, I wrote that, "the particular reasons that move us, along with the psychological predispositions, likes and dislikes, and other constitutive factors that make us who we are, themselves are ultimately the result of factors beyond our control." In reply, you said, "So what?" You then added that what really matters is autonomy, self-control, and moral competency. Of course, this is the standard compatibilist move. Compatibilists maintain that what is of utmost importance is not the absence of causal determination, but that our actions are voluntary, free from constraint and compulsion, and caused in the appropriate way. Different compatibilist accounts spell out requirements for free will differently but widely endorsed views single out responsiveness to reasons, self-control, or connection of action to what one would reflectively endorse. But before we get into a debate over whether the compatibilist view is capable of preserving free will, I would first like to get clearer on what, exactly, determinism entails with regard to human action and whether you accept those implications.

Do you accept, for instance, that if determinism is true, then all human behavior, like the behavior of all other things in the physical universe, is causally determined by antecedent conditions in accordance with natural laws? Do you also accept that determinism rules out or excludes an agent's *ability to do otherwise* in exactly the same set of circumstances? Consider, for example, the following everyday example. This morning, after I showered, I went to my closet, opened it, looked inside, deliberated for a moment (not very long), and then decided that I would wear one of my (many) black button-down collared shirts. If determinism is true, my choice would have been the *only* one I could have made in *exactly that situation*, keep everything in the universe exactly the same up until the moment of choice. That is because according to determinism, our choices and actions are the fixed result of a deterministic chain of events that trace back to factors ultimately beyond our control (i.e. events in the remote past and natural laws). Hence, if determinism is true, then for any given voluntary action we would end up with something like the following picture – where a myriad set of antecedent conditions determines our unique set of inner psychological states and processes, which in turn determines our subsequent choice and action.

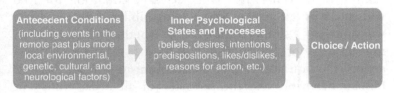

Figure 1

On this picture, keeping everything in the universe exactly the same up until a particular moment in time, say time *t*, the agent's choice would be causally determined such that they *could not have done otherwise* in exactly those circumstances.

Of course, some compatibilists have argued that terms

like *can*, *power*, and *ability* should be given a *conditional* or *hypothetical* analysis. These compatibilists maintain that when we say that an agent *can* (i.e. has the *power* or *ability* to) do something, we mean the agent *would* do it *if* the agent wanted (desires or chose) to do it. On this approach, to say "you could have done otherwise" would amount to the counterfactual claim that you would have done otherwise, if (contrary to fact) the past (or the laws of nature) had been different in some way. The problem, however, with analyzing *I could have done otherwise* as *I would have done otherwise if I wanted (or chose) to*, is that it only invites the obvious question: Do I have the freedom or ability to want (or choose) differently? For the compatibilist argument to work, it would have to show that the *ability to want otherwise* is itself compatible with determinism, and here the conditional approach will not help without causing a regress. Furthermore, this analysis would still fail to preserve the *unconditional ability to do otherwise* – hence, agents would still *lack the ability to do otherwise in exactly the same set of circumstances* keeping the laws of nature and antecedent conditions fixed. It would seem, then, that understanding the "ability to do otherwise" by means of conditional analysis would amount to nothing more than "the little *could* that *would* but *can't* so *won't*."

Setting aside for the moment the question of whether the "ability to do otherwise" is a necessary condition for free will, and without getting into a compatibilist defense of free will quite yet, I simply want to know whether you agree with my summary of determinism and what it means for human action. Do you accept that if determinism is true, then all human behavior, like the behavior of all other things in the physical universe, is causally determined by antecedent conditions in accordance with natural laws? And do you also accept that determinism rules out or excludes an agent's *ability to do otherwise* in the unconditional sense?

Dennett: You've given an admirably clear summary of the standard definition of determinism, Gregg, and your two closing questions make exactly the right distinction, so let me answer them. Yes, I accept that "if determinism is true, then all human behavior, like the behavior of all other things in the physical universe, is causally determined by antecedent conditions in accordance with natural laws." (And I have no quarrel with determinism; I see no reason at all to hope that human behavior is undetermined by those antecedent conditions.) But I do *not* accept your second claim, that determinism rules out or excludes an agent's ability to do otherwise. You add: "in the unconditional sense" and this clause, as I've argued for decades, is a huge mistake – and I'll say more about it in our debate. If what you are interested in is the *ability* of anything to do anything, you are *never* interested in what it does "in exactly the same circumstances." I'll try to make that clear as we go along. Let me add that I think your account of how "some compatibilists" interpret "could have done otherwise" in terms of certain conditionals about desires is accurate, but it shows that they, too, miss a key point. If you stick to these (quite standard but nevertheless misguided) readings of "could have done otherwise," then not only is free will an illusion, as you would claim, but so is life; nothing is *really* alive. I consider that a *reductio ad absurdum*, but tastes may vary.

Caruso: Thank you, Dan, for your direct and candid answers. They provide us with a good starting point. It seems we generally agree on the implications of determinism for human action, you just deny that the ability to do otherwise should be understood in terms of the "ability to do otherwise *in exactly the same circumstances*." (I assume you agree, though, that if determinism is true, we lack such an ability?) I'll give you an opportunity to explain your position further, but you may be surprised to learn that my primary reasons for rejecting compatibilism do *not* depend on *the ability to do otherwise* or presuppose that it is a necessary condition for free will. In fact, my main arguments against compatibilism focus on the causal history of an agent's actions and not on alternative possibilities. In our next exchange, I hope to spell out and discuss two of these arguments in detail, the *manipulation argument* and the *hard luck argument*. For the moment, though, I'll provide a few rough reasons for thinking that determinism is a threat to free will and (desert-based) moral responsibility.

First, consider the following argument for incompatibilism, which is independent of considerations regarding alternative possibilities and the ability to do otherwise. It comes from the American philosopher Peter van Inwagen, Professor of Philosophy at the University of Notre Dame. As he puts it:

> If determinism is true, then there is some state of the world in the distant past P that is connected by the laws of nature to any action A that one performs in the present. But since no one is responsible for the state of the world P in the distant past, and no one is responsible for the laws of nature that lead from P to A, it follows that no one is responsible for any action A that is performed in the present. (van Inwagen 1993: 182–183)

This argument captures one of the incompatibilist intuitions I have regarding determinism (see also Pereboom 2001: 34). The problem, I contend, is that if determinism is true, then there are conditions for which no one is, or ever has been, even partly responsible (in the sense relevant to free will), and these conditions determine the *actual sequence that brings about* the agent's action. This is why I endorse, along with my friend and fellow skeptic Derk Pereboom, the following incompatibilist intuition about determinism: "An action is free in the sense required for moral responsibility only if it is not produced by a deterministic process that traces back to causal factors beyond the agent's control" (Pereboom 2001: 34).

Second, so-called *folk intuitions* about free will indicate that ordinary people (or the "folk" as philosophers like to call them) think that their choices aren't determined. As the experimental philosopher Shaun Nichols explains: "It is not just that they don't have the belief that their choices are determined. Rather, they positively think that their choices are not determined. And this belief is implicated in their thoughts about free will" (2012: 203). For instance, when presented with a description of a deterministic universe, most participants say that in that universe, people don't have free will (see, e.g., Nichols and Knobe 2007). More specifically, in one classic study, participants were given descriptions of a deterministic universe (A) and another universe (B) in which everything is determined *except* human choices. Participants were asked, "Which of these universes is most like ours?" More than 90 percent of the respondents said that universe (B) – the indeterministic universe – is most like our own (Nichols and Knobe 2007: 669). Additional empirical findings indicate that, not only do people tend to *believe* that they possess indeterminist free will, people's *experience* of choosing and deciding is that they possess such indeterminist (or libertarian) freedom (see Deery et al. 2013). And, even when people *seem* to express compatibilist intuitions, there's evidence that this is largely explained by the fact that people import an indeterministic metaphysics into the deterministic scenarios they are given when making judgments about free will and moral responsibility (see Nadelhoffer et al. 2019). There is converging evidence, then, that ordinary thinking is at least *partly or largely* indeterminist.* This provides reason to think that the everyday conception of free will is not compatible with determinism (or at least that people's intuitions are unclear and confused). So, even if every-day folk tend to think that our ordinary desert practices are justified, this may be because they falsely presuppose that indeterminism is true.

Given these empirical findings, I have four questions for

---

* (Nichols 2004, 2012; Nichols and Knobe 2007 Feltz and Cokley 2009; Feltz, Perez, and Harris 2012; Deery et al. 2013; Knobe 2014; Nadelhoffer et al. 2019; Rose and Nichols 2013; Sarkissian et al. 2010)

you. First, how do you explain the widespread folk tendency to believe in indeterminist free will? Second, why think your compatibilist conception of free will is the one the folk care about? Third, if it's *not* the one the folk care about, why should we think that it's the *only* sense that matters to the free will debate? And lastly, are you at least willing to admit that your account is a *revisionist* one, i.e. it seeks to defend a notion of free will that is different than the one ordinary people believe in?

I have other concerns regarding determinism as well, but perhaps I should pause here and let you respond.

Dennett: I'll briefly answer your four questions, leaving the details for later in the debate. First, the widespread folk tendency to believe in indeterminist free will is due to *misunderstanding*. I will point out the mistakes of imagination that have led us to this curious state. For instance, determinism *does not prevent you* from making choices, from turning over a new leaf, from becoming less impulsive, from rethinking decisions, from learning from your mistakes, from resolving to do better and succeeding – or from taking advice on how to think about free will! If that's news to you, you have been mis-imagining determinism and you have lots of company. Second, I think my compatibilist conception of free will is the one the folk care about because it is not *inflated*. When people think something is really important – and free will is really important – they tend to exaggerate their account of what it is or must be; they don't just want powers, they want superpowers, or so they think. Third, the reason I think my conception of free will is the only kind of free will worth wanting is that I've been asking very smart people for decades if they can tell me why anybody should care about any concept of free will other than mine, and nobody yet has come up with a good answer. Why, for instance, would anyone want the ability to make "contra-causal" or strictly undetermined decisions? I can readily imagine good reasons for wanting to be able to fly by flapping one's arms, or the ability to travel to another galaxy, or to time-travel – what a trip that would be! – or, getting closer to home, the ability to undo a deed one regretted, but the attractions of indeterminism of choice have yet to be defended – I'll discuss later an apparent defense that proves (to me) that the quest is superstitious at best. Mostly people just *assume* that an inflated concept of free will is the only one worth thinking about – "Accept no substitutes! Look out for Dennett's *bait-and-switch* move!" Fourth, I am not just willing but eager to "admit" that my account is a *revisionist* one, that seeks to defend a notion of free will that is different than the one ordinary people believe in. One of the besetting foibles of much contemporary philosophy is its regressive reliance on everyday "intuitions" as the touchstones of truth.

Caruso: Thank you again for your candor and for acknowledging that your account of free will is a *revisionist* or *reformist* one. To be clear, I do not reject your account of free will *because* it seeks to revise or reform cur traditional notion of free will. I acknowledge that a revisionist account of free will is a legitimate position. Instead, I reject it because it fails to preserve the kind of control in action (i.e. free will) required for moral responsibility in the basic-desert sense. That is, I hope to show in the arguments to come that if an action is produced by a determinist process that traces back to causal factors beyond the agent's control, then it would be wrong to hold that agent morally responsible in the *desert-based sense* – the sense required for an agent to *justly deserve* to be praised and blamed, punished and rewarded. But perhaps we should delay no longer and just get directly into the argument. What do you say?

Dennett: Yes, let's get on with it.

Exchange 2

Going Deeper: The Arguments

Caruso: Dan, I would like to begin by clarifying a few points that came up in our last exchange before we jump back in where we left off. First, I maintain that we can have a secure, stable, and just society *without a system of desert* that is used to ground blame and punishment. You disagree. You think a system of desert is needed to maintain order, to respect the autonomy of individuals, and to punish wrongdoers. However, you also claim that *basic-desert* moral responsibility, the kind of moral responsibility I deny, is "a chimera fantasized by philosophers." But here is Derk Pereboom's helpful definition of basic-desert moral responsibility:

> For an agent to be morally responsible for an action in this sense is for it to be hers in such a way that she would deserve to be blamed if she understood that it was morally wrong, and she would deserve to be praised if she understood that it was morally exemplary. The desert at issue here is basic in the sense that the agent would deserve to be blamed or praised just because she has performed the action, given an understanding of its moral status, and not, for example, merely by virtue of consequentialist or contractualist considerations. (2014: 2)

I find this definition both intuitive and clear. I also think it captures exactly what has been of central philosophical and practical importance in the free will debate. One of its virtues is that it provides a neutral definition that virtually all parties can agree to – i.e. it doesn't exclude from the outset various conceptions of free will that are available for compatibilists, libertarians, and free will skeptics to adopt. By defining free will as the control in action required for basic-desert moral responsibility, all the traditional questions remain unsettled. If it turns out, as I think it might, that you agree with me that compatibilist control is not enough for basic-desert moral responsibility, then so much the worse for compatibilism!

Dennett: Gregg, the fact that you find Pereboom's definition "both intuitive and clear" and think "it captures exactly what has been of central philosophical and practical importance in the free will debate" nicely focuses a major point of disagreement. I see Derk's proposal as a classic example of philosophical *rathering* (for a definition and explanation, see Dennett 2013a: ch. 9). It rules out, "by definition" in effect, the prospect that a policy of *basic* desert might itself *depend on* "consequentialist or contractualist considerations." Well, you may say, Pereboom *means* to rule out by definition dependent varieties of desert and concentrate our attention on *basic* desert. But, I reply, that leaves unexamined the possibility that some kind of desert that is as basic as desert could be grounds for our convictions of desert precisely by being supported by indirect "consequentialist or contractualist" considerations. I see Pereboom as creating a will-of-the-wisp of no importance with his purer, more absolutistic definition.

I'm happy to grant you that Pereboom's "basic-desert moral responsibility" is incompatible with science. Moreover, so far as I can see it is just incoherent, in spite of its distinguished philosophical pedigree, but there is a respectable – in a strong sense – variety of *quite* basic-desert moral responsibility that will give us all the moral responsibility we should take seriously. You say that Pereboom's definition "doesn't exclude from the outset various conceptions of free will that are *available* for compatibilists, libertarians, and free will skeptics to adopt" but it does exclude mine.

Caruso: I agree with you that Pereboom's definition of basic desert nicely captures a major point of disagreement between us. You reject it because it excludes consequentialist and contractualist notions of desert, like your own. Fair enough. But I adopt it precisely *because* it does so. It's my contention that a *non-consequentialist conception of moral responsibility and desert* best captures what has been of central philosophical and practical importance in the traditional debate – hence, a definition that focuses our attention on such a conception is helpful. On this understanding, *free will* is a kind of power or ability an agent must possess in order to justify certain kinds of *basically deserved* judgments, attitudes, or treatments – such as resentment, indignation, moral anger, and retributive punishment – in response to decisions or actions that the agent performed or failed to perform. These reactions would be justified on purely backward-looking grounds – that's what makes them *basic* – and would not appeal to consequentialist or forward-looking considerations, such as future protection, future reconciliation, or future moral formation.

I favor this conception of free will and moral responsibility for two main reasons. First, if the issue were simply about whether or not there are good forward-looking reasons to engage in certain forms of moral protest when individuals act badly, and the inverse when they do good, it's hard to see what the substantive dispute is all about. I assume that most parties in the debate (i.e. most libertarians, compatibilists, and free will skeptics – present company excluded) think that there is more to the debate than that. In fact, free will skeptics can agree that certain forms of forward-looking responsibility are perfectly consistent with the rejection of free will and basic-desert moral responsibility. Insofar, then, as the kind of moral responsibility that interests you would also be acceptable to free will skeptics, your style of compatibilism ought to be rejected since it is not discernible from free will skepticism in any substantive way. This is why I think your view is much closer to that of the free will skeptic than you acknowledge.

Of course, one obvious difference between our views is that, as a free will skeptic, I reject various notions that you wish to retain. For instance, I reject the idea that individuals *justly deserve* to be praised and blamed, punished and rewarded for their actions, whereas you wish to keep the notion of *desert* in the lexicon. But this brings me to my second reason for defining free will in terms of control in action needed for basic-desert moral responsibility. I contend that the notion of *desert*, as traditionally understood, is too entangled with *retributive desert* and the *basic* notion of moral responsibility to serve as a useful concept on its own, separated from those foundations. That is, it's unclear to me whether a consequentialist, like yourself, should even continue to talk of *just deserts*, given its strong deontological and retributive connotations. What you appear to be advocating is the *practical necessity* of a system of desert, not that it's intrinsically good that, say, wrongdoers be blamed and punished for their actions. But the notion of "just deserts" strongly implies that it's intrinsically good that wrongdoers suffer in proportion to their wrongdoing *regardless of any forward-looking benefit this would have*. Given the canonical understanding of "just deserts" and how it is used to justify various retributive attitudes, judgments, and treatments, your use of the term lends itself to easy confusion and gives the mistaken impression that you are setting out to preserve something you are not.

Having said all that, I think it's important to pause for a moment and acknowledge that we appear to agree on one very significant point – i.e. that the kind of free will required for basic-desert moral responsibility is *incompatible* with (i.e. cannot be reconciled with) our understanding of the natural world characterized by science. If that's correct, then I think we're making real progress. It seems, then, that not only do we agree that libertarian accounts of free will are non-starters, we also agree that compatibilist control is not enough to preserve basic-desert moral responsibility. While normally I would see this as a victory for the skeptic, since the kind of free will we are most interested in doubting or denying is the kind required for basic-desert moral responsibility, it would be an empty victory if you were in fact correct that "some kind of desert that it is as basic as desert could be" could be grounded in consequentialist considerations. So, perhaps it's best that we acknowledge our agreement that compatibilist accounts fail to preserve basic-desert moral responsibility and move on to discussing your forward-looking (consequentialist) attempt to ground backward-looking desert and moral responsibility.

Dennett: Gregg, you say that "the notion of 'just deserts' *strongly implies* [my emphasis] that it's *intrinsically good* [my emphasis] that wrongdoers suffer in proportion to their wrongdoing *regardless of any forward-looking benefit this would have*." I just checked a few online dictionaries, and they all agree that, roughly, the phrase means "a fair and appropriate punishment related to the severity of the crime that was committed." That's what I mean by "just deserts." One definition does add that it is *sometimes* referred to as the "retribution type of sentencing" and I think that this is because philosophers – you and Derk being cases in point – have insisted on saddling the idea of justly deserved punishment with the "canonical" idea that it is "intrinsically good" to punish the guilty. I agree with you that (thanks to many philosophers) the idea of just deserts is badly "entangled with" the idea of "retributive" desert, but I think this damage can be undone by inquiring whether or not a concept of just deserts as "fair and appropriate *punishment*" grounded in non-intrinsic considerations can be defended, not as a revolutionary revision of our traditional concept of just deserts but as capturing the rationale that the concept has always had, whether or not people recognized it. So yes, "not only do we agree that libertarian accounts of free will are non-starters, we also agree that compatibilist control is not enough to preserve basic-desert moral responsibility," a concept that we all agree to be bad philosophy. (That is, Derk defined it in order to dethrone it.)

Caruso: Again, I'm glad to know we both agree that compatibilist control fails to preserve basic-desert moral responsibility. But I would also like to push back on your claim that the basic-desert notion of moral responsibility is "incoherent." Why think that? You make the charge without defending it. Immanuel Kant, for example, does a good job eliciting the basic-desert intuition, and explaining why it is practically important, in his famous island example. He asks us to imagine an island society that is dissolving its social contract "with the consent of all its members," where everyone has resolved to "separate and scatter themselves throughout the whole world." There is one remaining murderer in prison and Kant wonders whether we would be justified in giving them their *just desert* before leaving the island. This is essentially a question about basic desert, since Kant's example does a nice job in setting aside any forward-looking consequentialist or contractualist considerations. Here's Kant's own answer:

> Even if a civil society resolved to dissolve itself with the consent of all its members – as might be supposed in the case of a people inhabiting an island resolving to separate and scatter themselves throughout the whole world – the last murderer lying in prison ought to be executed before the resolution was carried out. This ought to be done in order that every one may realize the *desert* of his deeds, and that blood-guiltiness may not remain upon the people; for otherwise they might all be regarded as participators in the murder as a public violation of justice. (1785: Part II [italics added])

While I know we both oppose the death penalty and would therefore disagree with Kant on those grounds alone, there's no denying that Kant's example elicits a coherent intuition about basic desert. In fact, I've used Kant's examples for years in classes and talks, since it makes both contractualist and consequentialist considerations irrelevant, and almost everyone can understand the desert intuition involved in it.

Dennett: Well, I deny that Kant's notorious example elicits a coherent intuition. When Kant tries to explain his proposal and says "that blood-guiltiness may not remain upon the people; for otherwise they might all be regarded as participators in the murder as a public violation of justice," it looks to me as if he is trying to justify his recommendation in terms of how the people might wish to protect their reputations. He is using the poor murderer as a means to that end – a consequentialist reason not unlike my defense of punishment that considers only the backward-looking facts of the case: it is to preserve *respect for the law*, which is a practically necessary feature of a secure and happy state. But since Kant has stipulated that the "civil society" is to disband, he can't use that reason, so it looks like he's got to fall back on something drearily similar to "keeping their individual hands clean" (a selfish consequentialist reason indeed). And if nobody off the island knew of the fate of the murderer, then those folks wouldn't be *regarded* as public violators of justice – except by themselves! – so once again, it seems as if Kant is telling folks to keep their hands clean by executing a murderer for no other reason than to keep their hands clean. I agree with you, of course, that Kant's example nicely *illustrates* the idea of basic moral desert, which is why I am glad you raised it.

Caruso: Dan, you can easily drop out all those aspects of Kant's example you mention and focus instead on the core question: would we be justified in punishing a wrongdoer (e.g. a murderer) if they were the only other person left on a deserted island and there would be no forward-looking contractualist and consequentialist benefits in doing so?

Dennett: My answer to that question would be: No.

Caruso: Great, I'm glad we agree on that point – which for me is an important one! Your answer also reveals that there's nothing incoherent about the notion of basic desert, even if you wish to deny its importance to the free will debate. I think the real source of your unease with the notion of basic desert is this: you're not a traditional (or typical) compatibilist.

Dennett: True, I am not in many regards a traditional compatibilist, but I have been defending this brand of compatibilism – making it available in two books and many articles – for almost forty years.

Caruso: Indeed, you have. But unlike most traditional compatibilists, you do *not* set out to defend a non-consequentialist conception of desert. Rather, you offer a consequentialist defense of just deserts and maintain that it is the "forward-looking benefits" of the *whole system* of desert (praise and blame, reward and punishment) that justifies it, but it justifies the system while ruling out case by case consideration of the specific benefits or lack thereof accruing to any particular instance of blame or punishment. (I know of only one other mainstream compatibilist that holds such a view – Manuel Vargas (2007, 2013).) On your view, then, it is the consequentialist benefits of adopting a "*system* of desert" that justifies praise and blame, reward and punishment. But equally important, you also maintain that once we are internal to the system, judgments of blame and punishment remain backward-looking and grounded in the notion of *desert*. Given that your species of compatibilism is rather unique, it's easy for us to talk past one another. But I want to avoid that.

Dennett: So do I, and you've just given an excellent thumbnail account of my view. Thanks.

Caruso: If our disagreement were simply about terminology that would be unfortunate. But when you say that we should treat self-control as "our threshold for true desert," I assume you mean compatibilist self-control (i.e. a kind of non-libertarian control consistent with determinism) is enough to ground *truly deserved* blame and punishment. This seems to follow from your comments about culprits deserving punishment.

Dennett: Yes, Gregg. It is just as you say.

Caruso: It also seems to follow from what you say about blaming those who break their promises. According to you: "Autonomous people are justly held responsible for *what they did* because all of us depend on being able to count on them . . . So we can blame them for being duped, for getting drunk, etc. When we blame them, we are not just diagnosing them, or categorizing them; we are holding them *deserving* of negative consequences." Since you think that competent agents who knowingly (and without excuse) break promises are *deserving* of blame and punishment, you must (correct me if I'm wrong) view free will as the control in action required for *some kind* of desert-based moral responsibility. While this may not be "basic-desert" moral responsibility, it's a close simulacrum.

Dennett: Again, just so. Let me add a bit of evolutionary background (for a more detailed account see my *Freedom Evolves*, ch. 9). We don't have a full-fledged *instinct for retribution* that we inherit from our ancestors via our genes, but there is plenty of evidence for a powerful innate foundation of negative reactions (of anger, of the urge to retaliate ...) when mammals, especially social mammals, encounter recalcitrant individuals (see especially Forber and Smead, 2018, and Henrich and Muthukrishna, 2020). That is, there are patterns of "cheater detection" that involve rudimentary *mutual trust* (restricted to one's group

and family members) and *betrayal* of that trust, which typically leads to *ostracism* in extreme cases and *punishment*.
These are at best proto-moral dispositions, but they have
been harnessed, thanks to cultural evolution, turning what
David Hume called the *natural virtues* into moral virtues.
"If nature did not aid us in this particular, t'would be in
vain for politicians to talk of *honourable* and *dishonourable*,
praiseworthy and *blameable*. These words would be perfectly
unintelligible" (1739: 500). There are *good* (consequentialist) *reasons* why human cultures have adopted largely
consensual moralities and raised their offspring to honor
them. People don't have to reflect on, or even consider,
the *free-floating rationales* (see my *From Bacteria to Bach and
Back* (2017) for an account of these background reasons)
that ground their reactive attitudes – people can just take
them as part of human nature – but they are good design
features because they have had good consequences in the
evolutionary past. Now with changing times and changing
knowledge, we may decide we want to try to suppress or
redirect these very natural reactions, and in fact, we have
tempered them considerably in the last few hundred years,
largely abandoning the ideologies of retributivism that pur-
ported to justify them, but there is still a good case to be
made for maintaining the policy that *holds people who have
a certain kind of free will responsible*, blaming and punishing
them for their transgressions.

Caruso: I agree with you that *belief* in desert-invoking moral
responsibility may be grounded in a set of reactive attitudes,
emotions, and impulses that have been shaped by our evolutionary past. But even if these reactions served important
evolutionary functions in the past, that does not mean they
are *justified* or that the targets of those attitudes and emotions *deserve* them. There's no doubt that when we are
wronged, and when we observe another being wronged, we
feel a strong and immediate urge to strike back. According
to my good friend Bruce Waller, this strike-back emotion is

indeed one of the main sources of our strong, but stubborn, belief in moral responsibility:

> The deepest roots of our commitment to moral responsibility are in powerful emotions, rather than reason. There are many sources for the stubborn belief in moral responsibility, and some are quite subtle. But the most basic source has the subtlety of a barroom brawl, a back-country feud, or rats locked in a frenzied death struggle: the strike-back desire when we are harmed. (2015: 39)

Neil Levy also notes:

> Human beings are a punitive species. Perhaps because we are social animals, and require the cooperation of others to achieve our goals, we are strongly disposed to punish those who take advantage of us. Those who "free ride," taking benefits to which they are not entitled, are subject to exclusion, the imposition of fines or harsher penalties. Wrongdoing arouses strong emotions in us, whether it is done to us, or to others. Our indignation and resentment have fueled a dizzying variety of punitive practices – ostracism, branding, beheading, quartering, fining, and very many more. The details vary from place to place and time to culture but punishment has been a human universal, because it has been in our evolutionary interests. However, those evolutionary impulses are crude guides to how we should deal with offenders in contemporary society. (2016)

Crude indeed! In fact, when we look carefully at the strike-back emotion we share with rats and chimps, we often find that it overwhelms careful reflection and leads us to engage in inhumane and (from my perspective) unjustified practices and policies.

I acknowledge that the emotional reactions associated with the desire to strike back are *natural*, but at the same time challenge the claim that they are *justified*. Consider the reactive attitudes of resentment, indignation, blame, and moral anger. Since these reactive attitudes can cause harm, they can only be justified if the agent they are directed at *deserves* them. We can say, then, that an agent is *accountable* for her action when she deserves to be praised or blamed for what she did – i.e. she deserves certain kinds of desert-based judgments, attitudes, or treatments in response to decisions or actions she performed or failed to perform. But *if* free will skeptics are correct – something I doubt I will ever get you to agree to – then agents are never morally responsible in the desert-based sense, and hence expression of resentment, indignation, and moral anger would involve *doxastic irrationality* (at least to the extent it is accompanied by the belief that its target *deserves* to be its recipient). [The term "doxastic" derives from the ancient Greek *doxa*, which means "belief."]

Of course, one could ask, "But can we ever *really* relinquish these reactive attitudes? And would it be desirable if we could?" In response, I would first say that the moral anger associated with the reactive attitudes of resentment and indignation is often corrosive to our interpersonal relationships and to our social policies. I contend that the expression of these reactive attitudes are often suboptimal as modes of communication in relationships relative to alternative attitudes available to us – e.g. feeling hurt, or shocked, or disappointed (see Derk Pereboom's *Living Without Free Will* for more on this). On the question of whether it is *possible* to relinquish these reactive attitudes, my answer begins by first distinguishing between *narrow-profile* emotional responses and *wide-profile* responses (a distinction I borrow from Shaun Nichols, 2007). Narrow-profile emotional responses are local or immediate emotional reactions to a situation. Wide-profile responses are not immediate and can involve rational reflection. I believe it is perfectly consistent for a free will skeptic to maintain that expressions of resentment and indignation are irrational *and still acknowledge* that there may be certain types and degrees of resentment and indignation that are beyond our power to affect. If, for example, some serious moral wrong was done to my wife or daughter, I doubt I would be able to keep myself from some degree of narrow-profile, immediate resentment. Nevertheless, in wide-profile cases, we *do* have the ability to diminish or even eliminate resentment and indignation, or at least disavow it in the sense of rejecting any force it might be thought to have in *justifying* harmful reactions and policies. And since the wide-profile emotional reactions are most important when it comes to public policy – e.g. justifying legal punishment, etc. – I *do* believe philosophical arguments against free will and moral responsibility can change our practices and reactions.

My central point, then, is that an evolutionary account of our reactive emotions, attitudes, and impulses does not, itself, reveal that agents are *accountable* for their actions in the relevant philosophical sense. It may well be the case that these reactions, though natural, are philosophically unjustified. We still need to examine the philosophical arguments for and against free will to determine whether individuals truly deserve to be praised and blamed, punished and rewarded.

Dennett: Again, Gregg, there's a lot I can agree with in what you say. The "evolutionary impulses" are "crude indeed" – that's why, as Hume noted, we have to design institutions and norms that refine them, and we have done so, by two processes. The first is *cultural evolution*, a process that does not require human comprehension, but nevertheless can eke out good reasons for refining and redirecting our gene-founded impulses (for a new overview, see Henrich and Muthukrishna 2020). The second is reflective human assessment – philosophy, in short, and political science and jurisprudence – which aspires to *justify* the revised, harnessed, channeled attitudes and policies not just as "natural" but as, well, *just*. You say "it may well be the case that these reactions, though natural, are philosophically unjustified." Yes, it *may be*, but you have not yet given me any reason to think that this is so. This is exactly what I deny.

The Arguments for Free Will Skepticism

Caruso: Perhaps it's time, then, to fully spell out my arguments for free will skepticism. My own reasons for favoring free will skepticism do not depend upon the truth of determinism – I'm officially agnostic about the thesis of universal determinism. Instead, I maintain that the sort of free will required for desert-based moral responsibility is incompatible with *both* causal determination by factors beyond the agent's control *and* with the kind of indeterminacy in action required by the most plausible versions of libertarianism. That is, I maintain that we lack free will *either way*. I argue that since the various rival libertarian and compatibilist accounts all fail to preserve the control in action required for desert-based moral responsibility, the skeptical position remains the only reasonable position left standing. Since my view maintains that free will is incompatible with both determinism and indeterminism, I follow Derk Pereboom in labeling it *hard incompatibilism* so as to distinguish it from traditional *hard determinism*.

Against libertarian accounts of free will, I first distinguish between (a) views that maintain actions are caused solely by way of events, and some type of indeterminacy in the production of actions by appropriate events is held to be a decisive requirement for free will and moral responsibility; and (b) those views that appeal to *sui generis* kinds of agency or causation, where an *agent*, understood as a substance and not just a collection of events, has the power to cause various events (i.e. "free actions") without being causally determined to do so. Against the former view, which is known as *event-causal libertarianism*, I object that on such an account, agents are left unable to *settle* whether a decision occurs and hence cannot have the control in action (i.e. the free will) required for moral responsibility (see Pereboom 2014).

Imagine, for instance, that Farah is torn between two courses of action: (a) attending an important meeting at work tomorrow morning or (b) calling in sick and spending the day with a friend who is in town for just one day. She has good reasons for doing (a) but she also has good reasons for doing (b). Whatever she ends up doing, we can say that it was "intentionally endorsed" and that she had "reasons for doing it," since the action would be consistent with her general wishes, aims, goals, and intentions. If, however, indeterminacy is genuinely involved in the agential causal sequence, then it really is a matter of luck which action she ends up performing. To make vivid the lack of control agents have over genuinely undetermined events, consider what would happen if God rolled back the relevant stretch of history to some point prior to an undetermined event and then allowed it to unfold once more. Since events would *not* unfold in the same way on the replay as they did the first time around, since these are genuinely undetermined, and nothing the agent does (or is) can ensure which undetermined possibility is realized, the outcome of this sequence (in this case the agent's decision) is a matter of luck. Such luck, skeptics argue, is responsibility-undermining.

Against the latter view, which is known as *agent-causal libertarianism*, I argue that while it could, in theory, supply the control in action needed, it cannot be reconciled with our best physical theories about the world, since it requires a questionable notion of causation where an agent, understood as a substance and not just a collection of events, is capable of causing various events without being causally determined to do so. Agent-causal libertarians maintain that it is the agent him- or herself that causes "free" actions, though they, themselves, are causally undetermined by prior events and conditions. Roderick Chisholm, a leading defender of this view, describes this notion of self-determination in the following way:

> If we are responsible, and if what I have been trying to say [about agent causation] is true, then we have a prerogative which some would attribute only to God: each of us, when

we act, is a prime unmoved mover. In doing what we do, we cause certain events to happen and nothing – or no one – causes us to cause those events to happen. (1982: 32)

I think we both agree that there is no way to reconcile this view with our understanding of the natural world characterized by science. The notion of an agent, *qua* substance, capable of being an uncaused cause (or prime unmoved mover), is a magical notion indeed – one that has no place in our naturalistic world.

Dennett: I agree with you, Gregg, that all forms of libertarianism yet devised are "obscure and panicky metaphysics" (as P. F. Strawson once put it), and none of them stands a chance of being harmonized with what we already know from uncontroversial science. I devoted chapter 4 of my book *Freedom Evolves*, "A Hearing for Libertarianism," to the topic, concentrating on Robert Kane's intrepid attempt to sketch out a libertarian model of indeterministic free will (the best I have ever seen). While it has some interesting features, none of them require indeterminism! They do require the type of randomness you get from rolling dice or tossing coins, but that is not indeterministic in the quantum physics sense.

Caruso: Since we both agree, then, that the notion of libertarian free will should be rejected, let me now turn to the heart of our disagreement. Against compatibilism, I offer two distinct arguments. First, I maintain that there is no relevant difference between our actions being causally determined by natural factors beyond our control and our actions being causally determined by manipulators. The basic idea behind this argument is that if an agent is causally determined to act in a particular way by other agents – say, a team of neuroscientists who manipulate the agent's brain – then the agent is intuitively not morally responsible for that action, even if they satisfy all the prominent compatibilist conditions on moral responsibility.

Imagine, for example, that a team of neuroscientists manipulate an agent, let's call her Elizabeth, by means of a device implanted in her brain to kill an acquaintance named Donald. The neuroscientists manipulate her into killing Donald for self-interested reasons on her twenty-first birthday by directly causing in her various wants, desires, beliefs, and intentions via a remote control. (We could also imagine more distant forms of manipulation where instead of manipulating Elizabeth's brain directly, the team of neuroscientists programmed her at the beginning of her life so that her reasoning is often but not always egoistic, and at times strongly so, with the intended consequence that on her twenty-first birthday she is causally determined to engage in an egoistic process of deliberation that results in her decision to kill Donald.) We can also specify that Elizabeth's decision to kill Donald satisfies all the relevant compatibilist conditions. For instance, we can say that it satisfies David Hume's condition: i.e. Elizabeth's decision is not out of character, since for her it is generally true that selfish reasons weigh heavily – too heavily when considered from the moral point of view. In addition, the desire that motivates her to act is nevertheless not irresistible for her, and in this sense she is not constrained to act. The action also meets the compatibilist condition proposed by Harry Frankfurt – i.e. Elizabeth's effective desire (i.e. her will) to murder Donald conforms appropriately to her second-order desire for which effective desire she will have. That is, she wills to murder Donald, and wants to will to do so. In addition, the action satisfies the reasons–responsiveness condition advocated by John Martin Fisher and Mark Ravizza – i.e. Elizabeth's desire can be modified by, and some of them arise from, the rational consideration of her reasons, and if she believed that the bad consequences for herself that would result from killing Donald would be more severe than she actually expects them to be, she would not have decided to kill him. Finally, the action also satisfies the related condition advanced by Jay Wallace – i.e. Elizabeth has the general ability to grasp, apply, and regulate her actions by moral reasons. For instance, when egoistic reasons that count against acting morally are weak, she will typically act for moral reasons instead.

Even if we assume that Elizabeth's inner psychological states are causally efficacious, she does what she wants, she approves of her own behavior, she's moderately responsive to reasons, and she satisfies all the other compatibilist conditions for self-control you want to add, intuitively she would not be morally responsible in a desert-based sense for her criminal act. The argument then continues by maintaining that since such manipulation cases resemble, in the relevant ways, agents in the normal deterministic case – since in both cases, an agent's inner psychological states, reasons for action, and subsequent choices and actions, would be causally determined by factors beyond their control – we must conclude that if agents fail to be morally responsible in cases of manipulation, they also fail to be morally responsible in the normal deterministic case. (Manipulation arguments of this kind have been developed in detail by the likes of Al Mele (1995, 2006), Derk Pereboom (1995, 2001, 2008, 2014), Richard Taylor (1963/1992), Rosen (2002), Patrick Todd (2011, 2013), and many others.)

My second reason for rejecting compatibilism is one we've already discussed in our first exchange. I maintain that regardless of the causal structure of the universe, the pervasiveness of luck undermines the relevant notions of free will and moral responsibility. Following Neil Levy (see his excellent book, *Hard Luck*), I maintain that either actions are subject to *present luck* (luck around the time of action), or they are subject to *constitutive luck* (luck in who one is and what character traits and dispositions one has), or both. Constitutive luck is a problem since our genes, parents, peers, and other environmental influences all contribute to making us who we are, and since we have no control over these, it seems that who we are is at least largely a matter of luck. And since how we act is partly a function of who we are, the existence of constitutive luck entails that what actions we perform depends on luck. Present luck, on the other hand, is problematic since it includes any genuine indeterminism that may exist in the immediate causal chain leading to action, as libertarians posit, as well as any circumstantial or situational influences that may affect an agent's choice or action in a way that is outside their control. We can say that an agent's decision is the result of present luck if a circumstantial factor outside of the agent's control at or near the time of action significantly influences the decision. Such circumstantial factors could include the agent's mood, what reasons happen to come to them, what weight they give those reasons, situational features of the environment, and the like. Since all our morally significant actions are either constitutively lucky, presently lucky, or both, I argue that luck undermines the kind of moral responsibility needed to ground a *system of desert* since it undermines responsibility-level control.

In addition to these two more general arguments against compatibilism, there is one last reason for rejecting your more unique brand of compatibilism, with its forward-looking justification of backward-looking desert. I fear that your account is too instrumentalist about free will to justify the kind of practices you want to preserve, especially legal punishment which causes severe and intentional harm. By saying it's too instrumentalist, I mean that on your account, it seems that our practice of holding agents morally responsible in a desert sense should be retained, not because we are in fact morally responsible in this sense, but because doing so would have the best consequences relative to alternative practices. For instance, in the manipulation case sketched above, I imagine that all the same consequentialist reasons you would give for preserving a system of desert in the face of natural determinism would also favor holding Elizabeth morally responsible in the sense that she would deserve to be blamed and punished for her wrongdoing. But I would argue that this is unfair and unjust, since she does not *truly deserve* to be blamed and punished for her actions, since her decision to kill Donald was the result of factors beyond her control. I would also say the same in the case of natural determinism. I therefore think it beneficial to distinguish between two separate questions: (1) under the assumption of determinism, do agents *actually* have the control in action needed for them to be *truly deserving* of praise and blame, punishment and reward? And (2) under the assumption of determinism, is it *practically beneficial* to hold agents morally responsible in the relevant desert sense? My fear is that you are conflating these two questions, sacrificing the former to the latter. Unfortunately, doing so ends up turning important questions about genuine desert, fairness, and justice, into questions about instrumental value and utility.

Debating the Manipulation Argument

Dennett: Well, there's a lot there for me to work on. I think it best to discuss your three arguments one-by-one, starting with your example of Elizabeth, the manipulated murderer. Well done, Gregg, you've managed to package the whole literature on nefarious neurosurgeons and their manipulations into a couple of clear paragraphs, with the major citations included, giving me a handy target for this long-lived debate. There is one feature of these intuition pumps that is seldom discussed, and that you ignore as well: *whether Elizabeth knows about the manipulators' actions!* I think this is the key feature of all these examples, but you don't tell us. If she does know, if she has been given all the information about her unfortunate past that you have provided for us, then either:

(1) she hasn't had her basic capacity for rational thought destroyed (I guess this is Jay Wallace's "general ability" condition), and hence will be able to reconsider everything in her history and decide *for herself* whether she still approves or not. She can either change her course of action or decide to go ahead with it "of her own free will,"

or:

> (2) the manipulations have somewhat and somehow disabled
> her, preventing her from using her powers of reflection to
> deal with the issue.

In the first case, she acts of her own free will (supposing the thought-experimental situation is as cleanly presented as it must be if it is to count), and in the second case, her responsibility is at least mitigated and perhaps she should be completely exonerated since she has been disabled by other agents who *are* responsible for the murder.

This is not a tangential issue, but it has been oddly overlooked by those philosophers attacking the Frankfurt (1969) problem of the nefarious neurosurgeon, and its many descendants. It's been more than sixty years since a few philosophers and scientists pointed out that a predictor *who gives the prediction to the person whose choice is being predicted* destroys the epistemological warrant for the prediction.* You can't be a manipulator without being a predictor, and hence any manipulator whose presence and activities are known to the target *loses control over* the target's choice, in effect, because of the interaction. It is our ability to *learn* such things and then *act* on them that makes us such a challenge to any would-be controllers. If Elizabeth is informed about the manipulation, she will either call the cops and have them arrested (isn't that what you would do?) and demand that the manipulation devices be promptly removed, or she must have had her cognitive powers somehow disabled. Manipulation of thinking people depends on secrecy. What follows is an intuition pump of mine that turns that knowledge knob.

I am trying to lose weight, and not doing very well, so I pay a kindly neurosurgeon to implant a device in my brain that will act as a safety net: if I ever reach for the donut or

---

* (Versions due to Popper (1951) and MacKay (1960) are discussed in my *Elbow Room* (1984a: 112))

the cupcake (we can let these details vary widely) the neuro-surgeon and her 24/7 team will press the remote button and prevent me from lapsing. This is just like the Frankfurt cases, the Fischer cases, the Ravizza cases, except for my knowledge of the manipulation. Since I *know all this* and in fact put it all into effect myself, when I don't take a donut, I'm acting with prosthetically *enhanced* free will. Suppose further, that I find that the mere knowledge of the implant cures me of my weakness of will, my *akrasia*. They never have to push the button (just as in all the Frankfurt cases). Still, I'm getting good value for my money. Even if it doesn't cure me, it will help me avoid making choices that I don't want to (want to) make. My example fulfills all the conditions of your Elizabeth case and the examples you cite and yields the opposite intuition. I *am* responsible for my abstention whether or not the manipulation I have ordered is required. (Maybe you disagree, but I think you have to admit that it is far from obvious in my example that I am *not* responsible because I have been manipulated, which is the "obvious" intuition the other examples are supposed to pump.)

Here is another intuition pump that makes a somewhat different point about the role of knowledge in free will (drawn from my 2012 Erasmus Lecture: "Sometimes a Spin Doctor is Right"):

Case 1: My doctor, whom I know well, and trust, advises me to eat Bran Blobs for breakfast because it is the best way to lower my cholesterol. The effect of this audiovisual experience is that I go to the supermarket and buy a box of Bran Blobs.

Case 2: In the supermarket, I decide to try a new cereal. Never having heard of Bran Blobs before, I pull a box off the shelf and carefully read all the information on it (highlighted in bright yellow) about the nutritional value and zesty taste of Bran Blobs. Since I recognize that it is produced, according to the label, by a reputable cereal company known for its honesty, I decide to trust the information. I buy a box of Bran Blobs.

Case 3: In the supermarket I spot a box of Bran Blobs on the shelf with a fetching picture of Cameron Diaz on it. I buy a box of Bran Blobs.

Case 4: In the supermarket I approach a box of Bran Blobs which has a secret microchip transponder that tweaks the *nucleus accumbens* in my brain. I buy a box of Bran Blobs.

In each case, various features of the environment and its stimulation of my nervous system *cause me* to buy a box of Bran Blobs. Moreover, in each case, *there is an attempt to influence my choice by other agents*. But while the first two openly exploit my rationality and give me reasons I can endorse (or not) for making the purchase, the next two cases effectively bypass my rationality. Case 3 might be seriously manipulative if it were directed against some truly naive and sheltered person, but I am no babe in the woods; I know all about how companies use sex appeal to sell things, but for years I've been a fan of Cameron Diaz, who is as intelligent as she is beautiful, so I buy it as a souvenir. (If Bran Blobs had a picture of Carl Sagan or David Attenborough on the box, I'd buy half a dozen.) The chief difference between cases 3 and 4 is that in case 4 *I have no idea* that an attempt to manipulate me is occurring. Notice that if the world comes to be infested with such microchip persuaders, we will all be in the market for countermeasures, devices that will detect and disarm the secret manipulators so that we can maintain our integrity as rational agents. There has been for millennia an arms race between persuaders and their targets or intended victims. Folklore is full of tales of innocents being taken in by the blandishments of sharp talkers. This folklore is part of the defense we pass on to our children, so that they will become adept at guarding against it. We don't want our children to become puppets. If philosophers and neuroscientists are saying that it is no use – we are all already puppets, controlled by the environment, they are making a big, and potentially harmful, mistake.

The conclusion you draw from your first argument for rejecting compatibilism depends on the examples that purport to show that there is, as you put it, no "relevant difference" between having manipulation in the background and having some other causal history in the background. My counterexamples show that there is in fact a large and relevant difference. On my view, free will is *primarily* the ability to be self-controlled and to be able to detect efforts by other agents to manipulate you, to take over control and to destroy your autonomy. Control of a human being is actually very difficult (except in philosophers' fantastic thought experiments). If it were routinely possible, we – at least those of us controlled by other agents – would have no free will. But thank goodness, we aren't controlled by such agents, and we aren't controlled by "our past" either, whether it was benign or malign. The past is not an agent and can gather no feedback to aid in its efforts at control.

Caruso: Thank you, Dan. Those examples are very helpful. But I do not think they resolve or refute manipulation arguments against compatibilism for several reasons. For one thing, it's important to distinguish between so-called Frankfurt-style cases – named after Harry Frankfurt (1969) who first introduced them to the literature – and the kind of manipulation case I presented. Frankfurt-style cases are meant to show that the *principle of alternative possibilities* is not a necessary condition for being morally responsible, while the manipulation case I presented was an argument for *source incompatibilism* – which maintains that determinism is incompatible with an agent being the *appropriate source* of their actions or controlling them in the right kind of way.

For those unfamiliar with Harry Frankfurt's famous argument or the kind of *Frankfurt-style* cases they have generated, perhaps a brief summary would be helpful. Although there are numerous versions of Frankfurt-style examples in the literature, such examples typically involve a neuroscientist (or controller) who can make an agent do whatever the neuroscientist wants (perhaps by direct control over the agent's brain), yet the neuroscientist will not intervene if the agent is going to do on their own what the controller wants. In examples of this sort, an agent considers performing some action (say, voting for candidate *A* while standing in the voting booth), but the neuroscientist is concerned that they will not come through (they want the agent to vote for candidate *A* and will intervene, if necessary, to make sure they do). So, if the agent were to manifest an indication that they will not or might not perform the desired action (i.e. voting for *A*), the neuroscientist would intervene. But as things actually go, the neuroscientist remains idle, since the agent performs the desired action on their own. The idea is that even though the agent could not have avoided the action they performed, they are intuitively morally responsible for their action. Many contemporary compatibilists take such examples to show that the *ability to do otherwise* is *not* a necessary condition for moral responsibility.

While I am not convinced that Frankfurt and his followers succeed in refuting the *principle of alternative possibilities*, which states that a person is morally responsible for their action only if they could have done otherwise than they did, I would prefer to avoid that rabbit-hole here if possible. I only mention Frankfurt-style cases to point out that *they are different from the kind of manipulation case I presented.* Frankfurt-cases do not involve any *actual* manipulation, since the neuroscientist never intervenes. The Elizabeth example, on the other hand, does involve direct manipulation since the team of neuroscientists do in fact intervene in the proximate causal chain leading up to her decision to kill Donald. The case is meant to show that if an agent is causally determined to act in a particular way by other agents (i.e. a team of neuroscientists), then the agent is intuitively not morally responsible for that action, even if they satisfy all the prominent compatibilist conditions on moral responsibility. The argument then maintains that since such manipulation cases resemble, in the relevant ways, agents in the normal deterministic case, we must conclude that if agents fail to be morally responsible in cases of manipulation, they also fail to be morally responsible in the normal deterministic case. Now, I know you have responses to that last claim, which I promise to get to in a moment. I just want to flag the fact that your diet example – where a neurosurgeon has implanted a device in your brain that, when triggered, will prevent you from eating donuts and cupcakes, but they "never have to push the button" since you successfully resist eating them on your own – is more akin to a Frankfurt-style case than a manipulation case. Hence, it is not analogous to the kinds of cases I have in mind.

With that clarification in place, let me now turn to your main response. If I understand you correctly, your position is that: *if Elizabeth knows about the manipulators' actions*, then she is indeed morally responsible for her decision to kill Donald (assuming the manipulators have not prevented her from "using her powers of reflection to deal with the issue"). I find this reply odd, however, for three main reasons. First, manipulation cases, as they're typically presented, *assume the agent is not aware that they are being manipulated*. If I did not make that clear in my original statement of the Elizabeth example, then I should have. I therefore think we should consider the argument, at least initially, under that assumption that Elizabeth is unaware. Would your answer shift, then, regarding Elizabeth's moral responsibility if we were to assume that she is *not* aware of the manipulators' actions? If so, wouldn't this result in Elizabeth failing to be morally responsible even though she satisfies all the relevant compatibilist conditions – indicating that those conditions, either individually or collectively, are not sufficient for free will?

Perhaps to prevent this conclusion, you will simply insist on some kind of *awareness* or *knowledge* condition for moral responsibility, requiring that agents be aware of all the relevant information about their past *or* the (nefarious?) causal factors that may be influencing their reasoning and decision-making. Such a condition, however, would lead to a number of additional problems. For instance, can we ever be aware of all the relevant information? And what should we count as "relevant" here? Furthermore, do we only need to be aware of attempts at manipulation, or do we also need to be aware of other causal factors that influence our reasoning and decision-making? If you limit it to the former, isn't that question begging (since it assumes that other deterministic factors are not a threat to free will)? Before I could assess such a condition, I would need for you fully and clearly to spell out what kind of awareness or knowledge you think is required. Since I do not want to put words in your mouth or set up a straw man, I'll leave it to you to provide the details before I respond more fully.

Dennett: My claim is simply that if Elizabeth doesn't know that she's been adjusted somehow by these manipulative agents, then she is not responsible for whatever she does; they are responsible, for she is just a puppet whom they control.

Caruso: Okay, so you agree with me that if Elizabeth is unaware, then she is not responsible in the relevant sense. Great! That's all I was really hoping to show. That said, I will push further since you insist on the importance of knowledge and awareness. I would contend that *even if we assume* that Elizabeth knows about the manipulators' actions, it's not at all clear that this automatically undermines my first argument against compatibilism. Imagine, for instance, that, as before, a team of neuroscientists has implanted a device in Elizabeth's brain. But in this revised version, Elizabeth is aware that the neuroscientists are capable of manipulating her to do as they wish. We can imagine, for instance, that Elizabeth was duped by the team of neuroscientists into having the device implanted in her brain under false pretenses – i.e. they told her it was required for medical purposes. After the surgery, however, the neuroscientists come clean and tell Elizabeth that they can now directly control her brain remotely whenever they want. Unfortunately, Elizabeth does not know when she is being externally manipulated and when she is not. On her twenty-first birthday the team of neuroscientists trigger the device, realizing in Elizabeth a strongly egoistic reasoning process that deterministically results in her decision to kill Donald. As before, we can specify that Elizabeth's decision to kill Donald satisfies all the relevant compatibilist conditions (e.g. her decision is not out of character, she's moderately reasons-responsive, she approves of her decision to kill Donald, and she has the ability to grasp, apply, and regulate her actions by moral reasons, etc.). Is Elizabeth morally responsible in this revised case? My strong intuition is that she is not. If that's correct (and you may wish to challenge that conclusion), then the fact that Elizabeth is aware of the team of neuroscientists is not enough to make her responsible in the relevant sense.

Now, you may reply that what's missing in the above example is *awareness of the right kind*. But then I would again need you to spell out what kind of awareness you think is required for moral responsibility. I see no reason for demanding that Elizabeth also know when the device in her brain is actually activated. In fact, my example more accurately represents real-life cases of manipulation by advertisers, corporations, and the like. In such cases, we are *generally* aware that external agents are attempting to manipulate us into buying various things (etc.), but by no means are we aware of each and every *token* instance. In the real world, we have to live with the general knowledge that people are constantly trying to hack our brains. It would be unrealistic, however, for you to demand that for an agent to be morally responsible they must be aware of each and every attempt at manipulation.

Lastly, even if I granted you everything – i.e. even if we imagined that Elizabeth both knew about the team of neuroscientists *and* that they intervened on her twenty-first birthday – I do not see why this would, on its own, make her morally responsible for her decision to kill Donald. Such a scenario is consistent with the team of neuroscientists externally manipulating Elizabeth into *weighing that additional information* in such a way that she nevertheless "endorses" her decision to kill Donald and takes "ownership" for it, while still satisfying all the leading compatibilist conditions. Under such manipulation, I believe many would share my intuition that Elizabeth should *not* be held morally responsible for her decision to kill Donald – at least not in the sense under debate (i.e. the sense needed for Elizabeth to *justly deserve* blame and punishment). And the reason for this conclusion would be that both Elizabeth's egoistic reasoning process and her higher-order approval and endorsement were the result of factors beyond her control – i.e. the manipulation of the neuroscientists. The problem for the compatibilist, however, is that there is no relevant difference between such cases of manipulation and the normal deterministic case – since in both cases, an agent's inner psychological states, reasoning, and higher-order approval and endorsement, would be causally determined by factors beyond their control. I therefore maintain that we should reject compatibilism, since if agents fail to be morally responsible in cases of manipulation, they also fail to be morally responsible in the normal deterministic case. (Now, I know you will reject the antecedent in the previous sentence, but I just argued that your stated reasons for doing so fail to be convincing. If what I've argued is correct, then we should accept the conclusion of the manipulation argument.)

There is, however, one more move available to you. Instead of attacking the intuition that agents are not morally responsible in the manipulated cases, you could grant that Elizabeth is not morally responsible but then try to differentiate between cases of manipulation and cases of natural determinism. That is, you could argue that there are relevant differences that *would* account for why manipulated agents are not free and morally responsible, but non-manipulated and causally determined agents are. In fact you seem to suggest just such a thing when you write: "The past is not an agent and can gather no feedback to aid in its efforts at control." Here you seem to be suggesting that the relevant difference is that in cases of manipulation there are external agents who act as intentional manipulators, whereas no such agents are involved in cases of natural determinism. There are, however, two things I would say in response to this move. First, it is question begging to assume that this is a relevant difference. Incompatibilists would insist that it is completely irrelevant whether the inner states of the agent which (according to compatibilism) allegedly prompt my "free" activity are evoked by another agent or by perfectly impersonal forces. If free will and moral responsibility are to be compatible with the determination of our actions by factors beyond our control, as compatibilists maintain, it shouldn't matter whether those factors are personal or impersonal.

Second, while it is indeed correct that most extant manipulation cases involve external agents who act as intentional manipulators, new manipulation cases can be devised that avoid external agents altogether. For instance, imagine the following case:

> **Brain-Implant Malfunction Case:** Imagine that Elizabeth*
> has a device implanted in her brain for medical purposes
> (e.g. to control seizures or trembling due to Parkinson's dis-
> ease), not for the purpose of manipulation. When operating
> normally, the device does not affect Elizabeth*'s reasoning.
> One day the device malfunctions and ends up triggering in
> Elizabeth* an egoistic process that deterministically results
> in her decision to kill Donald. And it does so in a way that
> satisfies all the prominent compatibilist conditions (e.g. her
> decision is not out of character, she's moderately reasons-
> responsive, she approves of her decision to kill Donald, and
> she has the ability to grasp, apply, and regulate her actions
> by moral reasons, etc.). Here we have a case of accidental
> manipulation due to a malfunctioning device implanted in

Elizabeth*'s brain. (We could easily imagine variations on this case, where the triggering of the device was the result of a cat walking across a keyboard that remotely controlled the implanted device.)

The above case provides an example of a manipulated agent who is determined to commit a criminal action *without external agents acting as intentional manipulators*. And it would not aid the compatibilist to reply that since the device was intentionally implanted the case fails, since the fact that the device was intentionally implanted (for medical purposes) in no way undermines the main philosophical point: the malfunctioning of the device, and the subsequent manipulation, was *not* the result of external agents acting as intentional manipulators. Hence, the presence of intentional manipulation by external agents cannot be the relevant difference.

Dennett: First, let me say that once again you do an excellent job of categorizing all the different "moves" philosophers have made in dealing with both Frankfurt-style cases (where there is no *current* manipulation but just *secret* manipulation in the agent's past, setting up the implant) and cases where there *is* current manipulation. And then you nicely illustrate the process by which philosophers typically proceed in this literature: making more *intuition pumps* (Dennett 2013a): revising and pruning and shoring up their examples until they think they have closed all the loopholes and satisfied the ultimate test of their view: their *intuitions*. (But where did these intuitions come from? Why do philosophers have them? What grounds and explains those intuitions? That's what I'm trying to explain.) This leads you eventually to confront the issue I said has been routinely ignored: what Elizabeth knows and what effect this has on the case.

Let me begin by providing a bit more background on why I think this is the key mistake being made in this philosophical debate. (I don't *assume* that there is a difference between manipulation cases and ordinary determination cases. I argue for the difference, and I'll spell it out further now.) Stones and mountains and tides are not agents; bacteria, trees, wolves, chimps and human beings are agents; *all living things* are agents of one sort or another, and part of what distinguishes them from non-agents is that they are equipped (by natural selection) with *competences* that enhance their survival chances by *exploiting information* they are equipped to gather from the barrage of external stimulation raining down on them. Among organisms, the members of one species only, *H. sapiens*, have language, which *multiplies their self-control competences by many orders of magnitude.* Our general term for the normal level of competence human beings achieve is *comprehension* (for an extended discussion, see *From Bacteria to Bach and Back* (2017)). Chemists don't have to whisper in the lab about what tests they are running on their materials, and psychologists doing experiments with fruit flies or chimpanzees or dolphins don't have to be careful not to discuss in the presence of their subjects the manipulations they are planning or the effects they hope to discover on the dependent variables. But human subjects have to be treated with extreme care, to keep them "naive" and uninformed about the point of the manipulations they have agreed to undergo. Why? Because, as I pointed out earlier: if you give a human subject information about your manipulations or predictions, the subject is *no longer in your control.* Why not? Because the subject can not only reflect on the reasons for cooperating or not with you, but also consult other advisors, other sources of information over which you (unless you are an omnipotent and omniscient god) have no control and scant knowledge.

This has nothing to do with determinism. It is a straightforward implication of the "definition" of a well-functioning human agent. I put "definition" in scare quotes because there are, of course, lots of penumbral cases, where it isn't clear whether a particular human being *comprehends* what he/she is doing, or is competent *enough* to be held responsible, and this is just one more case where Darwinian gradualism throws a monkey wrench into philosophical arguments:

the attempt to define, as you demand of me, a complete list of "relevant factors" is as forlorn as the project of giving a counter-example-proof definition of a mammal. So instead of trying to list all the relevant conditions, I will describe the principle that generates them.

Part of the social contract, in effect, is that in return for political freedom – the right to move freely and form associations and expect the security and stability needed to engage in projects, for instance – human agents are obliged to protect their autonomy, by keeping an eye out for would-be puppeteers, manipulators who would usurp control and *destroy their responsibility*. Nobody is born morally responsible; it is an achievement that normally is assisted by rearing: the moral education provided by parents, peers, teachers, and the rest of society, its literature and entertainment, etc. There is no bell that rings when someone achieves the right level, so we have to have laws that ring artifactual bells, for instance in setting a minimum age for the freedom to consent to sex, drive a car, buy alcohol, vote ... These are arbitrary but movable by political persuasion and action as we learn more about human competences. When senility arises, we painfully and reluctantly *demote* people who no longer have the competence to protect themselves and others from would-be manipulators. Note that an ineliminable part of the rationale for these laws (and the unspoken moral codes and norms that lie behind them) is that *comprehension matters*. We are not born responsible, or guaranteed to maintain our responsibility throughout life, but once we are responsible we are *held* responsible for protecting that responsibility.

Now, if Elizabeth comprehends her situation, if she has not had her cognitive powers diminished by the manipulation, and if she knows the extent and likelihood of the manipulative influences on her, then if she does *not* resist the resulting urges, she is complicit in her wrongdoing, and deserves to be punished. (Otherwise the manipulators alone are the murderers and should be punished.) She knew better, and chose to act, and no other agent was in control of her. And her decision was *not* "due to factors beyond her control." Since this claim goes to the heart of the matter, I want to spell it out in a bit more detail. In our first debate, I quoted Ricky Skaggs: "I can't control the wind, but I can adjust the sails." He was noting that while there were many factors that had a bearing on his predicament over which he had no control, he *did* – thanks to other factors beyond his control – have control of the sailboat he was piloting. Since he'd learned to sail presumably (we may doubt this – a seasoned sailor would probably have said "I can *trim* the sails.") he had a competence that gave him control in this circumstance. Even if I grant that he became a competent sailor thanks to circumstances beyond his control, he was then able, lucky him, to trim the sails and control the boat. Similarly, if Elizabeth is cognitively intact and well informed about the manipulations, she can say, truly, "I can't control their efforts at manipulation, but I can try to anticipate and thwart them and if they think they have control of me, they're deluded." You and other free will skeptics make much of the fact that if we go back far enough we will find that her capacities for self-control were due to circumstances beyond her control. I claim that this does *not* show that she is not in control now, and it does not show that the nefarious neuroscientists can control her. They can't, unless they are practically omniscient and omnipotent.

As I said in our first exchange, philosophers have generally failed to notice the difference between causation and control. What is the important difference between being distracted from the thinking task you have set yourself by a beautiful sunset and being distracted from the thinking task you have set yourself by a YouTube video of a beautiful sunset? The latter is caused by a *controller*, a would-be puppeteer; the former just happens to happen. We are indeed responsible for improving and maintaining our undistractability (by sunsets, crowd noise, and our own daydreams, for instance), but we recognize that deliberate and persistent attempts by agents to capture our attention and thereby control us (to some degree) are particularly to be guarded against. Moreover, when they succeed, they are suitable entities for being held responsible. We get to pass the buck! Don't try to blame your automobile accident on the sunset, but if your GPS (which you glance at briefly periodically) were suddenly to display a few seconds of pornographic video that would distract almost anybody, you could well blame the GPS company and pass most of the moral responsibility to them. (And, Gregg, to deal with your example of the malfunctioning manipulation device, Elizabeth would indeed be absolved from responsibility, but the device manufacturers would not be. If it was deliberate, they are criminals and if it was due to poor design, they would be liable for the failure of the device; it might amount to criminal negligence.)

I claimed above that nobody is born morally responsible, so let me pause to short-circuit an argument that is often advanced at this point, most recently by Galen Strawson, who calls it the Basic Argument against "absolute free will and moral responsibility" (Strawson 2010):

(1) You do what you do – in the circumstances in which you find yourself – because of the way you then are.
(2) So, if you're going to be ultimately responsible for what you do, you're going to have to be ultimately responsible for the way you are – at least in certain mental respects.
(3) But you can't be ultimately responsible for the way you are in any respect at all.
(4) So, you can't be ultimately responsible for what you do.

The key move is (3). Why can't you be ultimately responsible for the way you are in any respect at all? In answer, consider an expanded version of the argument.

(a) It's undeniable that the way you are initially is a result of your genetic inheritance and early experience.
(b) It's undeniable that these are things for which you are not in any way responsible (morally or otherwise).

(c) But you can't at any later stage of life hope to acquire true or ultimate moral responsibility for the way you are by trying to change the way you already are as a result of genetic inheritance and previous experience.

(d) Why not? Because both the particular ways in which you try to change yourself, and the amount of success you have when trying to change yourself, will be determined by how you already are as a result of your genetic inheritance and previous experience.

(e) And any further changes that you may become able to bring about after you have brought about certain initial changes will in turn be determined, via the initial changes, by your genetic inheritance and previous experience.

Where's the fallacy in this argument? Strawson, like Pereboom and many other philosophers, insists on defining a notion of *ultimate* or *absolute* responsibility. As soon as you abandon "basic or ultimate" responsibility and consider the concept of partial or *sorta* responsibility (to use the term I champion in *Intuition Pumps*), everything falls into place. As we grow up we all begin just as Strawson says, as not responsible for anything at all – not even sorta responsible. It's the luck of the draw. As we mature, however, and become more competent, we are (normally) *held* responsible for *some* aspects of our own behavior. We are not (yet) even sorta responsible, our parents might grant, for being *held* responsible in this way, but we'll grow into it. Think of a thirteen-year-old boy who is asked to babysit his toddler sibling for an hour, for instance.

As you grow into responsibility, your *own actions* (for which you are now sorta responsible) become a larger and larger part of the causal background, the R&D that makes you you. You are not that imaginary being, the *causa sui*, or absolutely self-created thing, but you're something in the neighborhood; a *partially* self-made person, a person who has put a considerable amount of action – practice, practice, practice

– and reflection into refining and improving the child you were into the adult you are. In the same way we hold you responsible for any damage done by the model airplane you design, build, and fly under remote control, we hold you responsible for any damage you do more directly, with the body you have been learning how to control. You are not *absolutely* your own author, but you are more than the co-author of many of your aspirations, projects, attitudes, traits, dispositions, and weaknesses. You are also responsible for *not* having taken more care to improve yourself – by your own lights. *Blame me* if I forget to meet you at the promised time because I haven't taken your advice to set my alarm. My bad, as one says. But why blame me, if I "could not have done otherwise"? As Sarah Hladikova, a student of mine, put it in her essay the other day, "I could not have done otherwise, but I will certainly do otherwise the next time." One's self-creation does not end with one's initiation into adulthood.

To be sure, some unfortunate people are not good at this self-maturing process for reasons over which they have no control. If they are really defective, we don't hold them morally responsible at all. And yes, many of them have had terrible childhoods for which they were not at all responsible, but it is worth reminding ourselves that in some cases – maybe most cases – the very hardships and injustices and assaults they endured *hastened* their achievement of self-control and responsibility. The fifteen-year-old girl who was abandoned by her parents to care for her younger siblings for several years by herself is very likely to be a more responsible and reliable babysitter than the fifteen-year-old girl who has had a pony and a wise *au pair* in addition to kind and attentive parents.

I find it hard to believe that philosophers want to smother such important differences under the general metaphysical claim that if determinism is true, nobody is ever responsible for anything. I view that conclusion as a *reductio ad absurdum* of the very idea of ultimate responsibility, alongside David Sanford's comical proof that there are no mammals: every mammal has a mammal for a mother (that's *essential* or by definition), but there have not been an infinity of mammals, so there aren't any (discussed by me in *Consciousness Explained* (1991) and elsewhere). This is that old philosophical chestnut, the *sorites* or *heap* paradox, put to yet another (mis-)use: one grain of sand does not make a heap; adding a grain of sand to something that is not a heap does not turn it into a heap, so two grains of sand are not a heap . . . (repeat until bored).

Gregg, let me save you the effort of scouting out the further escape hatches: what if Elizabeth is *too busy* to reflect on her discoveries about her puppeteers, or what if she makes a huge goof, and just fails to appreciate the import of her new discoveries, or . . . We are familiar with many cases of this sort in the real world. You say at one point, "It would be unrealistic, however, for you to demand that for an agent to be morally responsible they must be aware of each and every attempt at manipulation." Indeed, it would be, but it is not unrealistic to demand that people *do their best* to thwart them, and to heed the best information on such topics. Who was *culpably ignorant* of the implications of the coronavirus reports coming out of the intelligence services in January 2020? There is no metaphysical or neurophysiological set of facts that could answer such a question. It is rather a matter of our deciding – ultimately a political decision – how strict we want to be in *holding* each other responsible. In the past, presidents have typically acknowledged and stoutly declared their responsibility for accidents, failures of anticipation, and ignorance of relevant factors ("I should have known."). We must not get used to the idea that moral responsibility is an obsolete concept.

Caruso: Dan, there's a lot there for me to respond to. Perhaps it's best if I just limit myself to making a few specific points. First, on your way of framing things, manipulation cases, like the Elizabeth example, can never satisfy all the relevant compatibilist conditions on action, since you insist that

Elizabeth be aware of the implant and the neuroscientists' nefarious activities *and* you insist that such information makes Elizabeth immune to manipulation (otherwise she lacks compatibilist control). Well, that's convenient! Of course, if you refuse to admit that manipulation cases are possible, even in the hypothetical sense philosophers want to use them, then we cannot appeal to such examples as an intuition pump to help clarify our intuitions in the natural case of determinism. But I thought the point of such "thought experiments" was to allow for there to be some stipulation of the facts. As such, the Elizabeth example states that Elizabeth satisfies all the relevant compatibilist conditions on free will and moral responsibility, and I've offered revisions of the case to explain how this can be so. Unfortunately, I think the entire discussion about knowledge of one's manipulation has distracted us from the core issue. If under the assumption of normal determinism, we knew the mechanisms of neural or physical causal influences on our actions, and had the ability to counteract them, then it's open that we'd be responsible for our actions despite those influences. *But in real life, we do not know about nor have the ability to counteract neural and physical influences.* That's why the Elizabeth case was originally structured as it was – i.e. Elizabeth doesn't know how she is being manipulated and does not have the ability to counteract the manipulation. As a result, the Elizabeth case and the ordinary case of determinism are relevantly similar, and the lack of responsibility in the former transfers to the latter. Would you agree that in the ordinary deterministic case, where we're not aware of how we're causally determined, agents are not morally responsible in the desert sense?

Dennett: Not at all. Your italicized sentence above is just false. In real life we responsible adults *do* have the ability to counteract neural and physical influences, and the obligation to keep vigilant about them and take reasonable steps to protect our puppet strings from others. (That's one of the points of my Bran Blobs intuition pump.) So, what I say is not just convenient; it's true. I don't think you and the other manipulation-imaginers have thought carefully enough about your own examples. There is a huge difference, as I have observed, between agents and non-agents, and another huge difference between adult human beings and all children and animals, no matter how clever they are. Normal adult human beings comprehend, and hence there is the option of *informing them* about efforts to predict and control them, and if they are so informed, this makes them *uncontrollable* by the manipulators – unless the manipulators bypass the intended victim's cognitive talents in one way or another. And in what you call "ordinary deterministic cases" (with no manipulators involved), it is quite normal for people to have ordinary confidence that they have not been secretly manipulated, and rightly so. Their past total history is, in a very strained and uninformative sense, "the cause" of who they are now, but this doesn't go any way at all to showing that they are not *now* responsible for being the responsible, self-controlled people they take themselves to be.

Caruso: While there's a sense in which I can agree with you, Dan, that we can sometimes "counteract neural and physical influences," you *also* have to admit that (under the assumption of determinism) whatever ability we have to counteract them would *itself be causally determined*. Let's say I'm addicted to chocolate, and so whenever there's chocolate in the house I end up eating it all. We can say that my desire for chocolate is due to various neural and physical influences (e.g. how the addictive properties of the chocolate affect my brain chemistry, all the chocolate commercials I see on TV, etc.). One day, however, I decide to join Chocoholics Anonymous. After attending a bunch of Chocoholics' meetings, I eventually gain the ability to resist my desire for chocolate. On your account, this successful exercise of self-control would make me morally responsible in the praiseworthy and blameworthy sense. I, on the other hand, would argue that, while there is a degree of self-control present here that is absent in those cases where my addiction to chocolate is left unchecked, such self-control is not sufficient to ground desert-based judgments of praise and blame. What I would want to know is the following: *where did the second-order desire to stop desiring chocolate come from*? Since compatibilists retain the assumption of determinism in order to reconcile it with free will, they would have to admit that *that* desire *itself* would have been causally determined by factors beyond my control – e.g. the cumulative effects of advice from my doctor, comments made by my wife about my weight, things I read in the newspaper, etc. So, when I say that determined agents, like manipulated agents, lack the control in action required for desert-based moral responsibility, what I'm saying is that they have no direct control over those proximate and distal causes that determine how they will ultimately deliberate and act. I do not deny that they have self-control in your sense. Instead, I argue that your sense is not the relevant sense when it comes to determining whether agents *deserve* to be praised and blamed, rewarded and punished for their action (in either the basic or non-basic sense). The manipulation argument and the luck arguments (which I'm sure we'll get back to eventually) are meant to show why.

Second, you go on to claim that there is "a huge difference . . . between agents and non-agents." I completely agree. But with regard to the manipulation argument, incompatibilists, like myself, would insist that it is completely irrelevant whether the inner psychological states of the agent, which causally determine my putatively "free" action, are themselves causally determined by another agent or by perfectly impersonal forces. As I said earlier, "If free will and moral responsibility are to be compatible with the determination of our actions by factors beyond our control, as compatibilists maintain, it shouldn't matter whether those factors are personal or impersonal." To insist that this distinction *is* the relevant difference would be question begging. I also introduced the Brain-Implant Malfunction Case as an example of a manipulated agent who is determined to commit a criminal action *without external agents acting as intentional manipulators*. Your reaction to that case was to agree that "Elizabeth would indeed be absolved from responsibility." But I think it's problematic for you (and other compatibilists) to admit that, since the case is designed such that Elizabeth *satisfies all the relevant compatibilist conditions*. By admitting that Elizabeth is not morally responsible in such circumstances, you are effectively admitting that those compatibilist conditions, viewed individually or collectively, are *not sufficient* for moral responsibility.

Dennett: We do have a fundamental disagreement here, Gregg. You agree that some agents have self-control in my sense, but argue that my sense "is not the relevant sense when it comes to determining whether agents *deserve* to be praised and blamed . . ." I've made the case for the moral relevance of "my" sense – which is the sense anchored in control theory and, more importantly, in the everyday decisions and distinctions we make when evaluating our own and others' behavior. If my drone crashes into your windshield, making you *lose control* and kill a pedestrian, you are not morally responsible; I am – unless I had also *lost control* of my drone due to circumstances *beyond my control* (it's the drone manufacturer's fault). We are responsible for what we control, which normally includes the actions of our bodies and we know that we will justly deserve the praise and blame (and reward and punishment) rightly assigned to the outcomes. This principle is independent of both determinism and its denial. I haven't seen any account of *your* sense of self-control, so I cannot judge whether it plays a more fundamental role in desert.

Caruso: While you may have "made the case for the moral relevance" of your sense of self-control, I have argued that you have not *successfully* made the case. I've attempted to show this by arguing that manipulated agents can satisfy *your* sense of control, yet fail to be morally responsible in the all-important desert sense. In fact, you seem to admit as much, at least in the case where Elizabeth is not aware that she is being manipulated and in the Brain-Implant Malfunction Case. Your main reply has been to insist that if Elizabeth were made aware of the neuroscientists' nefarious activities, then she would either be immune to their manipulation or fail to satisfy your compatibilist sense of control. But I'm not even sure that reply succeeds. Let me explain why.

Even if I were to play your game, which seems rigged from the start, it's not at all clear that awareness alone resolves the problem. You write: "Now if Elizabeth has not had her cognitive powers diminished by the manipulation, and if she knows the extent and likelihood of the manipulative influences on her, then if she does *not* resist the resulting urges, she is complicit in her wrongdoing, and deserves to be punished." The reason I don't find this reply satisfying is that it brushes aside (or views as irrelevant) the *source* of Elizabeth's desire or decision to *resist or not resist* the strongly egoistic reasoning process that was triggered by the team of external manipulators. As I said in my previous comments, even if Elizabeth is aware of what the external manipulators are up to, this is still "consistent with the team of neuroscientists externally manipulating Elizabeth into *weighing that additional information* in such a way that she nevertheless 'endorses' her decision to kill Donald and takes 'ownership' for it, while still satisfying all the leading compatibilist conditions." Imagine, for instance, that the team of neuroscientists trigger in Elizabeth *two distinct* states: (1) an egoistic reasoning process, and (2) a general apathy toward the actions of the neuroscientists, and that *together* those interventions deterministically result in Elizabeth's decision to kill Donald. Furthermore, we can imagine that Elizabeth's externally manipulated apathy (i.e. her lack of interest in, or concern for, the information regarding the neuroscientists), and her externally manipulated egoistic reasons for killing Donald, continue to satisfy all the prominent compatibilist conditions (e.g. her decision is not out of character, she's moderately reasons-responsive, she approves of her decision to kill Donald, she approves of her decision to weigh the information regarding the neuroscientists as she does, and she has the ability to grasp, apply, and regulate her actions by moral reasons, etc.). Here, I contend, we have an example that satisfies your demand that Elizabeth be informed about the neuroscientist's activities, yet (given the nature of the manipulation) Elizabeth would intuitively *not be accountable* for her decision to kill Donald – or so I would argue.

Now, I know you want to resist that conclusion and insist that, *even in this case*, Elizabeth has the control in action required for free will and moral responsibility. But I think your reasons for saying that are driven by a different set of intuitions. If I'm correct about your order of reasoning, your starting point is the conviction that agents *must* be free and morally responsible in the desert sense since society would fail to function properly if we relinquished that belief. You then proceed to argue that if manipulated agents, like Elizabeth, satisfy all the same conditions agents are required to satisfy in the case of natural determinism (according to compatibilists like yourself), then they too must be free and morally responsible in the desert sense. I, on the other hand, begin with examples like Elizabeth, so as to clarify our intuitions in a situation where it is clear that an agent's inner psychological states are causally determined by factors beyond their control (i.e. a team of external manipulators), and then I extend those intuitions to the case of natural determinism. Given our different starting points, it's not surprising that we come to different conclusions. But I tend to think your order of reasoning begs the question, since it begins by taking our normal moral responsibility practices as given (presumably because you find them essential), and then uses that stubborn belief in the moral responsibility system (to borrow a phrase from my friend Bruce Waller) to direct our thinking in manipulation cases like the Elizabeth example. I'll leave it to readers to decide which form of reasoning is more persuasive.

Dennett: You claim my analysis of the case "brushes aside (or considers irrelevant) the *source* of Elizabeth's desire or decision to *resist or not resist* the strongly egoistic reasoning process that was triggered by the team of external manipulators." I want to italicize two different words in your response: "*the* source . . ." and "*triggered*." What makes you think the actions of the manipulators are *the* source, and not just one of hundreds of sources of her decision to resist or not resist? If they can prevent her from listening to contrary advisors, for instance, they are disabling her rational abilities. Perhaps the manipulators can initiate ("trigger") a trajectory to Elizabeth's thinking (like firing a gun) but once you've fired a gun, the bullet *is no longer in your control*. It is a ballistic missile, not a guided missile. You have no feedback from the wind, the movement of the target, etc., that you can exploit to adjust that trajectory. In the case of Elizabeth, the same *inability to control* is magnified by many orders of magnitude (provided that she is allowed to go on thinking, an activity that has millions of degrees of freedom). You have now added manipulated *apathy* to the Elizabeth case, as if it weren't a sort of impairment of her system of self-control. This is to cut back, by stipulation, her degrees of freedom of thought. If somebody faced with the choice to murder someone was so apathetic she could not be bothered to review the pros and cons with some thoughtfulness – and wasn't surprised by her own apathy in the face of such a dire decision, and was unbothered by learning of her manipulators' activities, then the manipulators have definitely impaired her. Your latest version of Elizabeth is particularly useful, then, because all your "improvements" to the other nefarious neurosurgeon intuition pumps actually highlight the growing impossibility of such interventions, once the details are spelled out. (See Liam Clegg (2012) for arguments examining the prospects from the perspective of game theory.) Your goal is to construct an example "still satisfying all the leading compatibilist conditions." If it does satisfy them, so what? It doesn't satisfy my conditions, which I have defended in detail here.

You preface your last point by saying "If I'm correct about your order of reasoning . . ." but you are not. I do *argue* that my *non-basic* (you might say) concept of desert is both grounded in consequentialist considerations, and that your *basic* concept is at best only "intuitive" – grounded only in tradition. So, I am not begging the question. You say that your order of reasoning, in contrast, begins "with examples like Elizabeth, so as to clarify our intuitions in a situation where it is clear that an agent's inner psychological states are causally determined by factors beyond their control," and I am claiming that in doing this you are making a plain factual error: it is not "clear that an agent's inner psychological states are causally determined by factors beyond their control." Not only is it not clear; it is not, in general, true. There is, in fact, a tension or perhaps even a contradiction in your use of the term "beyond their control." Is there ever *anything*, according to you, that *is* in a controller's control? According to your argument, nefarious neurosurgeons *are* in control of Elizabeth. How can that be? Are neurosurgeons superhuman? (They do tend to have big egos, in my experience.)

You use Elizabeth's bizarre plight to argue for the conclusion, as you put it earlier: ". . . we should reject compatibilism, since if agents fail to be morally responsible in cases of manipulation, they also fail to be morally responsible in the normal deterministic case." If Elizabeth is not in control ever, then how can the nefarious neurosurgeons be exempt from the iron chains of their own pasts? If neurosurgeons can control her thoughts, why can't she control them herself – to some degree? The conclusion to the notorious Consequence Argument* of van Inwagen and others seems

---

* Although there are many different formulations of the Consequence Argument, we can follow van Inwagen in stating the basic idea as follows: "If determinism is true, then our acts are the consequence of the laws of nature and events in the remote past. But it is not up to us what went on before we were born; and neither is it up to us what the laws of

to me to imply that there isn't anything, ever, that is in control of anything. If you buy this conclusion, then simplify your argument: people don't have free will because nothing is ever in anybody's control, not their limbs, not their cars, nothing. Not really. Is that, then, your position? If not, you should give us a positive account of when an agent is in control of something.

Caruso: Let me briefly recap the dialogue thus far: In response to the manipulation argument against compatibilism, you insisted that Elizabeth (the manipulated agent) must be aware of the neuroscientists' nefarious activities *and* that this information makes Elizabeth immune to their manipulation (otherwise she lacks compatibilist control). I then presented you with a counterexample, one where Elizabeth *is aware* of the neuroscientists' activities and *nonetheless remains subject to manipulation*. Your reply to my counterexample is now to deny that this is possible. You write:

> You have now added manipulated *apathy* to the Elizabeth case, as if it weren't a sort of impairment of her system of self-control. This is to cut back, by stipulation, her degrees of freedom of thought. If somebody faced with the choice to murder someone was so apathetic she could not be bothered to review the pros and cons with some thoughtfulness – and wasn't surprised by her own apathy in the face of such a dire decision, and was unbothered by learning of her manipulators' activities, then the manipulators have definitely impaired her.

I have two replies to this. First, a general apathy toward certain information – or, more accurately, deciding to weigh that information less heavily than other considerations – need not be, and often is not, an impairment. *If it were*, that would

---

nature are. Therefore, the consequence of these things (including our present acts) are not up to us" (1983: 16).

seem to imply that anything less than perfectly rational deliberation (judged by whom? I do not know) would count as an impairment. That cannot be your view! On that standard, everyone who commits a crime would fail to be morally responsible, since they would have failed to be moved by the *right sorts of moral considerations* (a conclusion I think you want to avoid). In fact, isn't everyone who commits a violent crime (too?) apathetic to the relevant social and legal norms? The world is full of people making bad decisions. In my estimate, every single person who voted for Donald Trump failed to properly weigh the available information in front of them. Does that mean they all lacked compatibilist control since they were impaired? If not, then the fact that the neuroscientists cause Elizabeth to weigh the relevant information in a way that is suboptimal, when judged from the perspective of morality, does not itself mean she is impaired or fails to satisfy the relevant compatibilist conditions.

Second, are you suggesting that a counterexample along the lines I propose is *not* possible, even in principle? Or are you simply suggesting that such manipulation is not *easy* or *common* in real-life situations? If it's the latter, then sure. Fine. But that does not refute the argument. On the issue of control, itself, will you at least grant me that Elizabeth exercises no direct control over the neuroscientists when they cause in her the states and processes that deterministically result in her decision to kill Donald? Elizabeth's lack of control over the neuroscientists, I would argue, is analogous to the lack of control we have in the case of natural determinism when our inner psychological states are the result of events in the remote past and the laws of nature.

Dennett: Recall the joke about the philosophers who say "We know that it's possible *in practice*; we're trying to figure out if it's possible *in principle!*" I am suggesting that while it may be possible in the philosophers' sense of *consistently conceivable*, it is not possible in an important sense: if Elizabeth knows the facts about her implants and their powers, and if her normal human capabilities for rational reflection and inquiry are not impaired (a huge condition, of course) then her would-be manipulators would have no more likelihood of controlling her thought than of controlling the flip of a fair coin. If information is deliberately concealed from her, then she is not responsible; she is a puppet, through no fault of her own. If she doesn't notice the manipulators' intrusions because she is not up-to-date on the latest technological threats to autonomy, then she may be *culpably* ignorant, in which case she would share in the responsibility for the death, but perhaps not be considered an accomplice, more a useful fool. If there was no reasonable way for her to learn of her high-tech puppethood, then she is not, as your intuitions proclaim, morally responsible for what she does. You say, "They need only cause in her various reasoning processes ..." *Only?* Without dementing her in any way? Without preventing her from seeking advice? Perhaps you would like to borrow my perpetual-motion machine to power the manipulators' technology. Of course, if they surreptitiously shield her from all sources of contrary information or render certain reasonable trains of thought to strike her with revulsion, she is still a puppet. And remember, the past is not a team of high-tech puppeteers exploiting oceans of feedback to redirect their projectile. *It* does not control her, so in cases of what you call "natural" or "ordinary" determinism (determinism without manipulator agents), she is not a puppet.

Sam Harris, in his book *Free Will,* came up with his dismissive definition of compatibilism: "A puppet is free as long as he loves his strings." I have adopted his sentence and reinterpreted it as indeed a pretty good definition of free will. What we teach our children (and what Elizabeth knows, if she isn't damaged by the manipulation) is that if you are lucky enough to be a responsible agent, you have an obligation to *love your strings*, protecting them from would-be puppeteers. A wonderful old cartoon perfectly captures the idea of a happy autopuppet who loves his strings.

You may still be unconvinced. Do I really think that I, for

W Miller

Figure 2 Warren Miller, *New Yorker*, 1963

instance, could combat all efforts by nefarious neuroscientists to manipulate me? Of course not, if they took steps to conceal their manipulations from me. But if they share with me all the information they have about the steps they are taking to wrest control of me, I am confident that *unless they disable me from thinking clearly*, it will be child's play for me to take the obvious steps to foil their evil deeds. I'll arrange to remove the gadgets and walk away, a free auto-puppet. (Note that I am not succumbing to the philosopher's temptation to mount a formal argument along the lines of "An agent is mentally disabled (by definition) if . . . and autonomous

agents (by definition) know all the forces impinging on them
. . ." This isn't Euclidean geometry; it is about concrete phenomena that have lots of penumbral cases.)

Caruso: I'm not sure I have anything new to add to what
I've already said, Dan, especially since you want to insist
that manipulation cases are "not possible in an important
sense." I'll simply reiterate what I said earlier: "on your way
of framing things, manipulation cases, like the Elizabeth
example, can never satisfy all the relevant compatibilist conditions on action since you insist that Elizabeth be aware of
the implant and the neuroscientists' nefarious activities *and*
you insist that such information makes Elizabeth immune to
manipulation (otherwise she lacks compatibilist control)." I
think this is an uncharitable way to approach manipulation
cases. Manipulation cases are no more or less possible than
Frankfurt-style cases or any other philosophical thought
experiment. Furthermore, I've offered you a case where (1)
Elizabeth *is aware* of the neuroscientists' activities, (2) *she
nonetheless remains subject to manipulation*, and (3) she continues to satisfy all the relevant compatibilist conditions. While
you may want to deny that such a case is possible (at least
in "an important sense"), I see no non-question-begging
reason for prohibiting it as an intuition pump against which
the intuitive appeal and coherence of compatibilism can be
tested. That said, I see no benefit in continuing to debate
the matter. We've each had more than ample time to make
our case. It's time to move on. Perhaps we should turn to
my second argument against compatibilism, the one based
on luck?

Debating the Charge of Instrumentalism

Dennett: Before we turn to your second argument, I'd like
to dispose of your third point about my "instrumentalism"
because my answer fits quite well right here. You explain:

"By saying it is too instrumentalist, I mean that on your account, it seems that our practice of holding agents morally responsible in a desert sense should be retained, not because we are in fact morally responsible in this sense, but because doing so would have the best consequences relative to alternative practices." No, this misinterprets my position in a way that should be easy to make clear. I don't accept your "basic-desert" sense at all, as I've said, so I am not making the "instrumentalist" or (some would say) "fictionalist" proposal that we should, as it were, *pretend* to hold people responsible in *that* sense (because this would have good consequences), but should hold them *actually responsible* in the non-intrinsic, non-absolute sense I have defended because they *really are* responsible in that sense. Now if you are tempted to play the card that distinguishes *holding* people responsible from their *really* being responsible, let me point out that this is just the sort of appeal to "basic" or "absolute" or "intrinsic" responsibility I am criticizing as a philosophical inflation. A dollar doesn't have any intrinsic or basic or absolute value, but it definitely has value, real value, *in virtue of the role it plays in our economy.* Moral responsibility is similarly not "intrinsic" moral responsibility; it is dependent on the rolling, dynamical consensus of the society, just the way the value of a dollar is. We can devise steps to inflate or deflate its importance. I take you and the other moral skeptics to be arguing, whether you realize it or not, in favor of deflating the importance of responsibility in this non-intrinsic sense. I think we agree that intrinsic moral responsibility is a philosophers' mistake. So, what is the issue?

Caruso: First, let me say that I do *not* agree that the notion of basic-desert moral responsibility is a "philosophers' mistake." Far from it. My view has always been, both here and elsewhere, that basic-desert moral responsibility is what is of central philosophical and practical importance in the free will debate. What we *did* agree to (correct me if I'm wrong) is that "compatibilist control is not enough to preserve basic-desert moral responsibility." On that we agree. Hence, when it comes to the kind of free will needed for basic-desert moral responsibility, I consider us *both* free will skeptics. But just as one could be an atheist about the Judeo-Christian conception of God and still believe in other conceptions of God, it is possible for one to be a skeptic about the kind of free will required for basic desert yet still maintain that we can preserve *all the free will worth wanting*. In the spirit of accommodation, I therefore suggested that we investigate your own non-intrinsic, non-basic-desert notion of free will to see if, as you claim, it can preserve a notion of *desert* that "is as basic as desert could be." According to your view, "indirect 'consequentialist or contractualist' considerations" are capable of grounding a notion of desert where agents can be *truly deserving* of being blamed and punished. For instance, in our previous exchange you said we should treat self-control as "our threshold for true desert." My third argument was an attempt to challenge your non-basic conception of moral responsibility by contending that your account is too instrumentalist to preserve the kind of desert-based moral responsibility practices you want to preserve.

In response to that argument, you provide the following clarification: "I am not making the 'instrumentalist' or (some would say) 'fictionalist' proposal that we should, as it were, *pretend* to hold people responsible in [the basic-desert] sense (because this would have good consequences), but [instead I maintain that we] should hold them *actually responsible* in the non-intrinsic, non-absolute sense I have defended because they *really are* responsible in that sense." But what I still do not understand, and I'm not trying to be coy, is what it means on your account for an agent to be *really* and *truly* responsible. The best I can gather is that since you hold there are consequentialist benefits to adopting a "system of desert" (something I still disagree with since I contend that we would be better off without one), agents *internal to that system* should be treated *as if* they are morally responsible in a backward-looking desert sense. This is your forward-looking justification of backward-looking desert. Now, I know you'll take issue with the "as if" in the previous sentence. For you, such desert and moral responsibility are as real as real can get. But I disagree. There is, after all, a *realer* notion of desert and moral responsibility: the basic-desert notion. Perhaps this is why you have begun referring to the kind of moral responsibility your theory preserves as "*sorta* responsibility." But when we say that someone is "sorta responsible," is that like saying they *sorta* deserve life in prison?

Are you at least willing to admit that there's an important difference between the following two questions: (1) under the assumption of determinism, do agents actually have the control in action needed for them to be *truly deserving* of praise and blame, punishment and reward? And (2) under the assumption of determinism, is it *practically beneficial* to hold agents morally responsible in your *sorta* sense? I see your forward-looking defense of backward-looking desert as an attempt to answer the second question, but not the first. Furthermore, once we divorce the notion of desert from its retributivist and non-consequentialist connotations, as your theory attempts to do, what we are ultimately left with is an instrumentalist notion of desert. Such a notion, I contend, pales in comparison with basic desert and perhaps deserves a qualifier like "*sorta* desert" or "instrumentalist desert."

Dennett: I think you underestimate the force of my example of the parallel between desert and economic value. By parity of reasoning (or "parody of reasoning" as a student of mine once serendipitously wrote), you would maintain that with regard to money, "there is, after all, a *realer* notion of economic value: 'basic' intrinsic economic value. Perhaps, Dan, you should say that dollars have only *sorta* value, not real value." Shades of the Gold Standard! I do think we have outgrown that once useful myth and come to accept that money has value *only* because of the social and economic system and its shared practices. Our treating dollar bills and bank accounts *as if* they had economic value is what gives them whatever economic value they have. There is no such thing as intrinsic economic value. Nor, I hold, is there such a thing as basic desert. Still, there is money and it is really valuable, and there is real desert, and it is really valuable too.

I have used the same point to parody the existence of zombies in philosophy of mind (Dennett 2001a, "How much is that in *real* money?"). So, to make my position clearer, I am claiming that your insistence, with Pereboom, on couching the whole discussion of punishment and desert in terms of what you call "basic" desert, is parallel to insisting, in discussions of monetary policy, that all discussions be framed in terms of *basic* economic value, grounded in the Gold Standard: gold is absolutely and intrinsically valuable. That used to be a respectable argument. I am proposing that we should consider – and then adopt – the same perspective on "traditional" ideological arguments about the grounding of real moral desert. Perhaps the retributive, Kantian, entirely backward-looking view of just deserts was a useful crutch for the imagination, a handy myth to get people to take morality seriously and adopt a notion of guilt "in the eyes of God" as the true, real, basic notion of guilt and desert. What I am proposing is not that we switch to *sorta* desert as a pragmatically acceptable substitute for what would be *the real thing* if it existed; I am proposing that *there was never a philosophical need for "basic moral desert,"* but at best, a handy inflation or intensification of ideology to secure sufficiently devout allegiance. It keeps company with dogmas about burning in hell when omniscient God sees what you've done.

Finally, I'll respond to your surmise about my use of "sorta." Notice that I introduced the term to draw attention to the existence (in every empirical matter worth discussing – see my *Intuition Pumps*) of penumbral cases, and more particularly of gradual processes that defy *sorites* arguments. I didn't say that mammals in general are only *sorta* mammals (late therapsids were), and that normal *adults* are only *sorta* responsible for what they do; children and old folks on the shores of senility are only *sorta* responsible.

You challenge me to admit that there is a difference between two questions:

(1) under the assumption of determinism, do agents actually have the control in action needed for them to be *truly deserving* of praise and blame, punishment and reward?

(2) under the assumption of determinism, is it *practically beneficial* to hold agents morally responsible in your *sorta* sense?

I do admit that there is; it is the same difference we find between these two questions:

(A) do dollars actually have the property of having *true economic value?*

(B) is it *practically beneficial* to adopt the practice that holds dollars to have economic value of the *sorta* kind?

We should abandon the fantasies of intrinsic desert and intrinsic economic value. And to respond to another question of yours, if you will agree that since your dollars are only *sorta* valuable to you, I will agree that somebody who steals all of yours, only *sorta* deserves a long term in prison. He didn't do you any *real* harm, did he?

Caruso: What baffles me about your position, and your analogy with money, is that nothing remains fixed and agents can easily go from *having free will* at moment t to *not having free will* at t_2 if our social shared practices were to change. I agree with you that money gets its value from our social and economic systems and our shared practices. But it is also true that Confederate money went from having value for those in the south during the Civil War to not having value after. Likewise, if we treat *free will*, *desert*, and *moral responsibility* like money, then it's possible for our social systems and practices to change and for us to come to abandon those notions and adopt new ones. If that's possible – and I think you must admit that it is – then your account is instrumentalist through and through. Social and economic systems are human constructs that are malleable to our local needs and purposes, and therefore can, and often do, change over time. The same should be true for our moral responsibility practices.

I view that as a potential problem for your account. Here's why. A careful examination of cross-cultural anthropology, as well as moral psychology, reveals that different "moral ecologies" have evolved over time in response to different pressures and to serve different local needs and purposes. *Our* moral responsibility system, despite what some would have us believe, is not the only way to organize society, nor is it (in any absolute sense) the best. To think that it is, would be a Western bias – a byproduct of our WEIRD culture (where that means Western, Educated, Industrialized, Rich, Democratic). There are, as Owen Flanagan (2017) has persuasively argued, *varieties of moral possibility*. For instance, there are past and present cultures that feel completely justified in praising, blaming, and punishing people (sometimes severely) without requiring that those people satisfy the control conditions often associated with free will. *Honor cultures*, for example, often condone severely punishing, sometimes even killing, seemingly innocent individuals for the actions of the relatives. (For example: Hatfield-A wrongs McCoy-B, so McCoy-B sees fit to retaliate against *any member* of the Hatfield family.) Non-honor cultures, like our own, consider this fundamentally unfair and unjust. Furthermore, honor cultures shun third-party punishment, whereas third-party punishment is the norm in Western cultures. That is, it's very important in honor cultures that victims respond personally to perceived transgressions, and not necessarily to the person that harmed them. In honor cultures, individuals are obligated to protect their reputations by personally answering insults, affronts, and threats, oftentimes through the use of violence. In tribal societies, for instance, the punishment given for murder is often death. But as Tamler

Sommers (2012, 2018) describes, in such societies: "this punishment may not be given to him who has murdered. In his place, some other member of his family, group, or clan may be killed since the group is collectively responsible for the criminal acts of each of its members" (2012: 48). These cultural variations are the product of different ways of life resulting from adaptations to local ecological conditions. How would your account deal with these cultural variations? It would seem that on your account, if each moral ecology produced a system that worked effectively for those people, in those conditions, then they would be equally instrumentally justified.

Furthermore, I think the malleability of your approach provides a potential inroad for the skeptic to claim that the kinds of philosophical arguments we've been discussing, and other changes in societal perspective, can cause us to abandon our current practices and adopt better, more humane and effective ones. You've already admitted that our beliefs about desert can shift, since you argued that the notion of *basic* desert, though perhaps intuitive in the past when we had different needs and beliefs, is now (on your view) an antiquated notion. *If that were true*, then it's equally possible for society to decide that your notion of non-basic desert should also be abandoned and replaced with more effective attitudes, judgments, and practices. In fact, in our first exchange you agreed with me that it remains an empirical question whether, on balance, we would be better off without a system of desert. If it turned out we would be, then on your own account we would no longer be warranted in viewing agents as deserving of blame and praise, punishment and reward. Of course, you go on to add, "I cannot see how you can think we would be better off without a system of desert." But that's due to your own limitations and inability to see beyond the system of desert we currently occupy. The moral responsibility system is indeed a stubborn one (to quote Bruce Waller again), and it's difficult for many to move beyond it. But as an *optimistic skeptic*, I maintain that the practical implications of living without the belief in free will (and without the belief in basic and non-basic desert) would, on the whole, produce more positive consequences than negative.

You will, no doubt, disagree. But on what grounds? I contend that there are many historical precedents that support my optimism and very few that support your pessimism. An illustrative analogy here would be the unfounded concerns voiced in the past about disbelief in God. It was long argued (and perhaps still is in certain quarters) that if people were to come to disbelieve in God, the moral fiber of society would disintegrate, and we would see a marked increase in immoral and antisocial behavior. The reality, however, has turned out to be quite the opposite. Several studies have shown that murder and violent crime rates are actually *higher* in highly religious countries compared to more secular countries. Within the United States, we see the same pattern. Census data reveal that states with the highest murder rates tend to be the most religious. And these findings are not limited to murder rates, as rates of all violent crime tend to be higher in more highly religious states. And if one looks beyond crime statistics, one finds similar trends with divorce rates, domestic violence, and intolerance. Given how wrong people were about the putative harms of disbelief in God, I think we should view claims about the putative harms of disbelief in free will with a healthy dose of skepticism. Of course, you could argue that belief in free will is more essential to the proper functioning of society than belief in God was, but on what grounds would you make such a claim? In the past, people felt equally convinced that belief in God was essential.

Dennett: Your first concern is that "nothing remains fixed" according to my account of free will and responsibility. You are right, but this is a feature not a bug. I am embracing the view that sees morality as a (wonderful) social construction that has generated many species of morality in many different settings, and while there are clear signs of robustness or stability across many features around the world, there is constant adjustment, a dynamic process in which thinking people around the world reflect on their own culture's mores and norms, sometimes endorsing them wholeheartedly and sometimes devoting themselves to convincing their compatriots and others to change their minds. Obvious instances of the variation are the different attitudes cultures exhibit today toward eating meat, homosexual love, and capital punishment. There are even a few cultures that still don't vigorously condemn slavery. Is all this variation destined to resolve into consensus some day? Perhaps, and many people are devoted to trying to make that happen, but differences may persist in spite of centuries of persuasion and less benign forms of mind-changing.

I do not know of a culture that doesn't have any form of moral responsibility, blame, and punishment. That doesn't mean it must be eternally and necessarily justified, but it does strongly suggest that this is a feature of any viable society. As I argued in *Freedom Evolves* (2003a: 302ff), there are good examples of historical processes that have gradually and rationally homed in on best practices and – just as important – the mutually shared concept of *ideal* practices. From crude beginnings we now have straight edges that are accurate to within a millionth of an inch over long distances, a departure from perfection that we all understand and can even measure. This isn't obnoxious cultural colonialism; it is the spreading of a provably good idea. We can respect a culture's current mores and refrain from bullying those who were raised in it while still disapproving of many of its features *for good reasons*. Tolerance of different opinions is consistent with impassioned criticism of them. Witness the good practices of almost all committed vegans who know better than to harass and humiliate those of us who haven't yet been converted by their arguments.

I am amused by your claim: "Given how wrong people were about the putative harms of disbelief in God, I think we should view claims about the putative harms of disbelief in free will with a healthy dose of skepticism." You're pulling in my direction. You and Derk define "basic moral desert" as absolute, intrinsic, not grounded in best social policies, and then say it is incompatible with science. I wholeheartedly agree! *This* concept of desert used to be supported by religious dogma, but now that God's command has been removed from the scene (thank goodness), it has no warrant from any quarter aside from leftover "intuition." We both want to discard superstition and abandon antique versions of the truly important topics. We both want to give up God and libertarian free will, and we want to base morality on empirical differences that matter. You even grant me that there may be one or more defensible senses of responsibility ("take charge" responsibility, for instance), and contemplate the prospect of it being a requirement of any stable, secure society. You just don't want to think of this as *moral* responsibility, and don't want people held accountable and punished for any of their lapses with regard to it.

Caruso: Okay, Dan, I'll take your points in turn. You consider it a "feature not a bug" that "nothing remains fixed" on your instrumentalist account. Fair enough. But how do you then establish that compatibilist self-control is a necessary condition for desert-based moral responsibility? Consider again my example of honor cultures, which you side-stepped. The challenge of that example was that in the moral ecologies where honor cultures have evolved, people can be considered justified and appropriate targets of blame, punishment, and anger *even though they have not satisfied the control conditions associated with free will.* That is, in honor cultures the *group* is viewed as collectively responsible for the actions of each of its members. So, when Hatfield-A wrongs or harms McCoy-B, McCoy-B is justified in retaliating against *any member* of the Hatfield family since they are *all collectively responsible.* We still see examples of this kind of honor code in professional baseball. After one New York Yankee hits a grand slam to take the lead, the next Yankee up to bat is "beaned" in the head with a hundred-mph fastball by the opposing pitcher in retaliation – not for anything they did, but for the actions of their compatriot. In such a moral system, distributing just deserts is *not about* satisfying various compatibilist control conditions or restricting blameworthiness to only those individuals who have knowingly and voluntarily done wrong. How does your instrumentalism deal with such cases? If such honor systems function effectively for those societies that lack strong and stable third-party institutions of punishment, which is where they often evolve, wouldn't they be *equally justified* on instrumentalist grounds?

Second, your instrumentalism about free will and moral responsibility entails that an agent can go from having free will at moment t_1 to *not* having free will at t_2, *not because of any changes in the agent's abilities or capacities*, but because of changes in our shared social practices. Hence the problem of free will, on your account, becomes less about the abilities and capacities of agents and *more about* which social construct would produce, on balance, the best outcome for society. Sure, our shared social construct requires that agents satisfy a control condition on action to be held morally responsible in the desert sense, *but it need not do so*. The example of honor cultures reveals that. So does a moment s thought on all the varieties of moral possibility that have or could exist. Your instrumentalism therefore runs contrary to the widely-held view, which I thought we both shared, that *free will* is best understood as the power or capacity characteristic of agents, in virtue of which they *justly deserve* to be praised and blamed, punished and rewarded for their actions. On your account, the link between (self-)control and desert can only be a *contingent fact* unique to our own current shared social construct, since there can be *no necessary* link between the control in action associated with free will (on the one hand) and moral desert (on the other).

Third, by acknowledging that our moral responsibility practices are not fixed, you've opened the door (as I argued in my previous comments) for optimistic skeptics, like myself, to argue against the putative pragmatic benefits of adopting a system of desert. Since it remains an *open empirical question* whether, on balance, we would be better off without belief in free will and a system of desert, it also remains an *open empirical question* whether our current set of practices are justified on consequentialist grounds, as you claim. I do not see, then, how you can claim victory *even on your own terms*, since it is possible that adopting the skeptical perspective would produce better outcomes. And although you seem willing to acknowledge this possibility, at least theoretically, you're always quick to add some dismissive comment like: "[But] I cannot see how you can think we would be better off without a system of desert." According to you, prior cultural beliefs and practices "strongly suggest" that some commitment to free will and moral desert is going to be "a feature of any viable society." But why think that *must* be the case? In fact, you admit that we have no grounds (especially on your theory) for concluding that our current system of moral responsibility "must be eternally and necessarily justified."

Furthermore, I do not see why we should take prior cultural beliefs and practices as evidence for the need to retain our current system of moral responsibility. You write, "I do not know of a culture that doesn't have any form of moral responsibility and blame and punishment." You then go on to say this, "strongly suggest[s] that this is a feature of any viable society." First, note one important omission in your first sentence: you left out the notion of *desert* altogether. Free will skeptics do not deny that many forms of moral responsibility are consistent with the denial of free will (e.g. the *attributability* and *answerability* senses of responsibility, *take-charge* responsibility, etc.). Nor do they deny that certain forward-looking, non-desert-based, conceptions of moral protest and punishment could not be retained. I take it what you meant to say is that no culture has completely abandoned *desert-based* moral responsibility, blame, and punishment (where that is understood in either the basic or non-basic sense of desert). It's unclear to me, however, whether that stronger claim is completely accurate, since Buddhist cultures, or at least Buddhist teachings, largely reject the kind of reactive moral attitudes you want to preserve – i.e. resentment, indignation, moral anger, and blame (see my "Buddhism, free will, and punishment: Taking Buddhist ethics seriously," 2020a). That said, the real problem I have with your argument is the pride of place it gives to prior beliefs and practices. One can easily imagine an analogous argument for why we should retain religious beliefs: "I do not know of a culture that doesn't have any form of religious belief," hence this "strongly suggests that this is a feature of any viable society." I know you would quickly reject such an argument, as would I. But for similar reasons, I think we should reject your argument as well – sometimes change is good, and prior beliefs and practices become suboptimal over time.

Lastly, you have repeatedly made dire predictions about what would happen if we came to adopt the skeptical perspective. In our first exchange, for instance, you suggested that it would "return humanity to ... Hobbes's state of nature where life is nasty, brutish and short." You also suggested that in such a world: "There would be no rights, no recourse to authority to protect against fraud, theft, rape, murder. In short, no morality." While I think you are simply philosophically wrong about that latter point, your overall pessimism also seems unfounded. In an attempt to explain why, I pointed out how wrong people were in the past about the putative harms of disbelief in God, and why this should cast doubt upon similar claims today (by you and others) about the putative harms of disbelief in free will. While you may have been "amused" by that analogy, I think it also counts strongly against your pessimism. I see no reason for thinking society will collapse into a state of nature without the belief in free will. In fact, if I'm correct, there may be great benefit in adopting the skeptical perspective.

Dennett: If honor cultures did function effectively, they would make a good challenge. While I don't know much about honor cultures, I doubt you should lean on them to support your position. I've already pointed out that moralities evolve out of earlier social arrangements (some of which might better be called *amoralities*), and I doubt you can find any honor culture that is as "equally justified" as our culture of moral responsibility, which features both desert and punishment. Baseball's beanball tolerance is hardly a shining example (and perpetrators are duly punished when caught redhanded), and honor killings of daughters who have been raped is not a norm I think you'd want to defend. We have learned a few things in the last two millennia. Moreover, I am pretty sure you overstate your claim that such a system is "*not about* satisfying various compatibilist control conditions." I would be surprised to learn that there is any honor culture in which, if Hatfield-A pushed McCoy-B off a cliff, and McCoy-B lands on Hatfield-C, killing him, then the Hatfields take it out on the McCoys, since McCoy-B (though out of control) killed a Hatfield. Honor cultures may draw *different*, and *wider* and – I would say – ultimately *indefensible* boundaries around responsible parties, but if they don't look at self-control issues at all, then their local consensus might be called an *ethos* but I would suggest that they don't have anything worth calling morality.

Do any of them, for instance, treat very young children and adults just the same? Children by the age of three or four already appreciate the many degrees of freedom they have. AI's founder, John McCarthy once told me that his four-year-old daughter Sarah, when he asked her to do something, replied "I can, but I won't." John decided this was an excellent expression of free will and, inspired by his daughter's remark, he wrote a paper, "Free will – even for robots" which articulated, from the design stance, a compatibilist account of free will. "Free will does not require a very complex system. Young children and rather simple computer systems can represent internally 'I can, but I won't' and behave accordingly." The free will of a small child (or a relatively simple robot) is not enough for moral responsibility, of course, because it takes years of moral education to develop the skills to control all those delicious degrees of freedom well enough to be held responsible. I think every culture tacitly acknowledges this.

You say, Gregg, that on my account "the link between (self-)control and desert can only be a *contingent fact* unique to our own current shared social construct, since there can be *no necessary* link between the control in action associated with free will (on the one hand) and moral desert (on the other)." Once again, it is important to be explicit about knowledge. If somebody wanders into "our own current shared social construct" and doesn't know the norms, we don't hold them responsible (or fully responsible) when they violate them. And when we visit other cultures we are obliged to learn enough about differences to avoid gratuitously offending them, or committing grave sins (from their point of view) that pass muster in our culture. But if they know, and intentionally violate, our norms, they deserve (*really* deserve) our condemnation and, if it is severe enough, punishment for their deliberately antisocial behavior.

You are also ignoring the possibility that some *contingent facts* are the grounds for *practical* (but not logical) *necessities*. There is also no logically necessary link between eating and being alive, but it's a policy without exceptions. There is also no necessary link between being vigilant and staying alive, but it, too, is a practical necessity. My "instrumentalism," as you persist in calling it, is part of a large and distinguished body of what might be called "best practices" that have evolved over billions of years of trial and error testing. Put otherwise, I am claiming:

If you want to have a stable system of social order for groups larger than a family or small clan (of *H. sapiens*, that most autonomous, and hard-to-control species), you will need a system of morality – and codified law, if the group is very large – that is *respected*. And it won't be respected if it lacks sanctions or punishments proportional to the seriousness of violations of the rules, or if it lacks a distinction between those who are competent enough to understand and be guided by the rules and those who are not. Only the competent are to be held responsible, and only they are to be given the usual political freedoms, in return for which they accept, as justly deserved, the punishments they are due.

I agree with you that this is an empirical question, but I don't think it is a seriously open question. At least not as we are currently constituted. Maybe we will evolve culturally or genetically or both into a species that needs no laws and no free will; and perhaps we won't have to eat or be vigilant to stay alive: we'll become, perhaps, well-tended *growths* kept alive in large kettles by agents that find us enchanting, a variation on bonsai trees. More realistically, I am claiming that supposing that human beings don't change radically in their needs, including their psychological needs, by far the best sociopolitical arrangement (from a strictly consequentialist perspective) is a system of morality in which minors get elevated into full political freedom, with all its rights and responsibilities, when they exhibit comprehension of the norms and laws and the ability to control themselves.

Caruso: Dan, just a few quick points before moving on. I agree with you that our individualist system of desert is likely an improvement over honor cultures. If I were being honest, I wouldn't want to live in an honor culture. That said, since honor cultures evolved in contexts different than our own, it's conceivable that they functioned effectively in those contexts. I acknowledge, though, that there's lots of empirical questions regarding honor cultures that would need to be sorted out before we could determine how effective they were and how far they diverged from our own ways. I presented the case only to test how your instrumentalist approach would respond. I think I got my answer. There's also much I can agree with you on regarding the importance of morality. But there's no reason to think free will skeptics cannot preserve various forms of moral protest, forward-looking theories of moral responsibility, and axiological moral judgments concerning people's actions as "good" and "bad." The fundamental question is whether morality and a well-functioning society requires the kind of *desert-based* moral responsibility that I and other skeptics deny. I do not believe it does.

While I would love to respond further to some of your other points, I think it might be best to discuss my second argument against compatibilism, the one based on luck, before we run out of time. Perhaps we can then take up, in our third exchange, the key empirical question of whether a skeptical alternative to a system of moral responsibility and just deserts would be preferable – since we now agree that your consequentialist account is dependent on that empirical question.

Debating Luck (Again)

Dennett: Fair enough. I'll immediately turn, then, to your second argument. Once again, Gregg, the issue of knowledge interferes with your effort to distinguish two kinds of luck and show that one way or the other nobody can be responsible. First, of course, we are all spectacularly lucky just to be alive. More than 99 percent of all the living things that have ever lived have died childless, but not a single one of your ancestors or mine has suffered this overwhelmingly normal fate. And this has a remarkable corollary: we have evolved into creatures that are not just lucky but skilled, and not just skilled but skilled at making the most of our good luck and of arranging to minimize the bad effects of our bad luck. Now some of us are not so clever; these intellectually challenged folks don't have free will, through no *fault* of their own (they aren't *responsible* for not having free will, just unlucky) but because of infirmities bestowed upon them by their unfortunate pasts, they lack the self-control required. This is a good example of people who, because of events in their past over which they obviously had no control, have no free will. But those of us who are luckier than they, and have been born with normal human intelligence and hence the ability to reflect on our circumstances can:

(1) seek out and identify flaws in our own pasts ("constitutive" bad luck) that threaten to deprive us of free will unless we take steps to institute repairs (get some eyeglasses, for instance, and take our meds, if we have a treatable mental condition)
(2) plan our daily activities and long-term projects with an eye to minimizing the effects of "present" bad luck. This includes seeking counsel, avoiding tempting environments, hiring kindly neuroscientists when they become available, and *avoiding situations where our luck, good or bad, is likely to be the deciding factor*. We decline to play Russian roulette, for instance, and stay off the highway when black ice is forecast. That maturity is part of the competence of free will.

The thing about luck that makes it a poor player in the free will discussion is that *we all know about luck*, and hence can be held responsible for making allowances, making plans, and remembering about luck when we decide who is responsible and who isn't. Philosophers have carefully contrived cases where no amount of foresight or maturity could help you, otherwise blameless, from doing some terrible deed, killing an innocent bystander, for instance, when your car, driving at the speed limit, hits an unforeseeable bump, but in those cases we can agree that its bad luck, a tough break indeed, that you get branded for the rest of your life as a committer of involuntary manslaughter. And to alter the case, if you were knowingly *speeding* when you hit the bump, gambling, in effect, on your good luck on the highway, you may get convicted of something more serious. Somebody else, who was also speeding, but who got home without mishap is only lucky to have avoided your fate. Life isn't always fair. Not so surprisingly, there is no guarantee against bad luck intervening to spoil your trajectory as a blameless agent. That's one of the prices we all pay for our freedom. The idea that we should adjust our policies to prevent all such occasional meaningless tragedies is, in my view, shortsighted in the extreme; we can articulate our policies of praise and blame to *minimize* the role of *mere* luck, and then just grit our teeth when the outcomes go awry. Any other policy would be at best paternalistic and patronizing, and at worse unfair. When an obviously inferior tennis player wins a match he "shouldn't" win against a player who stumbles over a turtle that has wandered onto the court, we don't hesitate to declare the inferior player the winner. Tough luck, but that's the way it goes. In a much more serious context, when you assume *for very good reasons* that the gun in your hand isn't loaded, never imagining that, by some scarcely imaginable and entirely non-nefarious series of bizarre coincidences, your unloaded gun has been displaced in your tracking of the world by a loaded duplicate, and you fire the deadly shot thinking you're just innocently playing cowboy, you are guilty of a crime. Don't *ever* aim a gun at anybody and pull the trigger unless you are morally certain that it isn't loaded.

Caruso: Dan, I think you drastically underestimate how pervasive luck is and how difficult it is for agents to overcome certain inequalities and disadvantages that are purely matters of luck. It's purely a matter of luck, for instance, that I was born into a relatively stable society, during a relatively stable period in history, to a pair of relatively supportive and loving parents. I could have easily been born into a war-torn nation where my only options were to (a) pick up a machine gun and join group A at age thirteen and begin killing members of group B; (b) join group B and start killing members of group A; or (c) remain neutral and have my family massacred in front of my eyes as retaliation for not joining either group.

If that were the hand luck dealt you, would you be capable of murder? I think you would be. I think most would be. This is not to say, of course, that the skeptical perspective is not consistent with other conceptions of responsibility – e.g. causal responsibility, attributability, answerability, etc. Nor is it to deny that there remain good reasons for incapacitating dangerous criminals and engaging in forms of moral protest in the face of bad behavior. Rather, it is to insist that to hold people *truly deserving* of blame and praise, punishment, and reward, would be to hold them responsible for the results of the morally arbitrary or what is ultimately beyond their control, which is fundamentally unfair and unjust.

Your antidote to luck seems to be skill or moral competency. But, as I argued in our first exchange, I do not see how this helps, since the series of actions through which agents develop various skills and competencies are themselves either the result of constitutive luck (when they stem from an agent's endowments), present luck, or both. It is a matter of luck, for instance, that we're even capable of identifying "flaws in our past ('constitutive' bad luck) that threaten to deprive us of free will." It's also a matter of luck, both constitutive and present, that we can "take steps to institute repairs." I do not see how we can undo luck with more luck (Levy 2011).

The reason I care so much about these issues is that they have real-world implications for public policy. Consider, for instance, our attitudes toward criminal behavior. It is quite common both in criminal law and everyday attitudes to portray criminal behavior as a failure of moral character and a matter of individual responsibility. The retributive justification of legal punishment (and your quasi-retributive justification which provides a forward-looking justification of backward-looking desert) assumes, for instance, that, absent any excusing conditions, wrongdoers are morally responsible for their actions and *deserve* to be punished in proportion to their bad deeds. Since it focuses almost exclusively on the individual and their responsibility, and not on the social determinants of criminal behavior, retributive (and quasi-retributive) justice tends to favor punitive approaches to crime rather than policies aimed at targeting the social structures and causes of criminal behavior. Such an approach maintains that it's the individual who is responsible for criminal wrongdoing, and thus criminal justice is primarily about giving wrongdoers their *just deserts*. Perhaps nobody embodied this ethos of individual responsibility more than Ronald Reagan, who famously said: "We must reject the idea that every time a law's broken, society is guilty rather than the lawbreaker. It is time to restore the American precept that each individual is accountable for his actions."

The problem, however, is that the more we learn about criminal behavior, the more it becomes obvious that crime has more to do with places and circumstances than people. In fact, look closely and you will find that there are lifetimes of trauma, poverty, and social disadvantage that fill the prison system (for a detailed discussion of the relevant data, see my *Rejecting Retributivism: Free Will, Punishment, and Criminal Justice*). Failing to recognize this has profound consequences. People very rarely think about the social forces that are enormous contributors to criminal behavior, such as poverty, housing, educational inequity, racism, sexism, exposure to violence, etc. Instead, we attribute criminal behavior to a person's moral character ("They're just bad people") and assume they deserve to be punished. Importantly, these assumptions have consequences. When we think about someone's "badness" as an essential personal quality because we're ignoring the situational forces, we treat them worse and are less generous to them. We adopt punitive reactive responses to crime rather than targeting the social determinates and structural causes of criminal behavior. We need to radically change our assumptions about criminal behavior and focus instead on those situational forces and changeable behaviors when making policy decisions.

Hence, I propose that we reject retributivism (and your quasi-retributivism) and adopt a more holistic and systematic approach to criminal behavior. Unfortunately, belief in free will stands in the way, since it encourages punitiveness and is driven by a desire to blame and hold others morally responsible. It sees criminal behavior as primarily a matter of individual responsibility and as a result ends the investigation at precisely the point it should begin. The criminal law, with its assumptions about free will, encourages us to adopt what I call a *time-slice approach* to criminal behavior. It asks, at a particular moment in time (the time of the crime), was the agent competent? Were they reasons-responsive? Did they have a guilty mind or criminal intent? Did they understand that their actions were wrong or unlawful? etc. If the answers are yes, yes, yes, and yes, then they are legally and morally culpable and it is legitimate to punish them – all things considered and assuming there are no excusing conditions. Of course, the criminal law occasionally considers prior circumstances as relevant (e.g. in cases of domestic violence), but it is primarily focused on establishing *actus reus*, *mens rea*, and the state of mind of the offender at the time of the crime. Unfortunately, adopting such a time-slice approach abstracts individuals from their lived circumstances and the social systems they are embedded in. It blinds us to the social determinants of criminal behavior, the causes and systems that shape us, and *how* individuals come to acquire a particular state of mind.

Once we adopt the skeptical perspective, on the other hand, we realize that the myopic focus on individual responsibility, blame, and punishment is mistaken and counterproductive. The skeptical perspective tells us that the lottery of life is not always fair, we do not all have equal starting points, and individuals are embedded in social systems that shape who we are and what we do. In contrast with the time-slice approach, I encourage a *historical whole person approach* that sees individuals as byproducts of their histories and circumstances. It helps us to recognize that criminal behavior is often the result of social determinants and that the best way to reduce crime and increase human well-being is to identify and take action on these determinants. I know you'll disagree, but perhaps we can discuss my *public health–quarantine model* in our next exchange so as to hash out some of our differences in a longer conversation.

For the moment, I'll simply say that I find your solution to luck rather naive. You seem to suggest that one can easily "seek out and identify flaws in our own past" that are due to matters of bad luck, and then "take steps to institute repairs." But that is more easily said than done, especially when the disadvantages are systemic and difficult to overcome. I cannot help but think that the nature of the problem is an order of magnitude greater than your example of getting some eyeglasses to overcome my bad eyesight (a matter of bad luck) suggests.

Dennett: Luck is hard to think about clearly. You say "I could have easily been born into a war-torn nation . . ." and if that is true, it is also true, I guess, that you could have been born a starfish or a cucumber or never born at all. And if I had been born into a war-torn state, I might indeed be a cold-blooded murderer through no fault of my own, or, again, I might have been a machine gun, no more responsible for the deaths than the person with the finger on my trigger. This imagination game has few if any stable rules. I've already pointed to every living thing *sharing* in the incredible luck of being born at all. Every human being, to move closer to our issue, has the incredible luck of being a human being (and not a toad or an earthworm, though they are probably quite content to be what they are, utterly oblivious to the fact that they don't have free will). And I am agreeing with you that among human beings, many are extremely unlucky in their initial circumstances, to say nothing of the plights that befall them later in life. This is all common knowledge, and any system of morality must deal with it, *and they already do*, though not with equal fairness.

The law already deals quite effectively with "present luck" and so does everyday informal morality. We all make allowances for unlucky circumstances, where people "couldn't have known" about this or that circumstance that turns out to be pivotal. Even small children recognize effortlessly that it isn't fair to penalize or even criticize someone for something that is clearly *just* a bit of bad luck. The law has devised stronger principles for special cases: strict liability laws that explicitly rule out the excuse of bad luck. This keeps pharmacists and crane operators and others in high-risk occupations on their toes, but adults in general are expected to exercise normal caution and vigilance. Those who can't are not allowed the freedom granted to the competent.

You say "I do not see how we can undo luck with more luck." I agree; it takes work and skill to undo luck. And as you say, adjusting your life style is "easier said than done." But with a little luck (and all but the most unfortunate have a *little* luck) you can develop the skills and work habits that make luck less dominant in your life. Two Birds have nicely expressed this point. Alex Bird, a famous British "punter" (gambler) who made a fortune betting on horse races once said, "I've never thought of myself as lucky. I'm a coward. That's why I can't be a gambler. But I work very hard. The harder I work, the luckier I get" (*London Observer*, April 24, 1983). The last sentence has also often been attributed to the great basketball player, Larry Bird. No doubt many others have invented this morsel of wisdom. I suppose you will object that you still have to have the luck to have the personality that allows you to do this hard work. Not necessarily. Maybe instead, in spite of your feckless personality, you might have the luck to have an assiduous coach who helped you overcome your bad luck in the true grit department. Or you might have the luck (is it good or bad?) to suffer some near-death ordeal in your youth that shocked you into a more stalwart character, or ... There are uncountable ways to maturity and self-control, and while the prisons are indeed well-stocked with people who never encountered one of them, they are not the only people in prison. My goal is not to eliminate the prisons, but to reform them and make due allowances – much more than our current system does – for the differences in both luck and skill that you point to.

But here you walk right by my alternative without a glance because you indulge in another case of *rathering*. Perhaps we should blame Ronald Reagan, whom you quote so effectively:

> We must reject the idea that every time a law's broken, society is guilty *rather* [my italics] than the lawbreaker. It is time to restore the American precept that each individual is accountable for his actions.

Why not both accountability *and* concern for society's role in disabling so many for that role? You say "People very rarely think about the social forces that are enormous contributors to criminal behavior, such as poverty, housing, educational inequity, racism, sexism, exposure to violence, etc. *Instead* [my italics], we attribute criminal behavior to a person's moral character ('They're just bad people') and assume they deserve to be punished." Let's note that many of us see no contradiction in thinking that many (not all) of those convicted of crimes deserve to be punished, *and* that we should devote much more attention to providing the sorts of environments and programs that will diminish the number of those convicted, whether in the end we hold them morally responsible or not. I will grant you, of course, that there are self-righteous believers in punishment, ardent retributivists who tend to dismiss or at least not support the sorts of social programs that would humanize our system of punishment, but you mustn't tar the rest of us believers in just deserts with that brush. As I have been insisting for years, I entirely agree that our current system of punishment is obscenely cruel and unjust, and in desperate need of major, well-nigh revolutionary reform, but I still maintain that discrediting the concept of moral responsibility would be a foolish first step in that project. I agree with Reagan about that, if not much else. So, I guess this is a point of major disagreement between us, since you quote Reagan as if what he said was clearly pernicious. The only word I object to in it is "rather."

Maybe some believers in punishment see "'badness' as an *essential* personal quality," but not I. In part because I don't believe in essences but more directly in this context because I believe – as I've been saying – that almost all people are remarkably able to reconsider, to reflect, to reassess, to resist becoming puppets. Any attempt at humane reform that patronizes the unfortunate as *mere* products of their past history is bound to be not only ineffective, but cruel in its own way. As most parents know, the best way to make a child responsible is to *hold* the child responsible, and for those in our custody who have not yet made that transition, treating them as not capable of *holding themselves* responsible is a systematic assault on whatever self-esteem they have, and is bound to fail.

You insist on lumping me with retributivists, another instance of a kind of rathering. What exactly is quasi-retributivism, if it rejects, as my view does, the "intrinsic" value of punishment? Is it just the belief that punishment can be justified? But as you have noted, my defense of responsibility and punishment is "forward-looking" and "consequentialist or contractualist." Let's not have any more "quasi-retributivism" since it sounds dreadful and doesn't tell us why it is dreadful. You have acknowledged that a live issue between us is that I defend an account of just deserts that includes punishment and blame (appropriately tempered) and you disagree with it. Neither of us is a retributivist or quasi-retributivist, whatever that is.

Just one more point on this subject. You say that the "time-slice approach," unfortunately, "abstracts individuals from their lived circumstances and the social systems they are embedded in." I do not see this as unfortunate, but as an important principle of any remotely respectable system of law. We don't have different laws for rich and poor, educated and uneducated, clever and dull, or even impulsive and self-controlled. That would generate more dispute than a pair of spherical dice. Who would say what the standards were? Better to abstract individuals from their specific circumstances and talents, decide whether or not they have committed a crime, exhaustively consider the excuses and extenuating circumstances already built into the law (and any more special conditions we decide to add in our reforms), and then mete out punishment, acquittal, or modified disposition of the case. You say that this abstraction "blinds us to the social determinants of criminal behavior, the causes and systems that shape us, and *how* individuals come to acquire a particular state of mind." Maybe it often does today, but it need not.

Caruso: I think it may be helpful, Dan, to temporarily table the question of legal punishment and how best to revise our criminal justice system and take the issue up anew in our third exchange when we discuss the practical implications of free will skepticism. There's much I have to say on the matter and our second exchange is nearing a close. At that point, we can also take up the question of how best to describe your justification of punishment.

Dennett: That's fine with me.

Caruso: On the matter of luck, I just have only one final point to make. I think our fundamental disagreement is over the *extent* to which individuals are affected by luck and the *ability* of agents to overcome luck by means of skill and effort. I claim that "luck swallows all." You disagree. On our ability to overcome luck, I contend, as I've now argued many times, that the series of actions through which agents develop various skills and competencies are *themselves* either the result of constitutive luck (when they stem from an agent's endowments), present luck (when, e.g. they result from local factors, such as a helpful parent or encouraging teacher), or both. You seem to agree with me that agents cannot undo the effects of luck with more luck, yet you fail to realize that the very means by which you say we can combat luck (e.g. skill, effort, grit – whatever you want to call it) is *itself* subject to pervasive and all-encompassing luck! You seem aware of this when you write, "I suppose you will object that you still have to have the luck to have the personality that allows you to do this hard work." But then you go on to say: "Not necessarily. Maybe instead, in spite of your feckless personality, you might have the luck to have an assiduous coach who helped you overcome your bad luck in the true grit department. Or you might have the luck ... to suffer some near-death ordeal in your youth that shocked you into a more stalwart character." Do you notice what you just did there? You tried to do what you said cannot be done. You tried to undo the effects of constitutive luck by introducing compensating present luck. Your own example confirms my point: the series of actions through which agents develop various skills and competencies are themselves either the result of constitutive luck, present luck, or both.

Dennett: Actually, Gregg, it doesn't confirm your point at all. When I said I agreed that you can't undo luck with more luck, I went on to say "it takes work and skill to undo luck." Now it isn't just brute luck that most of the world's children, even in dire straits, acquire maturity and the development of skill through work of one sort or another. Societies put a strong incentive on parents and teachers to provide the conditions under which this takes place. You *could* say that almost every child has *the good luck* of being raised among other human beings, gradually being granted responsibility, until they reach a level of maturity that makes them safe enough to be granted the freedoms of adulthood. I'd rather say that a small minority of children are so terribly *unlucky* that this normal development doesn't occur for one reason or another. They clearly do not have free will, and we should make great allowances for them and take care of them and put them in restricted environments where they can thrive. And then there is a larger minority of children for whom maturity and self-control is a lifelong problem, and we have to make provisions for them, too. Happily, modern societies have developed serious programs for ensuring that this number is minimized – such as compulsory schooling and laws against parental abuse, for starters – and we should devote much more of our national resources to further such measures. Everybody knows this. Too many children are unlucky in just the way you say, and we should indeed take steps to remediate and reform our policies, economic, educational, and political, to diminish this number as best we can. But it just isn't true that it takes more than normal good luck to make the grade.

So luck doesn't swallow all. It doesn't even swallow most things, and it swallows much less today than back in the bad old days of, say, Old Testament ethics. We've made great progress in the last few millennia and a lot of that progress has been made in the last century. We have vastly diminished the reign of both constitutive luck and present luck. Worldwide, poverty is way down, as a percentage of population, and so is child mortality and starvation. See Hans Rosling's *Factfulness* (2018) for the latest encouraging news on these and many other fronts. And there is much more education, guidance for parents, and, of course, information about the world and how to live in it that is now available to all but the most unlucky. Suppose we lived in a terribly unlucky world where most adults were disabled for rational self-control by one bit of bad luck or another. Even in that world, I am not persuaded that we should abandon the policy of holding people morally responsible. There would be fewer people to hold responsible, but our best hope of improving that world would be by encouraging them to engage in morally responsible projects for which they took moral responsibility. Not "in the eyes of God" moral responsibility, because we've outgrown the need for that carrot and stick; just the kind of moral responsibility that people find worth wanting. People who could think would realize that being *held* responsible is one of life's greatest blessings.

Exchange 3

Punishment, Morality, and Desert

Caruso: I think it's time, Dan, that we discuss in more detail the issue of punishment, particularly legal punishment, and our respective views on criminal justice. Let's begin with some definitions. Punishment, we can say, is the intentional imposition of an unpleasant penalty or deprivation for perceived wrongdoing upon a group or individual, typically meted out by an authority. Everyday examples include a teacher giving a pupil a "time out" for disrespectful behavior and a university expelling a student for plagiarism. Legal punishment is a specific sort of punishment; it is the intentional imposition of a penalty for conduct that is represented, either truly or falsely, as a violation of a law of the state, where the imposition of that penalty is sanctioned by the state's authority. More precisely, we can say that *legal punishment* consists in one person's deliberately harming another on behalf of the state in a way that is intended to constitute a fitting response to some offense and to give expression to the state's disapproval of that offense. Are you okay with those definitions?

Dennett: That seems fine to me.

Caruso: In our previous exchange, I accused you of defending a form of quasi-retributivism and you took issue with that label.

Dennett: Indeed, I did. I am no retributivist; I insist upon it.

Caruso: Well, the reason I labeled you a quasi-retributivist is that, although you justify the system of desert on forward-looking consequentialist grounds, you also maintain that *once we are internal to that system*, we should distribute legal punishment in accordance with desert. That is, you retain (at least as far as I understand) the core retributive notion that, absent any excusing conditions, wrongdoers are morally responsible for their actions and hence *deserve* (in the backward-looking sense) to be punished in proportion to their wrongdoing. Isn't that correct? I do not understand you to be advancing a consequentialist justification of punishment that claims that internal to our system of practices, punishment can only be justified if it effectively deters, makes us safer, or rehabilitates offenders.

Dennett: Right – except for your insistence on calling this the core *retributive* notion of punishment. That is, you are right that I defend a concept of punishment that says that once we have established that a person is both guilty as charged and morally competent, we don't then further consider whether *punishing this convict in particular on this occasion* would deter, or reform, or rehabilitate them, or make us safer. We punish them because they are guilty as charged, and they knew better. A simpler example is the umpire's role in calling balls and strikes. He knows the rules, the pitcher and the batter know the rules, and it is strictly *irrelevant* whether or not *on this occasion* calling the pitch a ball or a strike would make a majority of the people happy, or make the pitcher a more accurate pitcher, or improve the attitude of an overconfident batter, or somehow make the game of baseball better, or even level the playing field in a game already marred with unfairness of one sort or another. We know perfectly well that there are many strong temptations to bend the rules and admit such exceptions, and there are notorious cases of umpires who seem to have succumbed to them, but we also know that the game of baseball would become like professional wrestling if officials adopted such a policy. The umpire should call balls and strikes *according to the rules*. That's what they are obligated to do, and it is what makes baseball a game worth playing.

It is mainly a question of maintaining respect for the law in the face of ever-changing circumstances. When a law passed in good faith no longer makes sense, no longer satisfies our intuitions of fairness because of something we have learned, we should *change the law*, not bend it for consequentialist reasons, because if we do, we sacrifice the confidence of the general populace that our laws mean what they say, and that is a very dangerous situation. Since balls and strikes are not, strictly speaking, penalties (in spite of how much the judgments may hurt and outrage the players involved), a better example might be the ice hockey referee sending a player to the penalty box for high-sticking. This really is a punishment, and may result in the loss of a championship, the loss of a bonus, the loss of reputation. It can hurt like the dickens. But the referee should not consider, in each case, whether inflicting the punishment would increase human welfare or happiness, etc. That would undermine the stability of the law.

I have often inveighed against doing philosophy by *ism-mongering* – as in "which brand of materialism is yours, eliminative materialism, reductive materialism, instrumentalist materialism, fictionalist materialism, illusionist materialism?" – since it invites *rathering* that hides the nuances and misses the possibility that there is an element of truth in several or even all the alternatives. But sometimes labels help locate a position in logical space. My view here is, I suppose, a *contractualist* variation on *rule utilitarianism* – so it is *consequentialist* through and through (and hence not *retributivist* at all) but it is entirely backward-looking when it comes to settling who deserves what. Hockey players know the rules and if they violate them without legitimate excuse, they accept that the penalty called was fair and just. What is a legitimate excuse? It wasn't really high-sticking because the accused was tripped by an opposing player, which sent him out of control, causing his stick to rise. *Not:* it wasn't high-sticking because the accused suffered a terrible childhood and has great difficulty controlling his aggressiveness. And certainly not: it wasn't high-sticking because determinism is true and he couldn't do otherwise! It seems to me that the obvious ridiculousness of this idea shows that philosophers have simply misdiagnosed our everyday convictions about when "could not have done otherwise" exempts from responsibility. What people care about, rightly, is whether or not the alternative was *within the control* of the agent, which is independent, once again, of determinism.

So the system of punishment is justified by *consequentialist* reasons – it allows those who love the game to play or watch ice hockey. Similarly, the laws of a well-ordered society allow all its members to live relatively safe and secure lives, trusting their fellow citizens and making long-range plans. Key elements of these systems are the concepts of moral agency and just deserts.

These considerations can be clearly seen in the case of written, codified laws of nations or rules of games, but they also apply to the largely unwritten norms of moral and immoral conduct, independent of official legality. We can sometimes identify a "dirty" player who slyly – and immorally – exploits or evades the official rules of a game, just as we can identify an immoral citizen who manages to find loopholes in the law that permit him to violate the unwritten norms of the society of which he is a member without doing anything *illegal*. We can agree that this kind of individual should be reformed, rehabilitated, deterred (by public disapproval or shaming, for instance), but above all, we think this kind of individual *deserves* to "pay a price" for willfully and knowingly disrespecting our moral rules. Why? Because when you enjoy the benefits of life in a community you implicitly promise to behave yourself, to know the norms, and to acknowledge the right of the community to punish you when you betray them. It's like belonging to a club, the Moral Agents Club, which makes the rules and enforces them. It is worth noting that this principle applies just as clearly in the case of societies very unlike ours – hunter-gatherer societies, for instance, with lots of norms we ourselves do not accept or even understand. When they punish one of their own for violating one of the honored norms of their society, they are justified in doing so, and their members – including, typically, the person punished – accept that the punishment was deserved. But was it *really* immoral to commit that act, and did the accused *really* get his just deserts? That may well be a question that will one day get a consensus answer, if the hoped-for unification of morality world-wide is achieved. If not, then this may be unanswerable, but it should be noted that we face the same unanswered, but conceivably answerable, questions in our own societies. Under what conditions is civil disobedience justified? Is it immoral, in the end, to block abortion, or to support abortion? A person with free will is capable of considering all this and taking one stand or another. Either way the person is morally responsible, and legally if that comes into it, for the choices made. If you want to hang out with the hunter-gatherer community, you should learn their rules and honor them. That's the price of admission. If you then find that you cannot tolerate some of their so-called sacred norms, you can decide to go missionary and try to educate them into a different mindset while still honoring their rules – or you can leave, forsaking their hospitality. That is how to respect cultural differences.

Caruso: Thanks, Dan. That's helpful. And as you say, I don't want to get wrapped up in *ism-mongering* by insisting on this or that label for your view. Getting clear on the commitments of your view is more important to me than determining what to call it. The thing I still want to get clear on, however, is what role *desert* is playing in your justification of punishment. On the one hand, your contractualist and consequentialist approach to punishment appears to be one a free will skeptic could easily adopt since it's not really dependent on desert at all. That is, I do not see why some backward-looking, non-desert-based notion of responsibility could not do all the work you need. Imagine that Fred kills Tony by shooting him with a gun. A free will skeptic could acknowledge, without contradiction, that Fred is *causally responsible* for the death of Tony. They could also *attribute* various motives, intentions, and character traits to Tony even if he's not responsible for them in the basic-desert sense, since the *attributability* notion of responsibility is also compatible with free will skepticism. Why aren't these kinds of backward-looking consideration enough to ground a contractualist or consequentialist justification of punishment? Why bring desert into it at all? And since free will skeptics need not reject all justifications of punishment, only those based on desert, why isn't your account available for a free will skeptic to adopt?

On the other hand, you seem also to want to insist that when an individual does wrong and breaks our contractualist and/or legal agreements, they "*deserve* to 'pay the price' for willfully and knowingly disrespecting our moral values." It is in claims like this that the notion of desert appears to be playing a quasi-retributivist role in your account. Unlike theories of punishment that aim at deterrence, rehabilitation, or incapacitation, retributivism grounds punishment in the *blameworthiness* and *desert* of offenders. As legal scholar Mitchell Berman, himself a leading retributivist (2008, 2011, 2013, 2016), describes the retributivist claim: "A person who unjustifiably and inexcusably causes or risks harm to others or to significant social interests deserves to suffer for that choice, and he deserves to suffer in proportion to the extent to which his regard or concern for others falls short of what is properly demanded of him" (2008: 269). Do you agree with that claim? If so, then I think the notion of desert may be doing some real work on your account.

My question, then, is what role do you see desert playing in *justifying* punishment? Consequentialist theories of punishment need not appeal to, nor presuppose, the existence of free will or the desert of offenders. So, when you say that your account is "consequentialist through and through," you seem to be implying that it's consistent with the denial of free will. That is why I wonder: Are you open to the more skeptic-friendly interpretation I offered, or do you insist that punishment must be grounded in backward-looking *blameworthiness* and *desert*?

Dennett: You ask me why bring up desert at all? Because it focuses the consideration of particular cases of both praise and blame, reward and punishment, on what matters if we are to continue relying, as we do, on our fellow citizens *taking* responsibility for what they do (and not taking responsibility for other folks' good works). Our norms and laws won't command our respect – won't *deserve* our respect – if they don't make these distinctions regarding the moral competency of individuals. I think you have saddled yourself with too narrow a definition of desert. I am happy to accept Michael Berman's definition quoted by you above, and I note that it alludes quite directly to its indirect consequentialist grounding: a state or society that endorses this concept will protect the important interests of both state and citizen.

Caruso: I'm not surprised by your answer, but I was hoping you might be open to my more skeptic-friendly interpretation. Let me try this one more time by framing the question differently: *Do you think all desert-based justifications reduce to consequentialist justifications? If so, does desert then drop out as a justification?* As I understand you, your concerns are primarily pragmatic in that you want to know how we can justify punishment in order to ensure a well-functioning society. As I suggested above, there may be purely consequentialist ways of doing this that do not invoke backward-looking desert at all – although they retain other backward-looking components (e.g. Was the agent causally responsible? Were they competent at the time of the crime? Did they have *mens rea* (the intention or knowledge of wrongdoing)? etc.)

Giving up the notion of desert, in either the basic or non-basic sense, *does not entail* that we need to give up important distinctions regarding the moral competency of individuals. If you think it does, then I think you're working with a straw man version of the skeptical view. There are important forward-looking, non-desert-based reasons for retaining these important distinctions. Neither free will skepticism nor my preferred non-retributive alternative to addressing criminal behavior (the public health–quarantine model) implies that the difference between agents who are reasons-responsive and those who are not is irrelevant to how we should treat offenders. On the contrary, free will skeptics typically claim that this difference is crucial for determining the right response to crime. On the public health–quarantine model I defend, for instance, the question of whether an offender is competent and reasons-responsive is relevant for at least two reasons. First, it's important in assessing what kind of threat an individual poses moving forward and whether incapacitation is required. An offender suffering from a serious mental illness, for instance, differs in significant ways from one who is fully reasons responsive. These differences will be relevant to determining what minimum restrictions are required for adequate protection. Second, if the capacities of reasons-responsiveness are in place, forms of treatment that take rationality and self-governance into account are appropriate. On the other hand, those who suffer from impairments of rationality and self-governance would need to be treated differently, and in ways that aim to restore these capacities when possible. Understanding the variety of causes that lead to impairment of these capacities would also be crucial to determining effective policy for recidivism reduction and rehabilitation. Hence, free will skepticism and the public health–quarantine model (which I hope we have time to discuss) acknowledge the importance of reasons-responsiveness, self-governance, and differences in degrees of autonomy. But, rather than see these as relevant for assigning blameworthiness and desert-based moral responsibility, they instead view them as important (in fact, essential) to determining the appropriate course of action moving forward.

Your resistance, then, to my friendlier interpretation of your view may be due to a misunderstanding of what the skeptical view entails and what resources it has at its disposal. Derk Pereboom, for example, has developed a forward-looking account of moral responsibility that is grounded, not in desert, but in *three non-desert invoking desiderata*: future protection, future reconciliation, and future moral formation (see Pereboom 2014). On such an account, when we call an agent to account for immoral behavior, at the stage of moral address we request an explanation with the intent of having the agent acknowledge a disposition to act badly, and then, if she has in fact so acted without excuse or justification, we aim for her to come to see that the disposition issuing in the action is best eliminated. In normal cases, this change is produced by way of the agent's recognition of moral reasons to eliminate the disposition. Accordingly, it is an agent's responsiveness to reasons – together with the fact that we have a moral interest in our protection, her moral formation, and our reconciliation with her – that explains why she is an appropriate recipient of moral protest in this forward-looking sense. While many compatibilists see some type of attunement to reasons as the key condition for desert-based moral responsibility, we skeptics instead view it as the most significant condition for a notion of responsibility that focuses on future protection, future reconciliation, and future moral formation.

So before moving on, I would just like to ask one last time why your pragmatic approach to punishment cannot get along just as well without backward-looking desert. If you think all desert-based justifications reduce to consequentialist justifications, then doesn't desert drop out as a justification? Why not embrace that conclusion completely and purge your account of any and all remaining remnants of retributivism? I would suggest that you do, not only because it would bring our views closer together, but because it would make your account less reliant on the highly controversial, and often pernicious, notion of *just deserts*.

Dennett: At this point, Gregg, I'm unable to evaluate your reassurances about how you and Derk can provide "non-desert-based reasons" for your proposed alternatives to the view I'm defending, because it appears to me that you are underestimating the difficult dynamics of (what I tentatively take to be) your proposal. So, let's get down to the details of your quarantine model and see if my suspicion is right.

The Public Health–Quarantine Model

Caruso: Fine. I'll get directly to it then. In our first exchange you wrote: "If you have some other vision of how a stable, secure and just state can thrive without appeal to [desert-based] moral responsibility, you owe us the details." While I was unable to sketch my non-desert-based approach to criminal behavior then, I would like to do so now. I'll briefly sketch what I consider to be the best non-retributive (and non-punitive) approach to criminal behavior, one that is consistent with free will skepticism but also ethically defensible and practically workable. I call it the *public health–quarantine model* and it's the model I develop and defend in *Rejecting Retributivism: Free Will, Punishment, and Criminal Justice* (2021a).

The model takes as its starting point Derk Pereboom's famous account (see 2001, 2014). In its simplest form, it can be stated as follows: (1) Free will skepticism maintains that criminals are not morally responsible for their actions in the basic-desert sense; (2) plainly, many carriers of dangerous diseases are not responsible in this or in any other sense for having contracted these diseases; (3) yet, we generally agree that it is sometimes permissible to quarantine them, and the justification for doing so is the right to self-protection and the prevention of harm to others; (4) for similar reasons, even if a dangerous criminal is not morally responsible for his crimes in the basic-desert sense (perhaps because no one is ever in this way morally responsible) it could be as legitimate to detain him preventatively as to quarantine the non-responsible carrier of a serious communicable disease.

The first thing to note about the theory is that although one might justify quarantine (in the case of disease) and incapacitation (in the case of dangerous criminals) on purely utilitarian or consequentialist grounds, both Pereboom and I have resisted this strategy. Instead, our view maintains that incapacitation of the seriously dangerous is justified on the ground of the right to harm in self-defense and defense of others. That we have this right has broad appeal, much broader than utilitarianism or consequentialism has. In addition, this makes the view more resilient to a number of objections and provides a more resilient proposal for justifying criminal sanctions than other non-retributive options. One advantage it has, say, over consequentialist deterrence theories is that it has more restrictions placed on it with regard to using people merely as a means. For instance, as it is illegitimate to treat carriers of a disease more harmfully than is necessary to neutralize the danger they pose, treating those with violent criminal tendencies more harshly than is required to protect society will be illegitimate as well. In fact, in all our writings on the subject, we have always maintained the *principle of least infringement*, which holds that the least restrictive measures should be taken to protect public health and safety. This ensures that criminal sanctions will be proportionate to the danger posed by an individual, and any sanctions that exceed this upper bound will be unjustified.

Second, the quarantine model places several constraints

on the treatment of criminals. First, as less dangerous diseases justify only preventative measures less restrictive than quarantine, so less dangerous criminal tendencies justify only more moderate restraints. We do not, for instance, quarantine people for the common cold even though it has the potential to cause some harm. Rather, we restrict the use of quarantine to a narrowly prescribed set of cases. Analogously, on the public health–quarantine model the use of incapacitation should be limited to only those cases where offenders are a serious threat to public safety and no less restrictive measures were available. In fact, for certain minor crimes perhaps only some degree of monitoring could be defended. Secondly, the incapacitation account that results from this analogy demands a degree of concern for the rehabilitation and well-being of the criminal that would alter much of current practice. Just as fairness recommends that we seek to cure the diseased we quarantine, so fairness would counsel that we attempt to rehabilitate the criminals we detain. Rehabilitation and reintegration would therefore replace punishment as the focus of the criminal justice system. Lastly, if a criminal cannot be rehabilitated and our safety requires his indefinite confinement, this account provides no justification for making his life more miserable than would be required to guard against the danger he poses.

In addition to these restrictions on harsh and unnecessary treatment, the public health–quarantine model also advocates a broader approach to criminal behavior that moves beyond the narrow focus on sanctions. It places the quarantine analogy within the broader justificatory framework of *public health ethics*. Public health ethics not only justifies quarantining carriers of infectious diseases on the grounds that it is necessary to protect public health, it also requires that we take active steps to *prevent* such outbreaks from occurring in the first place. Quarantine is only needed when the public health system fails in its primary function. Since no system is perfect, quarantine will likely be needed for the foreseeable future, but it should *not* be the primary means of dealing with public health. The analogous claim holds for incapacitation. Taking a public health approach to criminal behavior would allow us to justify the incapacitation of dangerous criminals when needed, but it would also make prevention a *primary function* of the criminal justice system. So instead of myopically focusing on punishment, the public health–quarantine model shifts the focus to identifying and addressing the systemic causes of crime, such as poverty, low social economic status, systematic disadvantage, mental illness, homelessness, educational inequity, exposure to abuse and violence, poor environmental health, addiction, and the like.

Furthermore, the public health framework I adopt sees *social justice* as a foundational cornerstone to public health and safety. In public health ethics, a failure on the part of public health institutions to ensure the social conditions necessary to achieve a sufficient level of health is considered a grave injustice. An important task of public health ethics, then, is to identify which inequalities in health are the most egregious and thus which should be given the highest priority in public health policy and practice. The public health approach to criminal behavior likewise maintains that a core moral function of the criminal justice system is to identify and remedy social and economic inequalities responsible for crime. Just as public health is negatively affected by poverty, racism, and systematic inequality, so too is public safety. This broader approach to criminal justice therefore places issues of social justice at the forefront. It sees racism, sexism, poverty, and systemic disadvantage as serious threats to public safety and it prioritizes the reduction of such inequalities.

Summarizing the public health–quarantine model, then, the core idea is that the right to harm in self-defense and defense of others justifies incapacitating the criminally dangerous with the minimum harm required for adequate protection. The resulting account would not justify the sort of criminal punishment whose legitimacy is most dubious, such as death or confinement in the most common kinds of prisons in our society. The model also specifies attention to the well-being of criminals, which would change much of current policy. Furthermore, the public health component of the theory prioritizes prevention and social justice and aims at identifying and taking action on the social determinants of health and criminal behavior. This combined approach to dealing with criminal behavior, I maintain, is sufficient for dealing with dangerous criminals, leads to a more humane and effective social policy, and is actually preferable to the harsh and often excessive forms of punishment that typically come with retributivism.

Dennett: Gregg, I am all for "prioritizing," as you say, concern for social justice and "attention to the well-being of criminals." Our past history in these regards is shameful, and I wholeheartedly endorse your desire to push for major reforms. And I will concede that sometimes defenders of our system of punishment have been "myopic" in their concentration on assuring that the principle of *just deserts* is supported, and have consequently had little to say about major efforts in social justice that could remedy the worst conditions that lead to criminal behavior in the first place. But I don't see why we can't cure the myopia while still maintaining punishment as a key feature of our society – and it's not because I want to indulge in "retributive" passions (I do wish you'd stop trying to brand my view retributive or quasi-retributive) but because I see punishment as a *necessary condition* for securing the very humane reforms you champion.

In short, I applaud all the emphasis you place on prevention of crime, education, minimal measures to protect our fellow citizens, security with as little imposed suffering as possible – but all of that can be emphasized in any reformed system of punishment, so far as I can see. That is, you haven't showed, or tried to show, as far as I can see, that these humane goals are *inconsistent* with a system of punishment. And I don't see how your public health-quarantine model deals with some familiar objections, so I'll just lay them out in simple form and let you show me what I'm missing. First, you declare that you and Pereboom improve on utilitarian or consequentialist treatments by endorsing "the *right* [my italics] to harm in self-defense and the defense of others." I suppose you would agree that we also have a right to freedom from interference by others (other citizens or the state) while engaged in non-harmful activities. Jeremy Bentham, the arch-utilitarian, notoriously called the concept of natural rights "nonsense upon stilts," and I agree, if by "natural" rights we mean something innate or intrinsic or "God-given" and inalienable. But there are plenty of good philosophical accounts that treat rights the way I am treating just deserts and moral responsibility, as socially constructed (or evolved) norms that have proven themselves worth respecting. So, I'm pleased to see you adopting rights talk, but wonder how you can have (moral?) rights without (moral?) responsibilities. They normally are seen as going hand in hand.

As I say, I have some doubts about the conceptual foundations you are building your model on, but I find it easier to see the practical problems confronting it. How does your quarantine model handle the treatment of those who resist being dealt with in the quarantine model? We have laws now that make it a crime, punishable by jail time or heavy fines or both, for anybody who is identified as rightfully quarantined and who resists going into the program. Whatever you call it, you're going to have to have incapacitation, incarceration, and, if need be, physical force imposed on anyone who won't go along with the quarantine. Then what happens? If "quarantine facility" is just your term for a prison with better living conditions and an emphasis on rehabilitation, then you're not proposing anything new. We're all in favor of that. Similarly, you cite a *principle of least infringement* when "treating those with violent criminal tendencies" but you say nothing about whether anyone who is deemed to have violent criminal tendencies is subject to *any* kind of treatment if they haven't yet broken the law. We quarantine people who haven't yet infected anyone but are known to be vectors, but we don't imprison people who haven't yet committed crimes but are predicted by experts to become criminals. You talk about your stress on directing attention and resources to ameliorating the social conditions that breed crime, but you are silent on the issue of whether among the steps that you would permit would be quarantining young people, for instance, who seem intent on a life of crime but as of yet have not been charged with any crimes. Again, if your system follows our current policy of requiring conviction of a crime before, um, institutionalization – to pick as neutral a term as I can find – then it seems that "quarantine" is just a euphemism for prison. The big difference, of course, is that one is not supposed to be put in prison unless one *deserves* to be put in prison. If you abandon this feature in the quarantine system it will not appear remotely defensible to most civil libertarians or ethicists or the general public. You speak above of those who are "a serious threat to public safety." That phrase is suspiciously ambiguous. Does it include those who have only made serious threats but not yet acted on them? This is the troubling issue of whether a citizen is free to strike the first blow before he can be arrested and charged. We deal with it, typically, and wisely, by enacting laws that reduce the risk to the rest of the citizenry by making it a crime to *own* nerve gas or an atomic bomb or a machine gun (in most sane states). We citizens are prepared to live with a moderate level of risk as the price of granting freedoms that we wish to enjoy ourselves. How does your quarantine model deal with this?

You stress rehabilitation and reintegration, and you suggest that this might "replace punishment as the focus of the criminal justice system" but this is another ambiguous phrase. Do you mean to replace punishment altogether, or leave some punishment in place and just beef up rehabilitation and reintegration as the *focus*? It makes a big difference. Suppose, to make it simple, thanks to your projects, a pill is invented that cures people of "violent criminal tendencies."

I haven't committed any violent acts yet, but I also haven't taken the pill. I decide to terrorize a neighbor I can't stand, threatening him with bodily harm, vandalizing his property, kicking his dog . . . until I drive him away – and then I take the pill. No need to quarantine me, right? I'm cured. No need to waste the taxpayers' money putting me into quarantine, and according to the principle of least infringement I should just go home and enjoy my life. And of course I'm not morally responsible for anything I've done, and I'm no longer a threat to society, so reintegration should be a snap. Does that seem right to you?

Your quarantine model, with its stress on danger and violence, is so far silent on all the crimes that are neither violent nor dangerous in the normal understanding of the term. Embezzlement is a gentle, painless affair, and typically risks no lives or limbs, and so is perjury, fraud, bribery, tax evasion, money laundering, libel, and even extortion, if it is limited to threats. How does the quarantine model handle these crimes? Public safety does not depend on holding these people in quarantine, so perhaps you will say that hefty fines should be used instead. What about those who are bankrupt (or have moved their money to offshore accounts) and can't or won't pay the fines? Maybe we'll have to "quarantine" them for "rehabilitation," but that sounds like punishment to me. Are white-collar criminals who are found guilty going to be allowed to run their businesses from their comfortable quarters in the quarantine facility? You insist that their lives may not be made more arduous than their confinement requires. Will you allow them to socialize via internet or daily visits from their friends? If Trump requests quarantine in Mar-a-Lago, what grounds will you have for denying him this location? He'll no doubt volunteer to put up the rehabilitation team in the hotel at his own expense. In other words – and this point has been made by others, such as Saul Smilansky – how are you going to prevent your quarantine system from becoming a free hotel, provided by the state, for all who choose to live there, taking their time getting rehabilitated and leaving when the spirit moves them? I'm all for making prison life less inhumane and soul-deadening than it currently is, but it's worth remembering that the idea that prison is a warm bed and free meals in times of trouble has occurred to many. Is it fair to law-abiding citizens who don't need rehabilitation and reintegration that they can't just check themselves into indefinite quarantine when they find themselves strapped for cash?

In short, until you give me a lot more practical details about how your quarantine system would work, it appears to be either just a humanized prison system (as in the Scandinavian countries, for instance), or utterly unworkable, a system that is vulnerable to exploitation and abuse by both citizens and the state, and unworthy of respect for all its good intentions.

Objections and Replies

Caruso: I appreciate your response, Dan, and I think there is much we agree on. You write: "Gregg, I am all for 'prioritizing,' as you say, concerns for social justice and 'attention to the well-being of criminals.' Our past history in these regards is shameful, and I wholeheartedly endorse your desire to push for major reforms." Great! I welcome any and all allies in the effort to reform our broken and excessively punitive criminal justice system. It's good to know we are on the same side. You also concede that "sometimes defenders of our system of punishment have been 'myopic' in their concentration on assuring that the principle of *just deserts* is supported." On this we also agree. You then go on to say: "But I don't see why we can't cure the myopia while still maintaining punishment as a key feature of our society – and it's not because I want to indulge in 'retributive' passions ... but because I see punishment as a *necessary condition* for securing the very humane reforms you champion." In answering this, I first need to make clear a distinction between my *own preferred* approach to addressing criminal behavior (the public health–quarantine model) and *other approaches that remain open to the free will skeptic.*

You are correct that the public health–quarantine model Pereboom and I defend is intended as a *non-punitive* alternative to retributivism – since the kind of incapacitation it licenses does not satisfy the definition of punishment introduced earlier (see also *Rejecting Retributivism* and my co-authored work with Derk Pereboom). Since legal punishment *seeks to make wrongdoers suffer* and requires the *intentional imposition of a penalty* for conduct that is represented as a violation of a law of the state, and since the public health–quarantine model does not involve punishment in this way, it offers a non-punitive alternative to treatment of criminals. When we quarantine an individual with a communicable disease in order to protect people, we are not intentionally seeking to harm or impose a penalty on them. The same is true when we incapacitate the criminally dangerous in order to protect society. The right of self-defense and prevention of harm to others justifies the limiting or restricting of liberty, but it does not constitute punishment as standardly understood. We do not punish, for instance, the quarantined ebola patient. This is important for several reasons. First, the model demands that we view individuals holistically and that we adopt a preventive approach – one that understands that individuals are embedded in social systems, that criminal behavior is often the result of social determinants, and that prevention is always preferable to incapacitation. Second, after a criminal offense has occurred, courts would need to work with mental health experts, drug treatment professionals, and social service agencies to seek alternatives to incarceration. Third, for those who must be incapacitated, they would need to be housed in *non-punitive environments* designed with the purpose of rehabilitation and reintegration in mind. Since most prisons in the US (as well as the UK and Australia) are inhospitable and unpleasant places designed for punitive purposes, we would need to redesign them so that the physical environments and spaces we inca-pacitate people in better serve the goal of rehabilitation and reintegration. In *Rejecting Retributivism*, I discuss this issue of prison design at great length. Lastly, we would need to end other punitive practices, like voter disenfranchisement, the use of solitary confinement, the death penalty, the banning of books in prison, three-strikes laws, and much more.

That said, free will skeptics *need not adopt a non-punitive approach* like the one Pereboom and I defend. Traditionally, in addition to retributivism there have been a number of other common justifications of (legal) punishment, includ-ing consequentialist deterrence theories and moral education theories. Consequentialist deterrence theories, for instance, maintain that we should only punish wrongdoers when it would augment social utility and the future benefits out-weigh its future cost. These future benefits primarily include deterrence and increased safety. According to these theories, then, the prevention of criminal wrongdoing serves as the good on the basis of which punishment is justified. But since consequentialist theories of punishment are forward-looking and in no way require agents to be morally responsible in the basic-desert sense, they are completely compatible with free will skepticism. It's possible, then, for a free will skeptic to agree with you about the necessity of punishment, *even if Pereboom and I prefer to go a different route.*

My own reasons for rejecting these other alternatives to retributivism is *not* that they are inconsistent with free will skepticism, but that they face several well-known inde-pendent moral objections (see Caruso 2021a; Pereboom 2001, 2014; Boonin 2008). For instance, consequentialist deterrence theories allow individuals to be *used as a means to an end* (i.e. the deterrence of others) and this runs afoul of the prohibition on manipulative use. Deterrence theo-ries also have the potential to justify punishments that are intuitively too severe. Three-strikes laws, for instance, were implemented across the US in the 1990s in an attempt to deter crime. It's important to note that their justification was largely consequentialist and *not* retributivist. Advocates of such laws maintained that, although some individuals who commit three felonies may not be much of a threat to public safety, having fixed and harsh penalties, like life in prison, for those who commit three felonies will help deter would-be criminals. Unfortunately, these laws ended up resulting in extremely harsh penalties for minor crimes. Consequentialist deterrence theories would also seem to allow for the punishing of innocent people if it were the only way to maximize utility. While there may be ways to overcome these concerns, I consider these problems significant enough to seek an alternative approach. And the public health–quarantine model is my preferred alternative. I hope that helps clear some things up.

Let me now turn to your more specific concerns about the public health–quarantine model. Since it would require a treatise-long reply to answer all the objections you raised at once, I hope you don't mind if we take them one at a time. To begin, you have repeatedly raised concerns about skeptics continuing to talk about "rights" and "justice" since you claim these notions require moral responsibility. For instance, you write: "So I'm pleased to see you adopting rights talk, but wonder how you can have (moral?) rights without (moral?) responsibility." First, I must reiterate once again that free will skeptics do not reject all notions of moral responsibility – they simply deny *basic-desert moral responsibility*. Since you, yourself, also reject basic desert, you must agree that a proper understanding of "rights" and "justice" in no way requires an appeal to basic-desert moral responsibility. Second, while some critics have argued that free will skeptics are not entitled to talk about justice and rights, since such talk presupposes deontological and/or desert-based claims that we are not entitled to, I've never quite understood this charge. Unless one were to think that *all* theories of justice had to be *desertist* (i.e. grounded in desert), there's no reason to think this claim has any merit. Yes, there are desertist theories of justice that hold that justice is fundamentally a matter of receipt in accord with desert. The idea seems to be present, for example, in certain passages in Aristotle, Leibniz, Mill, Sidgwick, and Ross. There are, however, several prominent theories of justice that are not desertist, including the theories of David Hume, John Rawls, and Robert Nozick.

In *Rejecting Retributivism*, I defend a *capabilities approach* to justice, like that of Martha Nussbaum and Amartya Sen (see references at end of book), according to which the development of capabilities – what each individual is able to do or be – is essential to human well-being. For capability theorists, human well-being is the proper end of a theory of justice. And on the particular capability approach I favor, social justice is grounded in six key features of human well-being: *health, reasoning, self-determination* (or *autonomy*), *attachment, personal security*, and *respect*. On this account, the job of justice is to achieve a sufficiency of these six essential dimensions of human well-being, since a life substantially lacking in any one is a life seriously deficient in what it is reasonable for anyone to want, whatever else they want. I argue at length in that book that this theory of justice is perfectly consistent with the kind of free will skepticism I defend. But I really don't think we need to get into all that here, since as long as we understand justice in terms of a non-desertist theory (whichever one you prefer), there is no reason free will skeptics cannot appeal to the notion of justice and all that it entails.

Before I go on, can we at least agree that there are available non-desertist theories of justice that are consistent with free will skepticism and the denial of basic-desert moral responsibility?

Dennett: My one misgiving with what you say here is your continued reliance on your pinched notion of desert. I consider my view – and that of others you mention – to involve a quite ordinary and familiar sense of desert, so calling them "non-desertist" seems to me to be trying to tip the scales in favor of your concept, which I've objected to from the outset. I'm largely in agreement with Sen and Nussbaum's vision of justice; I don't think it *deserves* – if I may put it thus – to be called "non-desertist."

Caruso: My point about non-desertist theories of justice was in no way reliant on a "pinched notion of desert." In *A Theory of Justice* (1971), for instance, John Rawls stresses the fact that inequalities of birth are types of undeserved discrimination and claims that desert does not apply to one's place in the distribution of native endowments, one's initial starting point in society, the familial or social circumstances into which one is born, or to the superior character that enables one to put forth the effort to develop one's abilities. Rawls's theory therefore suggests a kind of *metaphysical argument* against desert, according to which: "since most of who we are and what we do is greatly influenced by undeserved native endowments and by the undeserved circumstances into which we are born, one cannot deserve anything, or, at best, one can deserve very little" (Peter Celello's summary of Rawls in his entry on "Desert" in the *Internet Encyclopedia of Philosophy* 2014). For Rawls, desert (basic or non-basic) should not have any role in distributive justice, since these undeserved factors have a major influence on all would-be desert bases (see Rawls, *A Theory of Justice*, sections 17 and 48). Sen and Nussbaum's capabilities approach to justice is equally sensitive to matters of luck and, at least on my reading of them, is in no way grounded in desert.

Let me now turn to a second concern you raise. You worry that the public health–quarantine model will allow for the incapacitation of "people who haven't yet committed crimes but are predicted by experts to become criminals." While I take such concerns seriously, I maintain that there are several considerations that count against the incapacitation of dangerous individuals who haven't yet committed a crime. I spell these out in *Rejecting Retributivism* but will summarize them briefly here (see also Pereboom and Caruso

2018). First, the right to liberty, I contend, must carry significant weight in this context, as should the concern for using people merely as means – and these principles are consistent with free will skepticism. Second, the risk posed by a state policy that allows for preventative detention of non-offenders needs to be taken into serious consideration. In a broad range of societies, allowing the state this option stands to result in much more harm than good, because misuse would be likely. Third, while the kinds of testing required to determine whether someone is a carrier of a communicable disease may often not be unacceptably invasive, the type of screening necessary for determining whether someone has violent criminal tendencies might well be invasive in respects that raise serious moral issues. Fourth, available psychiatric methods for discerning whether an agent is likely to be a violent criminal are not especially reliable and detaining someone on the basis of a screening method that frequently yields false positives is seriously morally objectionable.

Given, then, that we are unable to assess with certainty the likelihood of future violent behavior, and given the potential for false positives, I maintain that significant weight should be given to protecting individual liberty. The burden of proof should always be on the one who wants to limit liberty. Imagine, for example, that the various social and neurological determinants of crime are like individual dials on a vast combination lock. Even if nineteen out of, say, twenty dials are in place, the lock will not open until the last dial (e.g. the last environmental or neurological trigger) is put in place. Of course, in real life the number of variables responsible for violent behavior is much greater. I therefore contend that since we are in a poor epistemic position to judge when (if ever) certain factors will trigger a violent episode, and since this will likely remain true for the foreseeable future, we should put a bright line in the sand in favor of protecting individual liberty and against preemptive incapacitation.

For these reasons, I propose we adopt an attitude of *epistemic skepticism* when it comes to judging the dangerousness of someone who has not yet committed a crime. Given the limitations of our current screening methods, their invasiveness, and the likelihood of false positives, our default position should be to respect individual liberty and prohibit the preventative detention of non-offenders. Following Jean Floud and Warren Young (1981), I have argued that anyone who has not yet committed a crime should be entitled to a *presumption of harmlessness*, much as a person should be entitled to a *presumption of innocence*. Just as the presumption of innocence protects the unconvicted person against punishment, so the presumption of harmlessness protects the unconvicted person against preventive detention. And not only is the presumption of harmlessness consistent with the attitude of epistemic skepticism, it's also a presumption that should be afforded all rational individuals since respect for persons and considerations of justice demand it. These considerations, I contend, will block preemptive incapacitation in all but the most extreme cases.

Dennett: I'm relieved to see that your view takes seriously the right to presumption of harmlessness. And if some misguided state officials start rounding up likely future criminals and putting them in quarantine, what do you propose to do with those state officials? Put them in quarantine? Are you going to have *laws* in your quarantine state, or just *policies without punishment for ignoring them*?

Caruso: Rogue state officials who decided to disregard the presumptions of innocence and harmlessness would represent a serious threat to society and should therefore be removed from office. In most cases, prohibiting them from holding positions of power again would be enough to protect public safety. But if it weren't, and depending on the particular circumstance, incapacitation might be justified. This might also be a good place to answer your earlier question about white-collar criminals. You asked: "Are white-collar criminals who are found guilty going to be allowed to run their businesses from their comfortable quarters in the quarantine facility?" First, I would say that most white-collar crimes are probably better dealt with by less restrictive means than quarantine. If a stockbroker were to engage in insider trading, the principle of least infringement might favor removing their license and ability to trade in the future – along with some process of restitution. We can say the same for a lawyer who abuses their position, or a doctor who illegally prescribes pain medication for profit. Of course, if removing an individual's license or prohibiting them from working in a particular field is *not enough* to protect society from harm, then and only then can we justify more restrictive measures.

As for your question about laws, of course I want to preserve them. No one is suggesting that we return to a Hobbesian state of nature where chaos reigns and life is "solitary, poor, nasty, brutish, and short." I wish you would stop suggesting, even in jest, that skeptics would recommend such a ridiculous thing. Laws are part of our shared social contract and they play an important role in keeping us safe. The main difference between our views is *not* that you consider laws necessary for a properly functioning society and I don't. Instead, the difference is that you see violations of the law as justifying the state's right to punish in accordance with desert, whereas I see violations of the law, especially for violent crimes, as justifying the state's right to sanction and incapacitate wrongdoers on the grounds of self-defense and defense of others.

Dennett: And I cannot see how your proposal for dealing with "rogue state officials" and other white-collar criminals differs from punishment, when push comes to shove (as it surely often would). You acknowledge that if taking away their licenses and prohibiting them from working in a particular field is "not enough" you would justify "more restrictive measures." So, it seems that you agree with me that *enforcing* your quarantine system will require you to threaten to *punish* those who break the laws – the state will "sanction and incapacitate" them. My position agrees with yours on the practical necessity, in a secure and happy state, of laws with sanctions and incapacitation. Where my policy differs from yours is that it restricts such sanctions and incapacitation to those who deserve it; yours restricts it to those who are deemed by some authorities to be a threat to public safety in the same way pandemic carriers are. Except that you do now also acknowledge some backward-looking factors are relevant – "causal" responsibility, *mens rea*, competence. It seems to me then that you acknowledge all the factors I have advanced but insist that they don't amount to requirements of *moral* responsibility.

Caruso: First, I do not agree with you that enforcing the public health–quarantine model will require *threats of punishment* for those who break the laws. Of course, if my model endorsed punishment, that might be true. But it doesn't. As I said earlier, while consequentialist and other forward-looking theories of punishment are consistent with free will skepticism, I reject them for independent moral reasons. For a full accounting of those reasons, see my *Rejecting Retributivism* (2021a) as well as David Boonin's *The Problem of Punishment* (2008) and Michael Zimmerman's *The Immorality of Punishment* (2011). Instead of threatening punishment, then, what my model proposes is that those individuals who violate laws designed to protect public safety will trigger the state's right to restrict their liberty on the grounds of self-defense and prevention of harm to others. And, importantly, this justification for restricting liberty is analogous to the justification for quarantine and in no way presupposes or appeals to free will, just deserts, or the kind of moral responsibility I deny.

As for the "enforcement" part of your question, I do not think my model needs to embrace "threats of punishment." Instead, what we need is *transparency about our policies* so that citizens know that the state will incapacitate violent criminals on the grounds of self-defense and defense of others (when no less restrictive options are available). Think about how it works in the public health arena. We require that the state (or its agencies) be transparent about, and make publicly available, their policies and rationale for quarantine. And we do not view this transparency as a "threat of punishment." For one thing, when we quarantine individuals with communicable diseases, we do not punish them. Punishment requires more than just limiting liberty – see Boonin (2008), Zimmerman (2011), Duff (2017), or really any of the philosophical literature on punishment. Second, such transparency would not amount to a "threat" – or, at least, it's not obvious that it would be correct to interpret it as such. Enforcing the public health–quarantine model in the realm of criminal justice would essentially be the same. The state would need to be transparent about, and make publicly available, its policies and rationale for any and all restrictions on liberty, but it would be wrong to say that it must threaten punishment (since what the model proposes does not constitute punishment).

Perhaps your real concern is about deterrence – i.e. that without the threat of punishment, the law will be unable effectively to deter would-be criminals. In response, I would say two things. First, while I understand this concern, my preference is to avoid giving deterrence any justificatory role in my theory. That's because deterrence-based justifications of punishment, while consistent with free will skepticism, face a number of well-known difficulties. I'll mention just one (for others see the books by Boonin and Zimmerman mentioned above). Concerns over so-called *manipulative use* are particularly acute with regard to general deterrence, since punishing a person in order to deter others from crime would be to use that individual as an instrument (or a means-to-an-end) to affect the behavior of others. To see why, it might be instructive to first consider a slightly different example: the problem of evil. Many find it hard or impossible to understand why an all-knowing, all-powerful, all-loving God would allow the suffering of, say, innocent children. For instance, a child born with Tay-Sachs disease, a genetic disorder that results in the destruction of nerve cells in the brain and spinal cord, will live a life of nothing but pain and suffering and die sometime in early childhood. Around three to six months of age, the baby will lose the ability to turn over, sit, or crawl, followed by seizures, hearing loss, the inability to move, and finally death. Some theodicies attempt to explain such suffering by pointing to the potential benefits it may have on others. For instance, the child with Tay-Sachs may be used to test the parents' faith, help us understand the contrast between good and evil, or challenge society to be more loving, compassionate, and cooperative. Such replies, however, are thoroughly unconvincing and morally problematic. They run afoul of what I like to call the *Jack and Jill problem*, since they're analogous to a parent beating the hell out of Jack to teach Jill a lesson, which does not explain Jack (pun intended)! That is, the use of Jack for the benefit of Jill does not explain the necessity of Jack's suffering (or the child with Tay-Sachs) and is intuitively wrong.

Consequentialist deterrence theories have a similar problem. Consider the example of Leandro Andrade, who, as a result of California's three-strikes law, was sentenced to twenty-five years to life in 1995 for stealing a few VHS tapes from Kmart.

On November 4, 1995, Leandro Andrade walked into a Southern California Kmart. Andrade – who had several past criminal convictions – was about to commit a crime that would lead to a prison sentence of twenty-five years to life. Two weeks later, still a free man, Andrade struck again. This time, the target was a Kmart just three miles to the west of his previous crime. His plan was identical and would result in another sentence of twenty-five years to life. In two weeks, Andrade had attempted to steal nine VHS tapes: *The Fox and the Hound, The Pebble and the Penguin, Snow White, Batman Forever, Free Willy 2, Little Women, The Santa Clause*, and *Cinderella*. The total cost of the movies was $153.54. The actual cost to Andrade was fifty years to life. (Enns 2006: 1)

Under California's three-strikes laws at the time, two counts of petty theft with a prior conviction carried consecutive sentences of twenty-five years to life. Note that the injustice of this sentence was the result of the fact that three-strikes laws were implemented across the US in the 1990s in an attempt to deter crime. It's important to note that their justification was largely consequentialist and *not* retributivist. Advocates of such laws maintained that, although individuals like Leandro Andrade may not be much of a threat to public safety, having fixed and harsh penalties for those who commit three felonies will help deter would-be criminals. Unfortunately, these laws ended up resulting in extremely harsh penalties for minor crimes. The case of Leandro Andrade is just one example, but there are many others. The core problem with three-strikes laws is that when individuals who are not a serious threat to public safety are sent away for life in an attempt to deter others, they are treated as a means-to-an-end to be used for the benefit of others. In this way, Leandro Andrade resembles Jack in that both are harmed severely, without their consent, for the sake of others and in a manner most would consider unacceptable.

My second reply to the deterrence concern would be the following. If we are transparent about our policies, which we must be, then a system based on incapacitation will produce, *as a natural side-effect*, a significant level of general deterrence for free. Pereboom calls this "free general deterrence":

> We have the right to know what the state does to its members, and why, when they are dangerous to others. But such a policy would serve to yield, as a side effect, general deterrence. Such preventive detention would not only have a deterrence effect on the actual unjust aggressors who are detained but also on others who are tempted to commit crimes. This general deterrent effect comes for free, so to speak, since it is a side effect of the state's satisfying a

publicity requirement on special deterrence. I call general deterrent effects justified as special deterrence on the basis of the self-defense right *free general deterrence*. (Pereboom 2019: 103)

Free general deterrence follows from the state's requirement to be transparent about its practices regarding the incapacitation of the seriously dangerous, *but it does not appeal to deterrence in justifying its practices*. In this way, the public health–quarantine model can produce a significant level of free general deterrence while still respecting the principle of least infringement, which demands the minimum harm required to eliminate a threat on the right of self-defense.

Dennett: If I understand you, Gregg, this is how you deny that your view requires threats of punishment: "I don't call it a *threat* because it's just the state's obligation to be transparent about treatment policy, and I don't call it *punishment* because even though it involves 'sanctioning' and 'incapacitation' that doesn't meet my definition of punishment." The state, according to you, isn't *threatening*, or even *warning*, it's just *informing* people of a certain contingency. And if people are thus informed, most will likely be motivated to adjust their projects in the light of that information. Or as the Godfather said, "I made them an offer they couldn't refuse." It's not a threat; it's a very generous offer, and anyone who thinks otherwise is being unfairly suspicious. Well played.

I also agree with you that some theodicies – I would say *all* theodicies – are "thoroughly unconvincing and morally problematic." But that's not a problem for my view; its insistence on desert (in my sense, not yours) explicitly rules out punishing the innocent to accomplish some "greater good" while accepting the principle of obligatory quarantine (with compensation) for those whose free movement would endanger others' lives. In other words, I have no quarrel with quarantine in its current role; I am just skeptical about your proposal to enlarge it.

Your major innovation, you claim, is replacing punishment with quarantine, and abandoning deterrence as a positive reason for any law. But citing abuse of the law's power to deter (as in three-strikes laws) is no argument against deterrence. It's a good argument against abuse. And I note that you continue to restrict the state's legitimacy in quarantining to those who are "violent" or "seriously dangerous," so I am still wondering how you handle not just "white-collar" criminals but others who are not often violent – I'm expanding my list – blackmailers, purveyors of child pornography, con artists who bilk innocent folks out of their retirement money, counterfeiters, cyber-pirates, voting-machine tamperers, retailers who falsely advertise bargains to get customers into their stores and then try to sell them other goods . . . the list is enormous. None of them are obvious candidates for *quarantine*, or so it seems to me. Do you imagine they won't be a problem in your utopia? Why not? How will you deal with them, without a system of punishment?

You are concerned with not giving deterrence a "justificatory role" in your theory. I am concerned that leaving out deterrence by leaving out punishment turns laws into mere recommendations. And, as I've suggested before, without the, um, promise of punishment, you won't be able to manage your involuntary quarantine system. As you have no doubt noticed, the current strong *recommendations* to self-isolate in the face of the COVID-19 virus pandemic have been augmented around the country with quickly passed local *laws* with significant penalties for violators. You must be deeply opposed to all these new measures, right? What would you do?

Caruso: Let's settle this issue of whether quarantine is a form of punishment once and for all, since it's not just "my" definition of punishment that it fails to satisfy – quarantine fails to satisfy *any and all* reasonable definitions of punishment. On no intuitive definition of punishment do we punish the individual with ebola when we quarantine them. At a minimum, *intended harm* is a necessary condition of punishment. As Leo Zaibert correctly notes, "whatever else punishment seeks to do, it seeks to make wrongdoers suffer (by somehow diminishing their well-being or by visiting upon them something they do not want)" (2018: 1). He goes on to write:

> To punish ... is to (try to) inflict suffering (or pain or misery or a bad thing, etc.) on someone as a response to her wrongdoing. Punishment without trying to inflict suffering is like gifting an object without intending to transfer any right over the thing gifted or like feeding someone without intending to give her some nourishment. (Zaibert 2018: 7)

The renowned legal philosopher H. L. A. Hart stresses this point in his definition of punishment, which he maintains "must involve pain or other consequences normally considered unpleasant" (2008: 4). Wittgenstein concurs, finding it perfectly "clear" that just as "reward must be something pleasant," punishment must be "something unpleasant" (1961: 78e; see also Tasioulas 2006; Boonin 2008; Zimmerman 2011; Zaibert 2018). The kind of harm, suffering, or harsh treatment meted out by the state in cases of legal punishment need not involve physical pain, but it must be unpleasant or diminish (at least temporarily) the well-being of offenders.

It must also be the case that the state (or someone acting on its behalf) deliberately intends the harm, since unintended harms do not constitute punishment. If I trip and knock over an elderly person, causing them harm, I do not thereby punish them. Punishment requires *intentional* harm. As Alec Walen writes:

> For an act to count as punishment, it must ... First ... impose some sort of cost or hardship on, or at the very least withdraw a benefit that would otherwise be enjoyed by, the person being punished. Second, the punisher must do so intentionally, not as an accident, and not as a side-effect of pursuing some other end. (2014, sect. 2.1)

Michael Zimmerman concurs with this second requirement and writes, "no accidental harming can qualify as punishment; if you punish someone, then the harm that you cause is something that you intended to cause" (2011: 7–8). He goes on to argue:

> This being the case, it might be thought that although no accidental harm counts as punishment, perhaps the harm that punishment involves needn't be intended either, as long as it is foreseen. But I think that a little reflection shows that that can't be right. We often knowingly cause harm without intending to do so. Indeed, the harm that we knowingly cause might be just the same kind of harm as that caused by punishment but, unless we intend to cause it, we cannot be said to be engaged in punishment. Compare incarceration with quarantine, for example. The extent to which one's liberty is restricted may be the same in either case, but only the former qualifies as punishment, for only in the former case is the harm caused by the restriction to liberty intended. In the latter case, the harm is foreseen but it is not intended – although the restriction itself is of course intended, for otherwise it could not be classified as a case of quarantine at all. (2011: 9–10)

The difference between punishment and quarantine is obvious to anyone who considers it for more than a moment, and Zimmerman is absolutely correct that quarantine is not a form of punishment since it does not intentionally seek to cause harm. Punishment, on the other hand, requires that the harms caused be intended. I could run through the other necessary conditions of legal punishment if you like as well – for instance, punishment also expresses the state's disapproval both of the offense and of the offender. So, what distinguishes punishment from other kinds of coercive impositions, such as taxation, is not only that punishment is intended to harm individuals, or reduce their well-being, but that it also aims at communicating disapproval and condemnation for perceived wrongdoing. Do you really mean to conflate such important (and dare I say obvious) distinctions? It seems to me that your real concern is over the *enforcement* of my proposal, but it's simply incorrect to say (or imply) that what is being enforced is punishment. It's not.

You also overlook or avoid (I don't know which it is) my core point about theodicies, deterrence, and the problem of manipulative use. You write, these are "not a problem for my view; its insistence on desert (in my sense, not yours) explicitly rules out punishing the innocent to accomplish some 'greater good' . . ." My point, however, had nothing really to do with punishing the innocent. Instead, I was raising the more general concern that consequentialist theories that aim to achieve some level of general deterrence are willing to treat people merely as a means in order to promote some further independent end. I used the example of three-strikes laws and the case of Leandro Andrade, who was not innocent. The point is that, if a harsh form of punishment were the only effective way to deter others, consequentialists are willing to *use* certain individuals (i.e. those punished) to *help deter others*.

I would also like to note that your desire for fixed punishments for those who break the laws/rules, was *exactly the motivation behind the "tough on crime" drive for fixed prison sentences and "truth in sentencing" laws that were enacted to reduce the possibility of early release from prison.* The idea behind these policies was that judges had too much discretion in varying their sentences for the same crime. Proponents of these policies also felt that parole boards should not be able to release someone for murder after only serving five or ten years of a twenty-five-to-life sentence. The concern was that allowing such discretion would be tantamount to your analogy of the umpire who calls balls and strikes based on *situational* and *local* considerations rather than the cold hard (equally applied) rules and consequences. Hence, it's easy for you to dismiss such examples as "an abuse of the law's power" rather than an "argument against deterrence," but I think you fail to realize just how problematic punishment justified on the grounds of deterrence really is. Do you favor fixed sentences for those who commit felonies? If the best (or only effective) way to deter would-be criminals was to give those who commit felonies a long sentence after they committed two or three (or four) felonies, wouldn't your view demand that we do so? How do you respond to the "use" objection (see Pereboom 2014)? It's a bit amusing that you want me to spell out the appropriate reaction to each and every crime under the sun, but you're not willing to do the same. If you filled in the details of your view or considered concrete examples and sentencing guidelines, I think you would quickly realize that the devil's in the details.

My theory, on the other hand, gives a straightforward answer to your question about non-violent crimes: restrictions on liberty should be proportionate to the danger posed by an individual, and any sanctions that exceed this upper bound will be considered unjustified. Since my theory favors flexibility and sensitivity to specifics, each case would need to be judged on its own terms. I see this as an advantage, since not all felonies are equal and not all individuals who commit felonies represent the same risk to society moving forward. As a general rule, though, I think most non-violent crimes can be better dealt with by less restrictive means than quarantine (e.g. monitoring, loss of license, counseling, drug treatment, mental health services, etc.). The right of self-defense and prevention of harm to others gives the state the right to limit liberty in these ways, without appealing to deterrence as a justification. The same, I would say, is true for those individuals who refuse to self-isolate in the face of the COVID-19 virus pandemic, at least in those places where there are laws against going outside or gathering in large groups. Individuals who disregard such restrictions are placing the public at risk, and the right of self-defense gives the state the justification to place them under mandatory quarantine – if no less restrictive measures are available. My recommendation would be that we first try mandatory *home* quarantine, where the use of an ankle bracelet or other means of monitoring (e.g. required periodic phone calls to/ from home) are used to ensure compliance. If the individual does not comply with these restrictions, then the right of self-defense may allow for additional steps, such as forced quarantine at a state facility. Note, though, that: (a) I'm answering your questions about enforcement, (b) these are rough recommendations (which I'm making on the fly) and are subject to revision in light of best practices, and (c) such "enforcement" is grounded in the right of self-defense and does not appeal to deterrence or desert in any way.

Punishment, Morality, and Deterrence

Dennett: I think your quotations from Hart and Wittgenstein say it all. Punishment, Hart observes, "must involve pain or other consequences normally considered unpleasant" and as you say, "Wittgenstein concurs, finding it perfectly 'clear' that just as 'reward must be something pleasant,' punishment must be 'something unpleasant.'" This is a truism that hardly needs the support of these great philosophers, but in the spirit of clarification they drew attention to it. Duly noted. And you are right when you say "It seems to me that your real concern is over the *enforcement* of my proposal." Exactly. But you go on to say "but it's simply incorrect to say (or imply) that what is being enforced is punishment. It's not." I didn't say or imply that quarantine is punishment; I said you can't have a system of quarantine that isn't *enforced* – that is, *backed up by* a system of *punishment* for those who do not cooperate. The state must threaten (or advise or promise or publicize the fact) that "those who don't comply with our quarantine system will suffer consequences normally considered unpleasant." Fines are unpleasant, the confiscation of property is unpleasant, involuntary institutionalization is unpleasant; these are punishments and are, as your legal scholars carefully enunciate, *intended* to be unpleasant. That's the point of them. Your suggestions for alternative ways of handling the situation just postpone the compliance problem. Earlier I asked you whether you were going to have laws or just recommendations. Laws without intended unpleasant consequences for violations aren't really laws, I'm saying.

You say I "overlook or avoid (I don't know which it is) my core point about theodicies, deterrence, and the problem of manipulative use." You're right. I don't think this familiar Kantian trope about not treating people as means is serious. (It's not a "move" I would want to make in a philosophical argument, and I didn't want to open that can of worms.) If we are meticulous in how we define our terms here, it turns out that we use people as means all the time, and there's nothing wrong with it. You're using me as a helpful contrast for your view, and I'm using you for the same purpose. But we're not treating each other *"merely"* as means (whatever *that* means). There are lots of well-known and respected boundaries in how we use others while respecting their dignity, their feelings, their autonomy, their rights, and so forth. If you want to object that *any* system of punishment must use those punished *merely* as means, I disagree. Framing an innocent person to "set an example" would be using that person merely as a means, and is strictly out-of-bounds in my justification of punishment, but publicizing the punishment of a duly convicted criminal is not only acceptable; it is obligatory. We can't have secret systems of punishment. You also say "The point is that, if a harsh form of punishment were the only effective way to deter others, consequentialists are willing to *use* certain individuals (i.e. those punished) to *help deter others.*" If you strike the word "harsh" I happily endorse this principle (as a good consequentialist). As I have said, effective law depends on the public having *respect* for the law, and if the law is *too* harsh, this will undermine respect. You may be saying that any *punishment* is too harsh, and I would disagree vigorously. (And no, my view does not require fixed sentences, or mounting sentences for recidivists. It requires even-handed justice that can be understood and respected.

Of course the system of punishment I'm defending *uses* those punished to deter others, but if those punished have truly committed the offenses for which they are being punished, and qualify as members of the Moral Agents Club, they have only themselves to blame; they accepted this consequence in advance as a fair price for the political freedom and security provided by the state.)

The reason I challenged you with a long list of non-violent crimes was not, as you contend, to oblige you "to spell out the appropriate reaction to each and every crime under the sun" but to invite you to sketch some general principle that would cover such cases. They don't appear to meet your conditions for quarantine. Taxation, as you point out, is not punishment, but going to jail for cheating on your taxes is. If you don't enforce the laws – with punishment – few people will pay their taxes. You say "most non-violent crimes can be better dealt with by less restrictive means than quarantine." I simply don't believe you, but I am curious about why you said "most" instead of "all." You must think then that at least *some* non-violent crimes have to be "sanctioned" with "incapacitation." Or as I would put it, if we want laws people will honor, they have to have penalties (punishments, normally unpleasant consequences) for violations. This is probably a good time to recall the claim I once made that set this whole debate in motion. I had said "A world without punishment is not a world any of us would want to live in" (Dennett 2008: 258). A number of philosophers were dismayed, shocked. Now, thanks to this debate, I have given my reasons in some detail, and you, Gregg, have resolutely resisted. I hope they will recognize that, after all, they don't want to live in a world without punishment.

Caruso: Let me begin with your points about punishment and its enforcement. First, you approvingly quote Hart and Wittgenstein, noting that punishment requires harsh treatment and consequences that are normally considered unpleasant. You then go on to write: "you can't have a system of quarantine that isn't *enforced* – that is, *backed up by* a system of *punishment* for those who do not cooperate. The state must threaten (or advise or promise or publicize the fact) that those who don't comply with our quarantine system will suffer 'consequences normally considered unpleasant.'" You go on to say that, "fines are unpleasant, the confiscation of property is unpleasant, involuntary institutionalization is unpleasant" and that these are forms of punishment. It seems, however, that you completely missed my point about punishment requiring *more than* harsh treatment – even more than *intentional* harsh treatment. Punishment, as standardly understood by legal scholars, requires that the state, or someone acting on behalf of the state, not only harm the punishee, but that the harm be *intentional* and include a *condemnatory* component – i.e. it must *express* the state's disapproval both of the offense and of the offender (see Zimmerman 2011). With regard to this last condition, Antony Duff writes:

> [I]t is widely accepted that what distinguishes punishment from mere 'penalties' [see Feinberg 1970] is their reprobative or condemnatory character. Penalties, such as parking tickets, might be imposed to deter the penalised conduct (or to recoup some of the costs that it causes) without being intended to express societal condemnation. But even if a primary purpose of punishment is deterrence ... its imposition (the conviction and formal sentence that the offender receives in court, the administration of the punishment itself) also expresses the censure or condemnation that the offender's crime is taken to warrant. (2017)

Duff goes on to write, correctly in my opinion, that:

> These two features, that punishment is intentionally burdensome and condemnatory, makes the practice especially normatively challenging. How can a practice that not only burdens those subjected to it but aims to burden them, and which convey's society's condemnation, be justified? (2017)

I maintain that the enforcement of the public health–quarantine model can be done without this reprobative or condemnatory component. In fact, if free will skeptics are correct, this condemnatory component would be unjustified – if, that is, we understand it as including judgments about desert-based moral responsibility and blameworthiness, and not just judgments about good and bad behavior.

Having said all that, I'm tired of fighting with you over the definition of punishment. If you want to continue to insist, contrary to common philosophical usage, that "punishment" simply stands for any practice that restricts liberty or imposes consequences normally considered unpleasant, then so be it. The fact still remains that your account differs from mine in significant ways. For one, you offer a mixed account of punishment that appeals to both consequentialist and retributivist components, one that retains the notion of desert, whereas I justify sanctions and liberty-limiting restrictions on the grounds of self-defense and defense of others. Second, my account in no way presupposes or appeals to free will, just deserts, or retributive blame, whereas your account presupposes that agents are morally responsible in a desert-based sense. Lastly, I want to rid our moral and legal practices of the condemnatory attitudes and judgments associated with free will – including resentment, indignation, moral blame, and *all forms* of retributive punishment – whereas you seem to want to preserve these (at least in part). Perhaps the following example will help.

Imagine a case where an agent *clearly lacks moral responsibility* yet rules still need to be *enforced*. Imagine, for instance, that Betty is suffering from advanced Alzheimer's and is placed in a nursing home/community because her family can no longer properly care for her. The rules of the community dictate that residents should not leave the building, walk the grounds, or leave the community without proper supervision. The rules are put in place to help protect the residents. We can say that the rules are part of the *contract* that residents, or their proxies, must agree to before moving in. The rules, however, are the rules and they need to be enforced. Betty, however, repeatedly violates the rules – for no fault of her own. On more than one occasion she leaves the home and wonders off the grounds without supervision. Luckily nothing happens to her and she is safely returned to the nursing home by the police. I think we would both agree that steps need to be taken to limit Betty's liberty. Perhaps alarms need to be put on the doors to notify the staff that someone is attempting to "escape." Perhaps Betty is required to wear a tracking device. Perhaps the staff repeatedly remind Betty of the rules and tell her that her liberty will be further limited if she does not comply (I'm assuming that Betty retains some reasons-responsiveness, albeit a severely diminished amount). Perhaps *all the residents* are called to a meeting, reminded of the rules, and told that if they break the rules there will be certain consequences. Here we have a case where those in positions of authority "advise or promise or publicize the fact" that there will be "consequences normally considered unpleasant" for breaking the rules, *yet* (a) it's unclear whether we should call this enforcement of the rules "punishment," and (b) *even if* we do, it would be a kind of enforcement that lacks (or *should* lack) the condemnatory component of punishment – since Betty is not morally responsible in the sense needed for such condemnation to be fitting or appropriate. If you agree, then this example shows that we can have the enforcement of sanctions *without assuming that wrongdoers deserve to suffer, without condemnation, and without presupposing free will.*

Moving on, I'm not convinced by your response to my objection that consequentialist theories permit individuals to be used as a means to an end. If I understand you correctly, your reply is simply to deny that there's anything morally wrong with using people in this way. You write: "I don't think this familiar Kantian trope about not treating people as a means is serious." I disagree. I contend that consequentialist deterrence theories run afoul of fairly intuitive moral principle. But before I can fully spell out my concern,

I first need to introduce a distinction made by Victor Tadros, Professor of Criminal Law and Legal Theory at the University of Warwick. In his book *The Ends of Harm* (2011), Tadros distinguishes between *manipulative use*, where someone is used in order to promote some further independent goal, and harming someone to *eliminate* a threat they pose. In cases of manipulative use, we use individuals as a means to an end. And Tadros cites a wide range of examples where it is intuitively objectionable to use someone manipulatively in this way. On the other hand, harming someone to *eliminate* a threat they pose is much easier to justify, based on the right of self-defense. As Tadros puts it:

> If the *means principle* is a principle that prohibits using other people as a means, it necessarily involves intentions. For we can be regarded as using a person to achieve some goal only if we intend to harm that person in order to achieve the goal. But not all intentional harming involves using. Sometimes we intentionally harm a person simply to eliminate the harm that they pose to us. This is often true in cases of self-defense. When I defend myself against an attacker I do not use the attacker as a means to avert a threat. That person is the threat. The *means principle* is best understood as a principle that prohibits a subset of the set of intentional harming: that where the person is harmed for some further goal. In other words, the *means principle* prohibits manipulative rather than eliminative harming. (2011: 14)

I maintain that the "use" objection to consequentialist deterrence theories is best characterized as an objection against manipulative use, not eliminative harming. The right of self-defense and defense of others permits certain harms that do not count as "manipulative use" (see Tadros 2011; Pereboom 2018; Shaw 2019; Caruso 2021a). Given the distinction between eliminating harm and manipulative use, I contend that consequentialist deterrence theories run afoul of the *prohibition on manipulative use*. In particular, concerns over manipulative use are uniquely acute with regard to general deterrence, since punishing a person in order to deter others from crime would be to use that individual as an instrument (or a means-to-an-end) to affect the behavior of others. And unfortunately, this is exactly what we do when we punish person A beyond what is necessary to protect society (from the threat posed by A) for the benefit of deterring persons B, C, and D.

Dennett: Perhaps it's time for me to put in a good word for deterrence, since you have argued so vigorously against it. First, it works, and has always worked – but of course not perfectly. Where you are concerned to ensure that your theory "does not appeal to deterrence or desert in any way," I am concerned to have a theory of morality and law that *works*. Your "theory" strikes me as a philosophers' sort of theory: a collection of interlocking definitions that is invulnerable to charges of inconsistency with "our intuitions." I am looking for – and presenting the sketch of – a theory that *explains how and why* our evolved system of morality and law, imperfect as it currently is, is the best game in town. It isn't justified by the mere fact that it is a product of genetic and cultural evolution; it is justified – to the extent that it is – by the fact that after several thousand years of intelligent, deliberate, well-intentioned criticism and reform, nobody has come up with anything else that looks as if it could work at all.

Morality is clearly a social construction in one sense; it is neither a gift from God nor an entirely genetically transmitted "instinct." It is a product of social activity. For several thousand years people have been actively and foresightedly trying to revise, reform, replace, improve our morality and our attitudes towards morality, but before that time the R&D that guided morality's *development* (not *construction*) can be viewed as an exploratory, semi-understood trial-and-error process that yielded local improvements, which became more or less stable or in equilibrium, and these in turn could on occasion migrate outside of local societies as memes do, mutating (getting distorted sometimes, getting improved sometimes), and always appealing to and exploiting the current psychological dispositions of their hosts, as tempered and influenced by the cultural immune systems we all acquire and harbor.

It is a fundamental mistake in evolutionary thinking to suppose that whatever ways (ideas, practices, concepts, policies) survived this process must have proven fitness-enhancing for the human species, the lineage, or even the individuals (or groups of individuals) who adopted them. Some, even many, of the established ways (of thinking, of acting) may have been cultural parasites, in effect, exploiting weaknesses in the psychology of their hosts. You would put retributivism in this category, and so would I.

All of this evolution was accompanied by, and occasionally given a boost by, the efforts of intelligent designers: political and religious leaders who precipitated more memorable, persuasive expressions of the opinions that were taking hold. As in boat-building and architecture, some of the "intelligently designed" innovations soon proved to be bugs, not features, but others earned respect, and then popularity and finally something close to consensus.

All of these phenomena taken together yield the current set of *intuitions* that "we" tend to share about both morality and law. *The law* is largely a recent – extremely recent, in biological perspective – product of deliberate, intelligent (re-)design, while *morality* is a much more bottom-up, semi-understood product of both memetic and, in response, genetic evolution. Hobbes's just-so story about the state of nature was very much on the right track, and his social contract is a time-lapsed and idealized sketch of the set of free-floating rationales (Dennett 1983, 2017) that has shaped our shared sense of right and wrong. We needn't worry about which aspects of it are genetically transmitted ("innate" morality) and which are socially, memetically transmitted (culturally endorsed morality).

Neither the genetic route nor the memetic route has any claim to legitimacy in virtue of the route taken, in any case.

Doing "what is natural" may turn out to be doing the right thing, or it may turn out to be doing something we should condemn, and try to undo or mitigate, using our culturally acquired leverage. Loyalty, friendship, a basic sense of fairness, and a narrow-range kind of compassion show signs of a genetic basis (recall Hume on the "natural virtues"), while revenge, slavery, treating women as possessions, xenophobia, and other ugly dispositions also have quite clear genetic traces.

Where, then, do we get the Olympian perspective from which to make these moral judgments about the moral judgments we have made in the past and are still inclined to make? From one of culture's greatest inventions: the forum of informed persuasion, governed by consensual rules of argument and persuasion. That's what we're doing right now. Philosophy, or more particularly *practical* philosophy, is the project where intelligent designers have attempted to assess, critique, improve, and ultimately *justify* the principles we all should live by. We might call this process *political science* if that term hadn't been appropriated. This process is, like science more generally, a fallible but self-critical, self-improving, self-conscious inquiry into the project of establishing and maintaining norms and laws that will optimize (in a sense which is itself very much subject to critical adjustment) the well-being of all. (All what? Another revisable category.)

What a Darwinian perspective can help us see is that the innovations we attempt in our effort to reform our policies constitute an arms race, an opponent process in which (to start with the simplest cases) each new law passed sets off a search for loopholes by those whose behavior provoked the passage of the new law in the first place. When loopholes are found and exploited, a revised law will be passed, or the law will fall into discredit and cease to be enforced, or its enforcement will have unintended and undesirable side effects. Since respect for the law is always a desideratum (avoiding the catastrophe of a failed state), finding laws that reasonable people will, in the main, abide by and respect is the chief task of legislators. Note that these rationales need not be articulated or represented in the minds of either loophole-seekers or loophole-closers for them to govern and describe the process; one can quite unreflectively discover and exploit a loophole without thinking of it in those terms, and one can dimly recognize the value of respect for law without having any clear ideas about why maintaining that respect is a foundational requirement of stability in a state. The same dynamic plays out in the more fundamental and informal arena of morality. As we raise our children, we want them to acquire respect for our rules and policies, to acquire the perspective of a reflective, non-impulsive, caring agent who *takes* responsibility for her choices and actions, accepting moral criticism and even punishment when it is due. The project of rearing and socializing our children so that they can enter the adult world with a good chance of success is well known to be a daunting challenge, requiring patience, persistence, judgment and flexibility, which would be too much to expect of many, if not most of us, were it not for the biases inherited with our genes: we normally find our offspring cute, cuddly, adorable, and worthy of considerable sacrifice. The natural, genetically endorsed tendency of all of us to love and protect our children has been wisely – if largely unwittingly – exploited by the processes that have generated our moral policies and their supporting intuitions.

In short, we try not to "spoil" our children. Some parents succeed better than others. It is a tightrope act, with mistakes and pitfalls on both sides. Too much blaming and scolding can create a guilt-ridden adolescent and adult, to say nothing of the excesses of corporal punishment and outright abuse. Too little "supervision" can produce young adults who, "through no fault of their own," are burdened with an unwarranted sense of entitlement, unable to summon the self-control required to negotiate the complex social world of adulthood without constantly falling into conflict with their fellow citizens and with authority.

Negotiating these opposing pitfalls is a delicate task, especially in light of the fact that every move we make is public, discussable, criticizable, likely to "telegraph our punches" to those we are trying to influence (for their own good, of course, but mainly for the good of society at large). I spoke above about "practical philosophy" because we cannot do the job right while sequestered in our ivory towers, outside the ken of the general populace, so we must factor in the predictable effects of our very proposals – and our supporting reasons – on those who would be affected by them. We are not considering the most effective and humane policies of cattle raising or fishing or, for that matter, bricklaying, where the objects of concern are oblivious to our reasoning. We are considering how *we*, language-using, comprehending adults should go about influencing *each other's* behavior. This fact is sometimes forgotten by proponents on one side or another.

For instance, when you propose to *abolish* blame and responsibility outright, you deny to everyone the respect due to an agent who undertakes to live a moral life and obey the just laws of her society. As Erin Kelly puts it, with appropriate directness, "It is arrogant and disrespectful to presume to be able to tell who has and who lacks basic moral competence" (2018: 83). Obnoxious paternalism aside, such positions never – so far as I can tell – provide plausible details for how even a minimally secure and stable state could be achieved under such a vision. Kelly alludes to such views only in passing: "More radically, we could refuse to blame by suspending the agential perspective altogether and concentrating on a view of persons as part of the natural causal order" (2018: 114). *Could* we do this? I doubt it, but in any case we shouldn't. We can't view *ourselves* as just part of the causal order without lapsing into some kind of passive stupor. And to treat others this way while maintaining an agential view of our own dear selves would be beyond disrespectful; it would be monstrous.

Since treating every man, woman and child (and infant

and mentally disabled ... human being) as fully morally competent would also be a travesty, incapable of securing the respect of any thoughtful person, we *must* make a distinction between those who are morally competent and those who are not. This, I have long held, is the fundamental pivot; *this* is the variety of free will worth wanting.

Taking the birds'-eye view of this larger process, we – we political scientists, we ethicists, we philosophers, we citizens – recognize the fact that *equality* and *uniformity* and *rules* must not be abandoned if we are to maintain respect for the system we are all relying on. If, however, we want to achieve a secure and happy state with as much political freedom as possible, we must temper justice with mercy, conviction with compassion, and we must administer punishment – which is necessary – with minimal suffering and maximal opportunity for rehabilitation. The obscene sentencing policies in force today in the United States are finally being recognized for the dishonorable failure they have been, and there is mounting public pressure for legislators to follow the lead of their constituents if not their consciences and dramatically reform our overly punitive "correctional" system. But just as troubling as our decades-too-long imprisonments under harrowing conditions is the impediment ("a life-altering social stigma" (Kelly 2018: 39)) of the retributive branding that now follows convicted felons through their whole lives, like the Scarlet Letter. There is huge scope for reform here. Disenfranchising felons has just been abolished by referendum in Florida, and other states will, one hopes, soon follow that lead, one small but important step in the right direction. Introducing assistance, not further obstacles, to those whose future depends critically on recovering their reputations is a long-recognized but patchily implemented policy.

There is a reason why rehabilitation has had such a checkered history, a reason made clear from the arm's race perspective, and perhaps best illustrated by the parallel arms race in parenting, in rearing a child to competent moral adulthood. When should we start treating children as responsible adults, and when should we give them a break? As one of my grandchildren recently said to her mother, "But Mom, it's so *hard* to be good!" And sometimes it is particularly hard, but if our forgiveness is automatic, the lesson drawn is apt to be that we never "mean it" when we reprimand. Only the preternaturally saintly fail to notice when prohibitions are never enforced, and everyone else soon adjusts their compliance accordingly. Of course it is not just pre-moral children who more or less innocently test the limits; adults less innocently but almost universally drive five or ten miles over the speed limit because they have made a calculation that tells them that just as they made pragmatic allowances for their children's misdeeds, the law can be counted on to err on the side of leniency, simply because it makes enforcement so much less unpleasant and costly. But there have to be unwanted consequences – even dreaded consequences – for bad behavior if children are to develop the habits of thought and action that make bad behavior all but unthinkable, and if adults are to be protected from their own weaknesses and passions.

Even if we reform our legal system – a *relatively* straightforward and practical legislative and judicial task – we will still have the punitive, retributive, reactive attitudes of morality to deal with, and what practical chance is there of reforming them? Some optimists, you among them, point to other non-Western cultures for examples of societies that get along quite well with muted or transformed if not entirely absent categories of blame. Here is where the arms race perspective has a particularly critical role to play, building on Kelly's sensitive exploration. We need to think about the whole process of enculturation, from infancy (and parenthood) through school and adolescence to adulthood, with its rites of passage and its myths.

Kelly notes that in tort law, in contrast to criminal law, moral *blame* is not always an issue (2018: 116). Her parallel with tort law is very instructive. Victims have the choice not to pursue their complaints, and often excuse or ignore (or just don't bother). But *fortunately*, some victims invest the time, money, and effort in getting their rights attended to. We all benefit from the efforts of victims who take their tortfeasors to court and win. We don't need everyone to be litigious, and can tolerate an ambient reliance on others to find the outrage and energy to defend their rights and ours. A stable society can absorb a substantial number of free riders if it is otherwise well run. Similarly, a parent who always excuses her child's bad behavior, who never blames, bears some of the responsibility if that child grows up to be an antisocial, morally incompetent agent. We don't *have* to assign responsibility to the parents, and if we place all the responsibility on the parents (who then may offload it to their parents, and grandparents, and the environment in general, etc.) we subvert the whole process of socialization on which societies depend. *What prevents this vicious regress from getting under way* is the simple expedient of letting (prospective) parents know that society will *hold* their children responsible when they reach adulthood, no matter how derelict in their duties their parents were. Society thus harnesses our innate concern for the welfare of our offspring to motivate conscientious efforts at moral education. It tends to work well, but not perfectly of course.

Then what shall we do with those unfortunate individuals whose early lives were blighted by inattention or worse? No matter how well informed and balanced our policies are, no matter how many social improvements we build into our world to remediate the disadvantages encountered by some, there will be problem cases, and, on the supposition that we have already decided in principle that it is better to let some guilty (and responsible) people go unpunished than to punish the innocent, the problems will be concentrated among the unlucky who fall afoul of the law and for whom being law-abiding has been, for various reasons, especially difficult. In the past I have expressed the view that luck tends to average out, that in a well-ordered state the benefits of being held responsible, even though it carries punishment with it, is preferable to being declared morally incompetent, with its dire diminution of the everyday freedoms of normal citizens. I have been convinced by you and several other recent critics (Tom Clark, Bruce Waller) that my earlier expression of this view was too harsh. The state is obliged to explore and institute ways of leveling the playing field, but I have *not* been convinced by any of you that you have an alternative, more humane vision of how to minimize punishment – or do without it altogether.

We should not have a general policy of excuse. It would, in effect, spoil us all rotten. We have to strike a balance. Which balance? That is not anything that can be determined once and for all. Neither *never punish* nor *always punish* is sustainable, and attitudes in society at large may shift considerably over time in response to the harshness or laxity of enforcement. In his insightful treatment of this issue of social engineering, Allan Gibbard (1990) draws a nice distinction between "imperious" and "diffident" designs of moral norms. Imperious norms (setting too high a demand on individuals) foster hypocrisy and suspicion and tend to involve "somewhat inefficient hectoring" while diffident norms appeal to a compromise between prudence and self-interest that is easier for individual citizens to endorse (Dennett 2003a: 278–280 has more to say on this important topic).

Suppose we redesign our current institutions of punishment to remove the "cruel and unusual" features that should sicken us all. And suppose we also decide in favor of a "diffident" policy regarding blame. Some of the negative sequelae of blame are simply not options that can be abandoned. Kelly discusses the *non-retributive* rationales of a list of blame responses: "disappointment, sadness, regret, grief, and a disposition to renegotiate, restrict, or break off a relationship, or to demand an explanation or apology . . . when a person's judgments or attitudes interfere with her reliable prospects for acting in conformity with morality, but not because we think a person deserves to suffer on account of her wrongdoing" (2018: 107). She cites Thomas Scanlon (2013), who "accepts that 'fitting' attitudes have negative social and

psychological consequences for wrongdoers that are justified and even desirable 'simply by the faults displayed in
the wrongdoer's conduct'" (2018: 107). Those found guilty
must have their reputations tarnished. Yet, as Kelly insists,
we need not make it the official business of the criminal justice system to tell us just which blaming attitudes we should
take toward criminal wrongdoers. Criminal conviction is
society's way of spreading the word about untrustworthy
persons. Secret conviction and punishment would be a travesty. (Retributivists should check their intuitions on that;
just why, by their lights, should secret punishment be strictly
forbidden – or are they comfortable with that prospect?) It is
not fair to those who manage to be good if they are treated
the same as those who fail, and it erodes the pressure that
should always exist.

It is interesting that we *do* find room for entirely confiden-
tial and thus secret admonishment and even punishment of
children, precisely on the grounds that we thereby protect
their reputations among their peers and others, giving them
a second (or third, or tenth) chance to reform themselves
before taking on full-fledged moral responsibility. Such
private arrangements should always carry with them a tacit
understanding that a choice is being offered: "Do you want
my mercy or my respect? Let me know when you're ready
for the latter. To the extent that I excuse you, demanding less
from you in the way of moral and self-controlled behavior,
I express my judgment that you are not yet a reliable moral
agent, not yet somebody who can be counted on." By eliminating the threshold of moral competence – responsible free
will – from your rehabilitation scheme, you deny to those
convicts who *want* to be reinstated to society the opportunity
to win membership in the Moral Agents Club. At best, they
can hope for a certificate declaring them safe to be allowed
to roam the streets. By eliminating punishment, you deny
to them the right to claim that they have "paid their debt to
society." There is much that is askew in this idea of paying
one's debt to society. We certainly wouldn't tell a person

who was unjustly imprisoned for a decade that on his release, he was entitled to commit the serious felony of his choice – he'd paid for it in advance. We mustn't reduce punishment to just a *cost of doing business.*

A large part of the dues one pays for admission to the Moral Agents Club is the prospect of having one's proven misdeeds made public. In a truly exemplary society, this might be the paramount punishment: the damage to reputation and hence the limiting of opportunities for work, for friendship, for the otherwise default presumption of good faith with which we normally meet strangers. So far as I can see, there is no effective way of mitigating this punishment, beyond arranging as many opportunities as we can for them to demonstrate their recovered reliability while simultaneously protecting the citizenry. This is, of course, a topic of current heated controversy. How – if at all – should we permit convicted child molesters to live anonymously after release? I would like to see the *details* of any proposals from those who argue for the abolition of punishment and guilt for dealing with such issues.

Caruso: As a fellow naturalist, Dan, I welcome your evolutionary sketch of the emergence of morality. I completely agree with you, for instance, that morality "is neither a gift from God nor an entirely genetically transmitted 'instinct.'" That said, I fundamentally *disagree* with you when you: (a) equate free will with moral competency, (b) falsely claim that skeptics fail to distinguish between those who are morally competent and those who are not, (c) suggest that respect for persons requires giving them their *just deserts*, and (d) insist that the only effective way of "influencing *each other's* behavior" is by retaining those reactive attitudes, judgments, and treatments associated with free will, i.e. *resentment, indignation,* and *moral blame.*

Consider, for instance, your claim that "when you propose to *abolish* blame and [desert-based] responsibility outright, you deny to everyone the respect due to an agent who undertakes to live a moral life and obey the just laws of her society." Here and elsewhere, your concern seems to be similar to that of Oxford philosopher P. F. Strawson's (1962), who famously distinguished between the *reactive* and *objective* attitudes. Strawson maintained that our justification for claims of blameworthiness and praiseworthiness is grounded in the system of human *reactive attitudes*, such as moral resentment, indignation, guilt, and gratitude. Strawson contends that because our moral responsibility practices are grounded in this way, if we were to abandon the notion of moral responsibility, we would be forced to adopt the cold and calculating *objective attitude* toward others, a stance that relinquishes the reactive attitudes. According to Strawson and his followers, the denial of all moral responsibility is unacceptable, self-defeating, and/or impossible, since to permanently excuse everyone would entail that "nobody knows what he's doing or that everybody's behavior is unintelligible in terms of conscious purposes or that everybody lives in a world of delusion or that nobody has a moral sense . . ." (1962: 74).

While I take these concerns seriously, I also maintain that they are misguided when applied to the kind of free will skepticism I defend. As Pereboom and I have both argued, Strawson may be right to contend that adopting the objective attitude would seriously hinder our personal relationships (for a contrary perspective, see Tamler Sommers 2007). However, a case can be made that it would be wrong to claim that this stance would be appropriate if determinism did pose a genuine threat to the reactive attitudes. While, for instance, kinds of moral anger such as resentment and indignation might be undercut if free will skepticism were true, these attitudes may be suboptimal relative to alternative attitudes available to us, such as moral concern, disappointment, sorrow, and moral resolve. It is important to keep in mind that adopting the skeptical perspective does not require us to relinquish *all* reactive attitude, only those associated with free will. And *optimistic skeptics* maintain that the attitudes that we would want to retain are either not undermined by a skeptical conviction because they do not have presuppositions that conflict with this view, or else they have alternatives that are not under threat. And what remains does not amount to Strawson's objectivity of attitude and is sufficient to sustain the personal relationships we value (see Pereboom and Caruso 2018: 201; see also Pereboom 2001, 2014).

Second, neither free will skepticism nor the public health–quarantine model implies that the difference between agents who are morally competent and those who are not is irrelevant to how we should treat wrongdoers. On the contrary, free will skeptics typically claim that this difference is crucial for determining the right response to wrongdoing (see Pereboom and Caruso 2018). Consider again Pereboom's forward-looking account of moral responsibility, or what some philosophers call *answerability* responsibility. According to this concept of responsibility, someone is responsible for an action or attitude just in case it is connected to her capacity for evaluative judgment in a way that opens her up, in principle, to demands for justification from others (see Scanlon 1998; Bok 1998; Pereboom 2014). Such responsibility requires moral competency. When we encounter apparently immoral behavior, for example, it is perfectly legitimate to ask the agent, "Why did you decide to do that?" or "Do you think it was the right thing to do?" If the reasons given in response to such questions are morally unsatisfactory, we regard it as justified to invite the agent to evaluate critically what her actions indicate about her intentions and character and request reform moving forward. According to Pereboom, engaging in such interactions is reasonable in light of the right of those harmed or threatened to protect themselves from immoral behavior and its consequences. In addition, we might have a stake in reconciliation with the wrongdoer and calling her to account in this way can function as a step toward realizing this objective. We also have an interest in her moral formation, and the addressing described naturally functions as a stage in this process (see Pereboom 2014). Such forward-looking responsibility grounds moral protest, not in desert, but in *three non-desert invoking desiderata* – i.e. future protection, future reconciliation, and future moral formation – and as a result is perfectly consistent with free will skepticism.

The question of whether an offender is morally competent and reasons-responsive is also relevant on the public health–quarantine model for at least two reasons. I discussed these earlier, but it seems I need to summarize them again. First, it's important in assessing what kind of threat an individual poses moving forward and whether incapacitation is required. An offender suffering from a serious mental illness, for instance, differs in significant ways from one who is morally competent and fully reasons responsive. These differences will be relevant to determining what minimum restrictions are required for adequate protection. Second, if the capacities of reasons-responsiveness are in place, forms of treatment that take rationality and self-governance into account are appropriate. On the other hand, those who suffer from impairments of rationality and self-governance would need to be treated differently, and in ways that aim to restore these capacities when possible. Understanding the variety of causes that lead to impairment of these capacities would also be crucial to determining effective policy for recidivism reduction and rehabilitation (Focquaert et al. 2020). Hence, free will skepticism and the public health–quarantine model acknowledge the importance of moral competency, reasons-responsiveness, self-governance, and differences in degrees of autonomy. But rather than see these as relevant for assigning blameworthiness and basic-desert moral responsibility, they instead view them as important (in fact, essential) to determining the appropriate course of action moving forward.

Third, while it is true that in justifying incapacitation the public health–quarantine model appeals to an analogy with quarantine, it is also important to recognize that what is analogous here is the *justification* of incapacitation and quarantine. The model does not require us to view wrongdoers as "ill" or "diseased." While some people who commit criminal acts do so because of mental illness or incompetency, many others do not. These distinctions matter exactly for the reasons just stated. I therefore strongly want to resist what Bruce Waller (2011) calls "excuse-extensionism" – the idea that the denial of moral responsibility only makes sense on the basis of characteristics that make one incompetent (and thus excused) as a moral being (2011: 219). Since you and Strawson start from the assumption of the moral responsibility system, you hold that the denial of moral responsibility is absurd and self-defeating. But the universal denial of desert-based moral responsibility does *not* start from the assumption that under normal circumstances we are morally responsible, and it does *not* proceed from that starting point to enlarge and extend the range of excuses to cover everyone (so that *everyone* is profoundly flawed). That is indeed a path to absurdity. Instead, global skeptics, like myself, reject the basic system which starts from the assumption that all minimally competent persons are morally responsible in the desert-sense. Hence, we challenge the entire system of desert and do not accept the rules of that system. It would therefore be wrong to interpret the skeptical view as claiming that "nobody knows what he's doing or that everybody's behavior is unintelligible in terms of conscious purposes or that everybody lives in a world of delusion or that nobody has a moral sense . . ." (Strawson 1962: 74). That's not what the position claims.

Fourth, I agree with you when you write: "It is a fundamental mistake in evolutionary thinking to suppose that whatever ways (ideas, practices, concepts, policies) survived this process must have proven fitness-enhancing for the human species, the lineage, or even the individuals (or groups of individuals) who adopted them. Some, even many, of the established ways (of thinking, of acting) may have been cultural parasites, in effect, exploiting weaknesses in the psychology of their hosts." I'm glad you included that proviso, since it's an important one. It also helps sharpen one key point of disagreement between us. While we would both put retributivism in this category (although I'm still unclear what that means for your backward-looking, desert-based notions of blame and punishments), I would go further and *also* include the reactive attitudes of resentment, indignation, and moral blame. As an optimistic skeptic, I not only think that these attitudes lack justification, I also think that we can effectively "influen[ce] *each other's* behavior" for the purposes of moral formation, reconciliation, and safety by means of alternative attitudes. (At a minimum, it's an open empirical question, which no amount of *a priori* reasoning can settle.)

Lastly, as an incompatibilist who maintains that free will and desert-based moral responsibility are incompatible with *both* determinism *and* luck, I reject your attempt to equate free will with moral competency. First, our current practices are not fixed and can change. As you, yourself, noted several times, our socially constructed system of morality is sensitive to the influence of "intelligent designers" – i.e. philosophers and others who use the "forum of informed persuasion" to convince their fellow members to revise and improve their practices. The philosophical arguments against free will, the ones discussed in our previous exchange, can and *should* (on my view) bring about a shift in our practices, attitudes, and judgments. Remember that the core philosophical question is whether our practices are *justified*, not whether they are natural. And for me at least (I've given up hope of trying to persuade you), the manipulation argument reveals that moral competency, while a necessary condition for free will, is not a sufficient condition – since an agent can be morally competent, yet externally manipulated (e.g. by a team of neuroscientists) in such a way that they would intuitively fail to be morally responsible in the basic or non-basic-desert sense.

Dennett: I think you tend to forget that I view your idea of "basic-desert moral responsibility" as a red herring. You introduced Kant's notorious island example, which we discussed in Exchange 2, and it shows clearly why I dismiss retributivism out of hand, and propose to replace it with a consequentialist justification of *a familiar concept of desert* which is *not* Kant's, but rather a justified element in a working theory of morality and punishment, which I have just sketched. The concept of free will that makes sense in that context is the concept of responsible, reliable self-control (also known as membership in the Moral Agents Club). You define free will as "the kind of control in action required for basic-desert moral responsibility." And what kind of control is that? If you think that determinism implies that "we could never do otherwise" and that *this* shows that we don't have the right kind of control, I have shown that the sense of the phrase "could have done otherwise" we actually use to excuse people from moral responsibility is not one that follows from determinism. We self-controllers with our many degrees of freedom (even in a deterministic world) do have an ability to do otherwise in a morally relevant sense. When we *can, but won't* (as young Sarah McCarthy said), we are exhibiting the free will that, once under control, amounts to "answerability," as Pereboom calls it, or moral responsibility, as I would say. You go on to say that free will skeptics

> acknowledge the importance of moral competency, reasons-responsiveness, self-governance, and differences in degrees of autonomy. But *rather* than see these as relevant for assigning blameworthiness and *basic-desert moral responsibility*, they instead view them as important (in fact, essential) to determining the appropriate course of action moving forward.

Here you are *rathering* again, it seems to me; especially in light of the fact that you have now conceded that sometimes "the appropriate course of action moving forward" is, well, punishment under one name or another. I would add that if your system is justly administered, then the appropriate course of action – including sanctions, incapacitation, involuntary institutionalization in some cases – will be *deserved* (but of course not in the Kantian "basic moral desert sense"

sense). Quoting again your expert witness, Mitchell Berman, "A person who unjustifiably and inexcusably causes or risks harm to others or to significant social interests deserves to suffer for that choice, and he deserves to suffer in proportion to the extent to which his regard or concern for others falls short of what is properly demanded of him." You say that this is the "retributivist" concept of desert, but I think it fits my consequentialist account to a T.

You raise a criticism of P. F. Strawson's views after noting that my view "seems to be similar to" his. You declare that Strawson and I both "start from the assumption of the moral responsibility system." I don't, obviously. I have just gone to rather great lengths to show how the moral responsibility system might naturally and justifiably arise from the state of nature. You must have some other debater in mind. You go on to add that Strawson and I "hold that the denial of moral responsibility is absurd and self-defeating," but again, I don't recognize anything I've said here or elsewhere as implying that. Aside from citing with approval Strawson's delicious verdict on much of the free will literature – "obscure and panicky metaphysics" – I haven't announced my allegiance to any of his views. I'm not sure your objection to Strawson has merit, but even if it does, you are tarring with a broad brush.

Caruso: First, Dan, I do *not* maintain that agents lack the kind of control in action required for basic-desert moral responsibility *because* determinism implies that "we could never do otherwise." Instead, I have all along defended a form of *source incompatibilism* (vs. *leeway incompatibilism*) which maintains that determinism is incompatible with an agent being the *appropriate source* of their actions or controlling them in the right kind of way. That is, I agree with Derk Pereboom that, "An action is free in the sense required for moral responsibility only if it is not produced by a deterministic process that traces back to causal factors beyond the agent's control" (2001: 34). I therefore maintain that the clearest and most plausible case for incompatibilism concerns the causal history of an action and not alternative possibilities. That is why, in our second exchange, the two incompatibilist arguments I defended – the manipulation argument and the hard luck argument – both focused on the causal history of an agent's actions and not on alternative possibilities. It surprises me that you're still confused about that.

Second, as an incompatibilist, I contend that the kind of control in action required for basic-desert moral responsibility would be the kind presupposed by libertarians, especially agent-causal libertarians. And unlike you, I do not think that such a notion is incoherent. Nor do I think that it's irrelevant to the issue of free will. Quite the contrary, it's the kind of control in action we typically believe ourselves to have (Nichols and Knobe 2007; Sarkissian et al. 2010; Deery et al. 2013). I therefore reject the libertarian notion of free will, not because I think it's incoherent, but because our best philosophical and scientific theories about the world count strongly against it.

Third, we may be talking past each other if the only kind of "free will" you want to preserve is the kind that "amounts to 'answerability,' as Pereboom calls it, or moral responsibility, as I would say." If, in the end, all you really want to preserve is an *answerability* notion of responsibility, not the more contentious *accountability* notion, then I think we're in general agreement. But then I also think that it's game, set, match for the free will skeptic! That's because, while the accountability notion of responsibility is generally believed to require the kind of free will under dispute, the answerability notion of responsibility arguably does not – for exactly the reasons explained above. But before I can determine whether or not your view simply collapses into a form of free will skepticism, I need to better understand your notion of *desert*. For instance, you claim that your account "dismiss[es] retributivism out of hand" and replaces it with "a consequentialist justification of *a familiar concept of desert* which is *not*

Kant's, but rather a justified element in a working theory of morality and punishment." But almost immediately after that you approvingly quote Mitchell Berman, who defends a kind of modest retributivism (2016), and claim that his retributivist concept of desert "fits my consequentialist account to a T." I cannot help feeling that there's a tension in your view. Either you mean something different by "desert" than Berman, or your account includes *both* consequentialist *and* retributivist components.

I suggest that we wrap up our discussion of my public health–quarantine model and move on to your view. In particular, I would like to drill down further into your notion of desert and your account of punishment.

Dennett: Well, just one request for the future. You maintain that "determinism is incompatible with an agent being the *appropriate source* of their actions or controlling them in the right kind of way." I have given an account of control – real control – that is independent of determinism. You "free will skeptics" owe us an alternative account of control that shows why you think determinism would prevent agents from controlling their actions in this "right kind of way," whatever that is. Everything that happens, if determinism is true, "traces back to causal factors beyond the agent's control," in Pereboom's words. But so what? The causal factors beyond the agent's control do not control the agent. Neither your own past nor prehistory could control you. No autonomous agent could be in control of the causal factors that preceded its existence, obviously, but that doesn't establish that the agent doesn't have control "in the right kind of way."

Caruso: I think we just fundamentally disagree on what type of control is required. The manipulation argument and the hard luck argument were meant to show why your notion of control is not enough – i.e. manipulated agents can satisfy the compatibilist conditions for control, yet it would be intuitively wrong to hold them morally responsible in the desert-based sense. But at this point, I think we should move ahead instead of revisiting those arguments. I just need to quickly address one final criticism you had of the public health–quarantine model, so as not to give the impression that I'm trying to avoid it. It's your *pill example*, which runs as follows: "Suppose . . . a pill is invented that cures people of 'violent criminal tendencies.' I haven't committed any violent acts yet, but I also haven't taken the pill. I decide to terrorize a neighbor I can't stand, threatening him with bodily harm, vandalizing his property, kicking his dog . . . until I drive him away – and then I take the pill. No need to quarantine me, right? I'm cured." To begin, let me say that this is indeed an interesting challenge, since my view maintains that individuals who pose no forward-looking threat to society should not be subject to liberty-limiting restrictions. That said, there are still several things I would like to say in response. First, I could (if I were so disposed) question the underlying assumption of the case, much as you did in our discussion of manipulation cases, by raising concerns about how such a pill might be ethically objectionable on a number of different fronts. Would this pill fundamentally change who you are? Would it override or undermine your responsiveness to reasons? Would it be ethical for the state to force violent criminals to take the bill as a form of "treatment" for "violent criminal tendencies"? Would it, for that matter, be ethical for the state to give violent criminals the "voluntary choice" to take the pill or continue to be incapacitated? I don't pretend to know the answers to these questions. And it's important to raise them, since the public health–quarantine model could, and probably would, oppose the use of such a pill as a "cure" for violent crime (see Pereboom and Caruso 2018 for more on this).

That said, I'll answer your question directly, since I hate it when philosophers play the avoidance game by raising more questions or changing the subject when a difficult question is put to them. If, after taking the pill, it was a hundred percent guaranteed that you would be no future threat to society, then I would have to bite the bullet and say that it would indeed be wrong to incapacitate you. Now, I understand that many people will share your retributive intuition that punishment is *deserved* in this case, but I would instead let the commitments of my theory drive my intuitions. All theorizing requires a kind of reflective equilibrium, where we let certain intuitions inform and drive our theorizing, but then we use our theories, in turn, to help guide our intuitions in the more difficult cases. I consider this a difficult case. And though you may think my theory comes out on the wrong side of the issue, that's not at all clear – at least not without begging the question.

There are, however, two remaining things I would like to say that might make biting the bullet more palatable for some. First, incapacitation is not the only issue here. For example, in terms of tort liability, you may still owe your neighbor some financial restitution for their hardship. Additionally, I would recommend some kind of restorative justice process, where both parties sit down and work toward reconciliation. So, it's not as if you just pop the pill and that's it. Secondly, and I think this is important, an individual who knowingly and premeditatedly commits violent acts and intentionally puts off taking the pill until *after* they achieve their desired ends, may *still represent a forward-looking threat to society*. That's because we can *attribute* to them certain character traits and predispositions that increase the likelihood that they will engage in similar criminal acts in the future (unless, of course, you design the example so that the pill completely alters their moral character and prohibits their ability to commit any criminal acts in the future). Perhaps, then, some form of monitoring may still be justified.

Dennett: Thank you for biting the bullet, Gregg. Like you, I have no desire to consider the dozens or hundreds of alternative versions of my example, though other philosophers may want to leap into the game. One of your suggestions is that my neighbor may want to sue me, but I will ignore the subpoena, because it isn't really a subpoena on your theory, there being no *penalty* or *punishment* for ignoring it. I would also ignore your *recommendation* of some kind of restorative process, and I daresay my departed neighbor might want to ignore it as well. I rest my case.

Caruso: Such defiance, Dan! Perhaps after you take the pill, you'll think differently and shed your rebel nature.

Dennett: Yes, I want to leave room for defiance, don't you? And if taking the pill would render me incapable of challenging the laws of my state with civil disobedience, I wouldn't take the pill. My system, unlike yours, has well-tried – and justified – ways of dealing with folks with a rebel nature. I just hope that in our current COVID-19 crisis they suffice to maintain a secure and healthy state.

Caruso: That's unfair Dan. The public health–quarantine model can deal just as well with rebels, it just does so in a less condemnatory and more restricted way.

Dennett: So you say.

Debating Desert and Compatibilism: One Final Time

Caruso: As I see it, the difference between our views is quite simple, Dan. My view is non-punitive, in that it does not satisfy the definition of *punishment*, and it in no way requires agents to be morally responsible *in the basic-desert sense* (the sense I care about). When we quarantine the patient with ebola, we do not punish them, although we do restrict their liberty. We can also justify quarantining them *without* appealing to any of the cluster of notions under dispute: free will, basic (and non-basic) desert moral responsibility, just deserts, or retribution! If, in the end, you are willing to take all that onboard, then the difference between our views would indeed be minimal and may even evaporate altogether. But in that case, I would also consider your view indistinguishable from that of the skeptic, since it would in no way require the kind of free will under debate. I'm almost certain, though, that you will not agree. And that's because you want to give the notion of desert an important *justificatory* role in your account of punishment.

It's also important that I respond to a point you made earlier. Earlier you wrote, "Where my policy differs from yours is that it restricts such sanctions and incapacitation to those who deserve it." It's extremely important, in fact essential, that we distinguish here between two different kinds of desert claims and how they factor into the debate over punishment. In the literature on punishment, they are known as *negative desert* and *positive desert*. As Alec Walen explains in his *Stanford Encyclopedia of Philosophy* entry on *Retributive Justice*: "Retributivism . . . involves both positive and negative desert claims. The positive desert claim holds that wrongdoers morally deserve punishment for their wrongful acts." Yet: "This positive desert claim is complemented by a negative one: Those who have done no wrong may not be punished. This prohibits both punishing those not guilty of wrongdoing (who deserve no punishment), and punishing the guilty more than they deserve (i.e. inflicting disproportional punishment)" (2014, sect. 3.1). In your sentence, quoted above, you clearly have the negative desert claim in mind. What I still want to know is whether you *also subscribe* to the positive desert claim?

This is an important question for a number of reasons. First, if it's *only* negative desert you want to preserve, then your account amounts to a kind of *desert-free consequentialism side constrained by negative desert*. But if that's the case, then desert plays no positive role at all in justifying punishment on your account – an issue I've been trying to nail down for a while. Why not, then, simply drop the notion of desert and adopt a fully consequentialist account of punishment and blame? Second, if it's *only* negative desert you're after, then I think the public health–quarantine model can provide many of the same protections you're after, but in a non-desert-based way. Desert is not the only or best source of proportionality restrictions on criminal sentences. Consider the prohibition on punishing innocent people. Retributivists will argue that this prohibition follows from the protections provided by negative desert since only individuals who deserve punishment should be punished – hence, innocent people should not be punished since they do not deserve it. The public health–quarantine model, however, could achieve the same prohibition on punishing innocent people who pose no threat to society by arguing that the right of self-defense only permits the limiting of liberty in those cases when an individual *actually poses a serious threat*, and only then in accordance with the principle of least infringement. Since innocent people pose no such threat, it would be wrong to incapacitate them.

In *Rejecting Retributivism*, I propose the following *conflict resolution principle*, designed to deal with conflicts between public health and safety (on the one hand) and individual liberty and autonomy (on the other). It states that:

> *The Conflict Resolution Principle*: When there is a significant threat to public health and safety, individual liberty can be limited but only when it is (a) in accordance with the right of self-defense and the prevention of harm to others, where (b) this right of self-defense is applied to an individual threat and is calibrated to the danger posed by that threat (not some unrelated threat), and (c) it is guided by the principle of least infringement, which holds that the least restrictive measures should be taken to protect public health and safety.

Let me discuss each of these components in turn. The first condition (a) maintains that liberty can be limited in cases of quarantine and incapacitation but only in accordance with the general right of self-defense and defense of others. This is significant because it distinguishes the

public health–quarantine model from more general utilitarian and consequentialist approaches to punishment. Rather
than appealing to an increase in some aggregate good (e.g.
pleasure) or the benefits of general deterrence as a liberty-
limiting justification, the conflict resolution principle states
that liberty can only be limited in accordance with the right
of self-defense and the defense of others. This, I contend,
avoids the objections raised earlier to consequentialist
theories – e.g. the "use objection" and cases where framing
innocent individuals or using harsh and severe punishment
would be the most effective way to deter crime.

Take the example of framing an innocent person to prevent a riot. Imagine you are the sheriff in a racially volatile
community. For years you have worked to calm racial ten-
sions and have achieved some small level of success. But one
day a crime occurs, and it is perceived by the community
to be racially motivated. You know that if you do not find
someone guilty of the crime quickly, a riot will occur. In your
expert opinion, the riot will cause immense pain and suffering for the community, much like the L. A. riots in 1992.
Individuals will be injured, businesses will be destroyed,
violent attacks will occur, and the community will suffer
long-term economic and psychological damage. You know,
however, that you can easily frame an innocent homeless
person for the crime. The person was near the scene of the
crime and by using footage from local surveillance cameras
and, perhaps, some planted evidence, you can easily make
your case. We can even add that the individual has no close
family or friends, so no one but them will suffer. Despite the
fact that the individual is innocent, a consequentialist may
have to conclude that the pain and suffering caused by the
riot would far outweigh the pain and suffering experienced
by the innocent homeless person.

While consequentialists may argue against the practicality
of engaging in such practices, claiming that it would erode
important protections and produce poorer outcomes in the
long run, they must nonetheless allow for the possibility of

exceptions. Furthermore, such a reply would remain insensitive to the fundamental unfairness of punishing an innocent person, pointing only to practicality as a reason to avoid it. While some critics (yourself included?) may worry that the public health–quarantine model would likewise allow for the framing of an innocent person, the conflict resolution principle reveals why this is not the case. First, and perhaps most importantly, innocent people do not pose a threat to society, and as a result the right of self-defense would not justify incapacitating them. Second, condition (b) of the conflict resolution principle states that the right of self-defense and prevention of harm to others only applies to the danger posed by individualized threats, not general threats. That is, the right of self-defense only applies to the source of an individual threat and must be calibrated to the danger posed by *that* threat, not some unrelated threat. Accordingly, it would be wrong to incapacitate an innocent person because *that* person, being innocent, is not a danger to society nor are they the source of the threat posed by the impending riot. To limit the liberty of an individual because of concerns about the safety of society that emanate from a *different source*, would be a violation of the conflict resolution principle and any intuitive understanding of the right of self-defense.

Conditions (a) and (b) are also consistent with the *prohibition on manipulative use principle*, which maintains that it is generally wrong to use someone merely as a means in order to promote some further independent end – in contrast to harming someone to eliminate a threat they pose based on the right of self-defense. According to legal philosopher Victor Tadros (2011), *eliminative harming* is much easier to justify than *manipulative harming* since the former is based on the right of self-defense, whereas there are a wide range of cases where it is intuitively objectionable to use someone manipulatively. The prohibition of manipulative use principle therefore provides an additional explanation of why framing an innocent person is wrong and unjust – it involves using that individual as a means in order to promote some further independent end. On the other hand, harming someone to eliminate the harm they pose does not involve manipulative use. This is because in cases of self-defense, a person is typically harmed to avert a threat emanating from themselves, and not as a means to some independent end. Common examples include using physical force to defend oneself against attack. Such harming is widely perceived to be justified.

I contend that this right of self-defense, in accordance with the conflict resolution principle, extends to cases of state action where it is justifiable for the state to restrict the liberty of individuals who pose a serious threat to public health and safety. And the state's right to restrict liberty on the grounds of self-defense and defense of others in no way requires that agents are free and morally responsible in the basic-desert sense. As Derk Pereboom has argued, "if in order to protect society, we have the right to quarantine people who are carriers of severe communicable diseases, then we also have the right to isolate the criminally dangerous to protect society" (2001: 174). This is because in the case of contagious disease:

> If the danger to society is great enough, it is acceptable to deprive carriers of their liberty to the degree that the safety of society requires it. This is true irrespective of the carriers' moral responsibility for the disease. If a child is a carrier of the Ebola virus by its being passed on to her at birth from her parent, quarantine is nevertheless intuitively legitimate. (Pereboom 2001: 174)

The same is true for incapacitating the criminally dangerous: they need not be morally responsible in the basic (or non-basic) desert sense to justify restricting their liberty. Importantly, though, the state's right to incapacitate on the grounds of self-defense and defense of others, does not extend to manipulative harming. Hence, conditions (a) and (b) of the conflict resolution principle do not violate the intuitive prohibition on manipulative use. Yes, they allow for the limiting of individual liberty, which causes harm, but only in cases of eliminative harming.

Condition (c) of the conflict resolution principle simply reiterates that while the right of self-defense and defense of others may justify limiting liberty, such infringements of liberty should be guided by the principle of least infringement, which holds that the least restrictive measures should be taken to protect public health and safety. To successfully implement the public health–quarantine model in the criminal justice system, then, we would need to reevaluate the harms posed by various crimes so as to determine the appropriate reaction. Justice and fairness demand that we undertake this reevaluation so that liberty is limited no more than is absolutely necessary. Condition (c) provides the public health–quarantine model with a kind of proportionality principle of its own. It ensures that the sacrifice of autonomy and liberty will be proportionate to the danger posed by an individual, and any sanctions that exceed this upper bound will be considered unjustified. As for the case of "victimless crimes" where no one is harmed save the person engaged in the act, assuming such cases exist, my model would recommend decriminalization. The private use of marijuana may be such a case. But even if it's not, one thing is clear: many of the low-level crimes we currently incarcerate people for (sometimes for many years) would be judged from the perspective of the public health model as excessively punitive and unjustified.

Hence, if it's only the protections provided by negative desert that you care to preserve, then I think the public health–quarantine model can preserve those same protections by other means. If, however, you *really do want to preserve positive desert claims as well*, then your view is (despite your denials) committed to a kind of quasi-retributivism. Of course, it's totally legitimate for you to defend a quasi-retributivist account, under whatever label you wish to give it, it's just important for you to be upfront about the positive role desert plays in *justifying punishment* on your account.

Dennett: It seems to me that you're beating on an unlocked door, Gregg. You say that the difference between our views is "quite simple" and go on to say that your view "is non-punitive . . . and it in no way requires agents to be morally responsible *in the basic-desert sense* (the sense I care about)." Since I reject "the basic-desert sense" in any case, you ask me "Why not, then, simply drop the notion of desert and adopt a fully consequentialist account of punishment and blame?" But I do adopt a fully consequentialist account of punishment and blame! It is your insistence that "desert" must mean "basic desert" (which implies *retributivism*, in one of its senses), that is getting in the way. (It is interesting that the distinction you cite from Walen is in a section of his encyclopedia article entitled "Retributive consequentialism versus retributive deontology." Philosophers have taxonomized many varieties of retributivism, all labeled, wrapped – and ready for the trashcan, in my opinion.) As I said before, the concept of *desert* that I am employing is not the sense you care about; it is a very familiar one that children learn by the time they are in grade school. It lives in the evolved social reality of adults raising children to be responsible adults themselves by the time they reach their majority. Kids recognize that it *isn't fair* to make Tommy have a time out when it was Susy who drew with crayons on the wall, but it *is* fair to make Susy have a time out: she knew she shouldn't do it, and yet she went ahead and did it.

I'm not saying anything innovative here; I'm following John Rawls's great idea of *justice as fairness*. As he pointed out in his last statement of the view:

> These fundamental intuitive ideas are viewed as being familiar from the public political culture of a democratic society. Even though such ideas are not often expressly formulated, nor their meanings clearly marked out, they may play a fundamental role in society's political thought and in how its institutions are interpreted, for example, by courts and in historical or other texts regarded as being of enduring significance. (Rawls 2001: 5–6)

In my terms his project can be seen as a part of the effort to clarify, improve upon, and ultimately justify (politically, not "metaphysically" (Rawls 1985)) a set of widely shared norms and practices that are products of cultural evolution, and turn them into an intelligently designed ideal system of justice that could win the respect of all. It is misleading when you say that I "want to give the notion of desert an important *justificatory* role" in my account of punishment. The excellence of the system (in consequentialist terms) is what plays the justificatory role, and *desert* is simply the concept in that system that identifies who may be justifiably punished or rewarded.

Another model I have provided of the concept in action is the notion of who deserves penalties in games with rules; it's not at all a metaphysical category, and in this case not even a "political" category. It's only a game, but the game has rules and the rules describe conditions in which a participant *deserves* to be treated like other participants, penalized for infractions and rewarded with points for legitimate acts of scoring. If the game is a good game, with rules that "level the playing field," and if everybody plays fair, everybody gets what they deserve; the winners deserve to win, the cheaters deserve to be penalized or even ousted from the game. Civil society isn't a game, as Rawls acknowledges:

> Again, political society is not, and cannot be, an association. We do not enter it voluntarily. Rather we simply find ourselves in a particular political society at a certain moment of historical time. We might think our presence in it, our being here, is not free. In what sense, then, can citizens of a democracy be free? (1971: 4)

I am trying to answer that question, because I see free will and political freedom as closely intertwined. A child born into a society has not entered it voluntarily, but then grows into the privileged role of a free citizen – or doesn't; it all depends on whether the child develops the self-control and reflective imagination we require for moral responsibility.

If the child doesn't reach the threshold for membership in the Moral Agents Club, then society should make provisions for accommodating the person in one or another kind of guardianship – like quarantine in your model, non-punitive and as comfortable as feasible. If the child makes the grade (as almost all do, thanks to society's systems of education and protection), then political freedom is granted, with its rights *and responsibilities*. Some people, as you emphasize, may not be disabled but still have a much harder time controlling themselves and overcoming various circumstances. Bad luck does play a big role in this. You propose a "one size fits all" solution: treat the lucky and the unlucky, the skilled and the unskilled alike, declaring that *nobody* passes the test for moral responsibility and nobody ever deserves punishment. My proposed solution, in contrast to yours, is to take steps to minimize the size of this ineliminable set of problem cases by (1) reforming the social conditions that still leave many with an unfair share of bad luck, (2) tempering justice with mercy (see Kelly 2018), and (3) making the benefits of political freedom so attractive that just about everybody of sound mind would voluntarily accept membership, *accepting the risk of punishment if they break the laws* as a small price to pay for the security and stability of political freedom. Even psychopaths are in favor of this bargain, since it gives them the political freedom in a secure state in which to pursue their often amoral or immoral projects. Life in a failed state is too perilous and unpredictable to nourish ambitious schemes.

Caruso: Finally, I have an answer to my question! It took a while, much longer than it should have, but you have now finally made clear that on your account the notion of desert *plays no role in justifying blame and punishment*. You write, "It is misleading when you say that I 'want to give the notion of desert an important justificatory role' in my account of punishment. The excellence of the system (in consequentialist terms) is what plays the justificatory role, and desert is simply the concept in that system that identifies who may

be justifiably punished or rewarded." There it is, clear as
day – the answer I've been after since our first exchange!
The problem has not been my "insistence that 'desert' must
mean 'basic desert.'" Rather, what has been "getting in the
way" is your failure to distinguish between negative desert
and positive desert, and your obfuscation of the fact that by
"desert" you really only mean to be making a negative desert
claim. Any confusion that has arisen, then, has had less to
do with the basic/non-basic distinction, which I've made
major accommodations for in this conversation, and more to
do with your vagueness over the positive/negative distinction and your failure to make crystal clear that what you
really have in mind is a watered-down, anemic, and purely
negative conception of desert. That is exactly why I've
repeatedly asked about the justificatory function of desert in
your account – i.e. what role desert plays in justifying blame
and punishment. Until now, you've danced around a direct
answer. But now we have it.

Your answer makes a number of things clear to me. First,
instead of offering a consequentialist defense of retributive
blame and punishment, which preserves the justificatory role
of the positive desert claim that wrongdoers morally deserve
to be blamed and punished for their wrongful acts, your
account offers us only "a desert-free consequentialism side
constrained by negative desert." That is, on your account,
desert is simply that thing, internal to our consequentially
justified system of practices, that identifies who may be
justifiably punished or rewarded. But that brings me to my
second point. Those free will skeptics who prefer a consequentialist justification of punishment, over my non-punitive
alternative, can easily say the same thing. As I suggested earlier, when offering a skeptic-friendly interpretation of your
view, your notion of negative desert can easily be replaced
with some other less-contentious backward-looking feature.
For instance, you write: "the concept of *desert* that I am
employing ... is a very familiar one that children learn by
the time they are in grade school ... Kids recognize that it

isn't fair to make Tommy have a time out when it was Susy who drew with crayons on the wall, but it *is* fair to make Susy have a time out: she knew she shouldn't do it, and yet she went ahead and did it." Here it would seem that the notion of *causal responsibility*, which everyone agrees is consistent with free will skepticism, can essentially do the same job you want negative desert to do. A free will skeptic who opts for a consequentialist account of punishment would agree with you that, since Susy is the one who is *causally responsible* for drawing on the wall, it is *her*, and not Tommy, who should be punished. For the forward-looking consequentialist – a view which is completely compatible with free will skepticism – punishing Susy by giving her a time out would be justified on the grounds of forward-looking moral formation, reconciliation, and special and general deterrence.

It's important to keep in mind that there are really two different conversations going on here. On the one hand, I have my own preferred non-retributive, non-punitive approach for addressing criminal behavior, the public health–quarantine model, which is perfectly consistent with free will skepticism. On the other hand, free will skeptics are *not required* to adopt my model. Consequentialist theories of punishment are equally consistent with free will skepticism. I just reject them for other reasons. As far as I can see, your account is essentially indistinguishable from that of the skeptic who opts for a consequentialist justification of punishment. In fact, my suspicion all along has been that your position is much closer to that of the free will skeptic than you wish to acknowledge. But now that you've clarified that desert, for you, plays no role in justifying blame and punishment, I see no real substantive difference between you and the skeptic. Hence, I would like to repeat something I said in our second exchange: "it's unclear to me whether a consequentialist, like yourself, should even continue to talk of *just deserts*, given its strong deontological and retributive connotations . . . Given the canonical understanding of 'just deserts' and how it is used to justify various retributive attitudes, judgments, and treatments, your use of the term lends itself to easy confusion and gives the mistaken impression that you are setting out to preserve something you are not." I feel even more strongly now that you should drop the notion of desert altogether, since you have just made it clear that what you mean by desert is something that can be cashed out in less controversial terms and in no way plays a *justificatory* role in grounded positive desert claims.

Of course, differences still remain between our two approaches to punishment, but now they seem more like a family squabble between two skeptics: one who favors a consequentialist justification of punishment and one who favors a non-punitive approach like the public health–quarantine model. I would be happy to continue to discuss those differences, but it seems to me the entire tone of the debate has shifted in favor of the free will skeptic.

Since we're nearing a close to our exchange, I would like to conclude by distinguishing between a few possible interpretations of what the *compatibilist thesis* ultimately is. While free will skeptics are pretty unanimous on what they are doubting or denying, I've always found it amusing that compatibilists cannot agree on exactly what the compatibilist claim is. There are almost as many *compatibilists theses* as there are compatibilists. And not only do compatibilists disagree on what it is they are setting out to preserve, they also tend to disagree on exactly what conditions are necessary to preserve it – e.g. some say the "ability to do otherwise" is a necessary condition for free will, others disagree; some point to reasons-responsiveness as the key requirement, others point to connection of action to what one would reflectively endorse; etc. Focusing, though, on the compatibilist thesis itself, we can (at a minimum) differentiate between five possible compatibilist claims:

Thesis 1: Determinism is compatible with free will and moral responsibility, but we may still lack free will and moral responsibility for other reasons. [The free will skeptic

Neil Levy defends a view like this. He maintains that, while free will is compatible with determinism, the pervasiveness of luck is incompatible with free will and moral responsibility and ultimately undermines both.]

Thesis 2: Determinism is compatible with free will, but the notion of free will is independent of the issue of moral responsibility. [Bruce Waller, a skeptic about moral responsibility but not free will, maintains such a view.]

Thesis 3: Determinism (and presumably luck as well) is compatible with agents having the kind of free will required for *basic-desert* moral responsibility. [I take it that this is what most compatibilists have in mind, although they are not always clear about it.]

Thesis 4: Determinism (and presumably luck) is compatible with agents having the kind of free will required for *non-basic-desert* moral responsibility, where non-basic desert is justified on consequentialist or contractualist grounds and is understood as *justifying* the *positive desert claim* that wrongdoers morally deserve to be blamed and punished for their wrongful acts. [This view amounts to a consequentialist or instrumentalist defense of retributive blame and punishment.]

Thesis 5: Determinism (and presumably luck) is compatible with agents having the kind of free will required for *non-basic-desert* moral responsibility, where non-basic desert is justified on consequentialist or contractualist grounds and is understood as *a negative desert claim*, one that limits who can justifiably be blamed and punished, and where the *positive justification* for blame and punishment comes from its *forward-looking* benefits.

Am I correct in assuming that you are a *thesis 5-compatibilist*? Your remarks above would strongly suggest so. Note, though, that thesis 5-compatibilism is about as close to free will skepticism as one can possibly get without changing teams. And one may rightly wonder why it would not be better to simply eliminate the notions of *desert* and *free will* altogether, since they come with lots of historical baggage and are likely to confuse readers into thinking you're defining a stronger thesis than you are. Why not, then, adopt something like the following thesis instead: Determinism (and luck) is compatible with agents having the kind of *autonomy* and *control* required for the kind of *forward-looking* moral responsibility sketched earlier, where moral protest is grounded, not in desert, but in *three non-desert invoking desiderata*: future protection, future reconciliation, and future moral formation. Should I inform my fellow free will skeptics that we have a new member of the team? (I'll prepare your jersey just in case.)

Dennett: No, Gregg, I am not a "thesis 5-compatibilist" because I don't accept your suggestion that I am restricting myself to what you call a "negative desert claim." Walen says: "The positive desert claim holds that wrongdoers morally deserve punishment for their wrongful acts." I am happy to endorse that claim, so I am not making any use at all of Walen's distinction between positive and negative desert claims. It occurs to me that the miscommunication that is still dogging us has to do with how you understand the distinction. One more time: I am saying that people do really and truly and non-instrumentally *deserve* to be punished for their crimes because they have accepted a bargain – a promise, a contract – that stipulates that they will be treated thus. The existence of the contract and its justification is to be explained on consequentialist grounds, of course, but once it is part of a society, the desert of all participants is as real as the money in their bank accounts. There is no such thing as basic desert, just as there is no such thing as basic economic value.

Seeking to diagnose our failures to communicate, I have been puzzled by your frequent allusions to what is consistent

with, or available to, the "free will skeptic." Who might want
to be a free will skeptic? Not I. These claims are guaranteed
to fall flat when addressed *to me*, since only those who still
think that free will (in a sense that matters) is threatened or
challenged by determinism should be interested in this possibility at all. The sense of "free will" appearing in your term
"free will skeptic" is one of the senses of free will that I have
argued for decades is *not worth wanting*. Why not point out
while you're at it that these positions you recommend to me
are available to those who are skeptical about the existence
of Satan? I am of course a "Satan skeptic" but I would not
be tempted to take seriously an invitation to join the Satan-
Skeptics Club. You seem to assume, without argument, that
of course I am wrong to turn my back on the kind of free will
you are so interested in being skeptical about.

Caruso: Your position, Dan, is like wrestling an eel – every
time I have a grip on it, or think I do, it slips out of my
hands. You provided me with that I thought was a clear and
unambiguous statement: you do *not* want to give the notion
of desert an important *justificatory* role. But now you say
that you *are* willing to embrace the positive desert claim of
retributivism, which maintains that punishment is *justified* as
an appropriate, *because deserved*, response to wrongdoing. Do
you see my confusion? Perhaps the great legal philosopher
Antony Duff can help clarify the distinction I'm after:

> Theorists have distinguished "positive" and "negative"
> forms of retributivism. Positive retributivism holds that an
> offender's desert provides a reason in favor of punishment;
> essentially, the state should punish those found guilty of
> criminal offences to the extent that they deserve, because
> they deserve it. Penal desert constitutes not just a necessary,
> but an in-principle sufficient reason for punishment (only in
> principle, however, since there are very good reasons – to
> do with the costs, both material and moral, of punishment
> – why we should not even try to punish all the guilty).
> Negative retributivism, by contrast, provides not a positive

reason to punish, but rather a constraint on punishment: punishment should be imposed only on those who deserve it, and only in proportion with their desert. Because negative retributivism represents only a constraining principle, not a positive reason to punish, it has been employed in various mixed accounts of punishment, which endorse punishment for consequentialist reasons but only insofar as the punishment is no more than is deserved. (Duff 2017)

My problem, then, is that I do not see how you can "happily endorse" the positive desert claim of retributivism, which is what provides the justification needed for retributive punishment, while at the same time denying that desert plays an important justificatory role on your account. Secondly, I do not see how you can maintain that your account "is *consequentialist* through and through (and hence not *retributivist* at all)," while at the same time embracing the dual desert claims of retributivism!

To be perfectly blunt, and despite your constant claims to the contrary, I think your view *either* collapses into a form of free will skepticism, *or* it amounts to a kind of consequentially justified retributivism about blame and punishment. You cannot have it both ways and you still haven't settled which it is. If it's the former, I find it hard to see what the substantive dispute is really about. If it's the latter, there *would* be a substantive disagreement between us, but I contend there are good reasons for rejecting such a view. I think things comes down to how *thick* or *thin* we are to interpret your notion of desert.

On the thinnest possible interpretation, all desert-based claims about blame and praise, punishment and reward, would reduce to consequentialist justifications, and as a result the notion of desert would drop out as a justification altogether. But if this is what you mean, then I think your view is indistinguishable from the skeptic who adopts a forward-looking account of moral responsibility and a consequentialist or contractualist account of punishment. On the thicker interpretation, however, desert would play an important role in justifying various backward-looking, desert-based, and (quasi-)retributive attitudes, practices, and treatments. While this thicker notion of desert would not amount to full-blown *basic desert*, since the system of desert itself would be adopted on consequentialist/contractualist grounds, it would still be thick enough to ground a kind of (quasi-)retributivism about blame and punishment. It's sad that we are now at the end of three rather long exchanges and I still do not know which of these interpretations (if either) is correct.

There's also an ambiguity in your claim that your view "is *consequentialist* through and through," since consequentialists can go about justifying punishment in two different ways. On the first approach, which is consistent with free will skepticism, punishment is justified on the purely forward-looking grounds that it's necessary to deter crime and increase safety. Jeremy Bentham, one of the fathers of modern utilitarianism, articulated and defended a consequentialist theory of punishment along these lines. It's important to note, however, that he also famously remarked that "all punishment in itself is evil...[I]f it ought at all to be admitted, it ought only to be admitted in as far as it promises to exclude some greater evil" (Bentham 1823: ch. XIII.2). The reason why it's an evil, according to Bentham, is that punishment is a practice that inflicts, indeed intentionally seeks to inflict, significant hardship or burdens. There is, however, an alternative consequentialist approach to punishment, one that does not see punishment as an evil. As you, yourself, noted earlier, there are *consequentialist forms of retributivism* – i.e. accounts that give consequentialist arguments for adopting retributive practices and policies. About such accounts, you said: "Philosophers have taxonomized many varieties of retributivism, all labeled, wrapped – and ready for the trashcan, in my opinion." But instead of consigning such views to the trashcan, you may actually be proposing one yourself since you (now) say that you are "happy to endorse" the positive desert claim of retributivism. Again, I do not think you can have it both ways. At a minimum, I think you defend a *mixed account of punishment*, one that includes both consequentialist *and* retributivist components.

Lastly, with regard to the taxonomy of compatibilist views I offered above, you deny that you're a thesis-5 compatibilist. Okay, fair enough. But where does that leave us? Are you then a thesis-4 compatibilist? Or, perhaps, a combined thesis-4-and-5 compatibilist? Or do you reject *all five* of the compatibilist theses outlined above? And don't you find it odd that it's so difficult to nail down *exactly what* your compatibilist view amounts to? I do! The skeptic's thesis, on the other hand, is unambiguously clear: it maintains that we lack the kind of control in action, i.e. free will, required for basic-desert moral responsibility. That's it. It's simple. There's no ambiguity or slippage in what the position is denying. There's also no confusion as to what *basic-desert* moral responsibility amounts to – i.e. it's the kind of moral responsibility needed for an agent to deserve to be praised and blamed, rewarded and punished for non-consequentialist, non-contractualist reasons. It's a perfectly coherent notion. But since *you agreed*, rather early on, that determinism (and naturalism more generally) is *incompatible* with the kind of free will required for basic-desert moral responsibility, I decided to see if you could deliver on your promise to defend a "kind of desert that it is as basic as desert could be." But when I followed you down your preferred path – where free will is understood, not in terms of the control in action required for basic-desert moral responsibility, but in terms of non-basic desert or desert justified on consequentialist/contractualist grounds – I found myself in a thicket of contradictions, ambiguities, and questions. Unfortunately, I have very little hope, especially at this late hour, that we'll ever be able to untangle the thicket and come to an agreement.

Dennett: This is what happens, I think, when philosophers try to taxonomize *isms*, confident that they have covered all the possible nuances and done no *rathering*. As you see it, my view "*either* collapses into a form of free will skepticism, *or* it amounts to a kind of consequentially justified retributivism about blame and punishment." It is neither.

Working from the end of this disjunctive sentence to the beginning, you are here using "retributivism" in a sense that is clearly broader than Kant's, as exemplified in the island example. It is broader because, as you put it, it is *consequentially justified* "retributivism." Why call it retributivism at all, since Kant went way out of his way to exclude any consequentialist reason for executing the murderer? Is it because a properly labeled "retributivist" (Mitchell Berman – I'm taking your word for the claim that he considers himself a retributivist) offers a definition of desert that I accept? My view is not that *retributivism* is consequentially justified (which I would have thought was a contradiction in terms) but that *punishment* (defined by Hart and Wittgenstein) is consequentially justified. Are you using "retributive" to characterize *any* defense of punishment? That would seem to be the way the great legal scholar Antony Duff understands the term, according to the citation you provide, and I've certainly seen others who treat "retributive" and "punitive" as practically synonymous. I was initially baffled when I read your statement: "As you, yourself, noted earlier, there are *consequentialist forms of retributivism* – i.e. accounts that give consequentialist arguments for adopting retributive practices and policies." I was quite sure I had said no such thing! Looking back, I can now see that I have aided and abetted the confusion by parenthetically noting – with suppressed amusement – that Walen's encyclopedia article cited by you has a section entitled "Retributive consequentialism versus retributive deontology." You missed the intended irony – I should have added an exclamation point – but you did go on to quote my suggestion that all these nicely sorted and labeled positions be put in the trash.

Looking to the first half of your disjunctive sentence, thanks for reminding me how you define the free will skeptic's position: "The skeptic's thesis, on the other hand, is unambiguously clear: it maintains that we lack the kind of control in action, i.e. free will, required for basic-desert moral responsibility. That's it. It's simple." I've tried to show you, in this debate, that it is not so clear and simple after all. You haven't given a positive account of the "kind of control" you have in mind, or why it is "required for basic-desert moral responsibility," whereas I have had quite a lot to say about control and self-control, and have argued that determinism doesn't threaten our normal capacity for self-control *at all* – unless of course you want to argue that van Inwagen's Consequence Argument (see fn.1 in previous exchange) establishes that nothing controls anything, ever. In the novel *Gravity's Rainbow* (Thomas Pynchon 1973) a character portentously speaks of:

> The illusion of control. That A could do B. But that was false. Completely. No one can *do*. Things only happen. (1973: 34)

If you adopt this view, you are heroically biting yet another bullet, or maybe a hand grenade. If control is an illusion, then so is metabolism, so is life, so is inquiry, so is knowledge. There's just atoms and the void. Then what are we doing – excuse me, what is happening (we aren't *doing* anything) – and why?

Caruso: Dan, you seem to think that retributivism can only come in one form and that there's no such thing as a *mixed theory* of punishment. You're simply wrong about that. There are plenty of mixed theories in the literature, ones that incorporate *both* consequentialist *and* retributivist components. To quote Antony Duff again:

> Given the challenges faced by pure consequentialist and pure retributivist accounts, some theorists have sought to make progress on the question of punishment's justification by incorporating consequentialist and nonconsequentialist elements into their accounts. Perhaps the most influential

example of a mixed account begins by recognizing that the question of punishment's justification is in fact several different questions, which may be answered by appeal to different considerations: we can argue, first, that the "general justifying aim" (Hart 1968/2008: 8–11) of a system of punishment must lie in its beneficial effects, but second, that our pursuit of that aim must be constrained by nonconsequentialist principles that preclude the kinds of injustice alleged to flow from a purely consequentialist account. (Duff 2017)

Mixed theories of this kind can take different forms. The first, and most basic, is to appeal to negative desert as a kind of *constraint* on pure consequentialism, where this constraint is seen as forbidding the deliberate punishment of the innocent and excessively harsh punishment of the guilty. The most famous advocate of this kind of mixed theory was the renowned legal philosopher H. L. A. Hart (1968/2008). Critics, however, have charged that this strategy is ad hoc or internally inconsistent (see Kaufman 2008: 45–49; Duff 2017: sect. 6). In addition, retributivists argue that it relegates retributivism to a merely subsidiary role since it amounts to nothing more than desert-free consequentialism side constrained by negative desert. Another key worry about such accounts concerns the grounding of these side-constraints. As Duff explains, "If they are derived from a 'negative' retributivism that insists that punishment is justified only if it is deserved…, then they face the thorny problem of explaining this retributivist notion of desert…: but it is not clear whether they can be justified without such an appeal to retributivist desert" (Duff 2017; see also Hart 1968/2008: 44–48; Feinberg 1988: 144–155; Walker 1991: ch. 11). Nevertheless, I don't think this is what you have in mind since you (a) embrace the positive desert claim of retributivism, and (b) deny that you're a thesis-5 compatibilist.

From here, mixed theories can embrace more and more robustly retributive commitments. For instance, one can posit a two-step justification of punishment. There are different ways this can be done – for a description of some of these views see Duff (2017: sect. 6 on mixed accounts) and David Boonin's *The Problem of Punishment* (2008: ch. 4). On one version, the first step would appeal to retributivism to argue that the commission of a criminal act renders the offender eligible for, or liable to, the kinds of coercive treatments that punishment involves. The second step would then offer a positive consequentialist reason for imposing punishment on those who are eligible for it or liable to it. Here's another option:

> A somewhat different attempt to accommodate prudential as well as moral reasons in an account of punishment begins with the retributivist notion that punishment is justified as a form of deserved censure, but then contends that we should communicate censure through penal hard treatment because this will give those who are insufficiently impressed by the moral appeal of censure prudential reasons to refrain from crime; because, that is, the prospect of such punishment might deter those who are not susceptible to moral persuasion. (Duff 2017)

This kind of account differs from the first account, on which retributivist prohibitions on punishment of the innocent and excessive punishment of the guilty constrains the pursuit of consequentialist aims, since on this account the retributivist imposition of deserved censure is part of the *positive* justifying aim of punishment (Duff 2017: sect. 6). Beyond these options, there are many other proposals for mixed theories of punishment, theories that combine consequentialist and retributive considerations (see, e.g. Hampton 1991, 1992, 1994; Braithwaite 1999; Matravers 2000; Duff 2001).

From my perspective, you've failed to spell out your view clearly and sufficiently enough for me to understand the details of your account, which still strikes me as not a version of pure retributivism, but still retaining certain retributive components. And without the details I have no way of fully judging the role you want to give desert. I offered you the opportunity to adopt a pure consequentialist theory of punishment, free from desert, but you rejected it. I then offered you the opportunity to adopt a mixed account that views desert only as a negative constraint on punishment, but you rejected that as well. I'm therefore left thinking that you must adopt a mixed account that views desert as providing some kind of *positive* justification. But, of course, that's exactly the kind of claim that needs defending! And my view is that *all* forms of retributivism, both pure and mixed, are unjustified.

Dennett: I'm disappointed that I haven't been able to explain to you my rather straightforward and detailed proposal: societies are like clubs (or games) with rules. There are good consequentialist reasons to make the laws or rules respectable, and good consequentialist reasons for people to endorse them: it makes for a stable and secure society where opportunity and political freedom can be counted on, and visible paths to improve these precious features are abundant. Participants in such a society understand that if they choose to disobey the rules/laws without excuse, they will be held by society to *deserve* the unpleasant consequences stipulated in the rules, just as they *deserve* the fruits of their legitimate actions. That's not your concept of desert, because it is independent of determinism and indeterminism, and it is not touched by your claims about luck. But it is a familiar one, and I claim that it is just what we need for grounding moral responsibility, which is, as you agree, a social construct. It presupposes that normal people are capable of *taking* responsibility for controlling themselves and preventing others from turning them into puppets – which is the only variety of free will worth wanting. If there is a "retributive component" in this view, you have indeed failed to show me what it is.

Sadly, though, we've come to the end of our debate. We'll have to leave it to readers to decide which of us has made the stronger case and offered the more coherent theory.

References and Suggested Readings

[For suggested readings: useful introductions to the problems of free will are indicated by the symbol ¹ (for individually authored books) and ^C (for collections)]

^C Baer, John, James C. Kaufman, and Roy F. Baumeister (eds.) (2008) *Are We Free? Psychology and Free Will*. New York: Oxford University Press.

Bedau, Hugo (2015) Punishment. *Stanford Encyclopedia of Philosophy*. https://plato.stanford.edu/entries/punishment/

Bentham, Jeremy (1823/1948) *An Introduction to the Principles of Morals and Legislation*. New York: Macmillan.

Berman, Mitchell (2008) Punishment and justification. *Ethics* 18: 258–290.

Berman, Mitchell (2011) Two kinds of retributivism. In *Philosophical Foundations of Criminal Law*, eds. R. A. Duff and S. Green. New York: Oxford University Press.

Berman, Mitchell (2013) Rehabilitating retributivism. *Law and Philosophy* 32: 83–108.

Berman, Mitchell (2016) Modest retributivism. In *Legal, Moral, and Metaphysical Truths: The Philosophy of Michael S. Moore*, eds. Kimberly Kessler Ferzan and Stephen J. Morse. New York: Oxford University Press.

^C Berofsky, Bernard (ed.) (1996) *Free Will and Determinism*. New York: Harper & Row.

Bok, Hilary (1998) *Freedom and Responsibility*. Princeton, NJ: Princeton University Press.

Boonin, David (2008) *The Problem of Punishment*. New York: Cambridge University Press.

Braithwaite, J. (1999) Restorative justice: Assessing optimistic and pessimistic accounts. In *Crime and Justice: A Review of the*

Research, ed. M. Tonry, pp. 241–367. Chicago: University of Chicago Press.

ᴵ Campbell, Joseph Keim (2011) *Free Will*. Malden, MA: Polity.

Caruso, Gregg D. (2008) Consciousness and free will: A critique of the argument from introspection. *Southwest Philosophy Review* 24(1): 219–231.

Caruso, Gregg D. (2011) Compatibilism and the folk psychology of free will. In *An Anthology of Philosophical Studies, Vol. V*, ed. Patricia Hanna, pp. 215–226. Athens, Greece: ATINER.

Caruso, Gregg D. (2012) *Free Will and Consciousness: A Determinism Account of the Illusion of Free Will*. Lanham, MD: Lexington Books.

ᶜ Caruso, Gregg D. (ed.) (2013) *Exploring the Illusion of Free Will and Moral Responsibility*. New York: Lexington Books.

Caruso, Gregg D. (2014a) Précis of Derk Pereboom's *Free Will, Agency, and Meaning in Life*. *Science, Religion and Culture* 1(3): 178–201. [Part of a book symposium w/Derk Pereboom, John Martin Fisher, and Dana Nelkin.]

Caruso, Gregg D. (2014b) (Un)just deserts: The dark side of moral responsibility. *Southwest Philosophy Review* 30(1): 27–38.

Caruso, Gregg D. (2015a) Free will eliminativism: Reference, error, and phenomenology. *Philosophical Studies* 172(10): 2823–2833.

Caruso, Gregg D. (2015b) If consciousness is necessary for moral responsibility, then people are less responsible than we think. *Journal of Consciousness Studies* 22(7–8): 49–60.

Caruso, Gregg D. (2015c) Précis of Neil Levy's *Consciousness and Moral Responsibility*. *Journal of Consciousness Studies* 22(7–8): 7–15.

Caruso, Gregg D. (2015d) Kane is not able: A reply to Vicens' "Self-forming actions and conflicts of intention." *Southwest Philosophy Review* 31(2): 21–26.

Caruso, Gregg D. (2016a) Free will skepticism and criminal behavior: A public health–quarantine model. *Southwest Philosophical Review* 32(1): 25–48.

Caruso, Gregg D. (2016b) Review of Bruce Waller's *Restorative Free Will*. *Notre Dame Philosophical Reviews*.

Caruso, Gregg D. (2017a) Free will skepticism and the question of creativity: Creativity, desert, and self-creation. *Ergo* 3(23): 591–607.

Caruso, Gregg D. (2017b) Moral responsibility and the strike back emotion: Comments on Bruce Waller's *The Stubborn System of Moral Responsibility*. *Syndicate Philosophy*, 2/19/17.

I Caruso, Gregg D. (2018a) Skepticism about moral responsibility. *Stanford Encyclopedia of Philosophy*. https://plato.stanford.edu/entries/skepticism-moral-responsibility/

Caruso, Gregg D. (2018b) Consciousness, free will, and moral responsibility. In *The Routledge Handbook of Consciousness*, ed. Rocco J. Gennaro, pp. 78–91. London: Routledge.

Caruso, Gregg D. (2019a) A defense of the luck pincer: Why luck (still) undermines moral responsibility. *Journal of Information Ethics* 28(1): 51–72.

Caruso, Gregg D. (2019b) Free will skepticism and its implications: An argument for optimism. In *Free Will Skepticism in Law and Society*, eds. Elizabeth Shaw, Derk Pereboom, and Gregg D. Caruso, pp. 43–72. New York: Cambridge University Press.

Caruso, Gregg D. (2020a) Buddhism, free will, and punishment: Taking Buddhist ethics seriously. *Zygon* 55 (2): 474–496.

Caruso, Gregg D. (2020b) Justice without retribution: An epistemic argument against retributive criminal punishment. *Neuroethics* 13(1): 13–28.

Caruso, Gregg D. (2020c). Why free will is not real: A reply to Christian List. *The Philosopher* 108(1). [An exchange with Christian List about his book, *Why Free Will is Real*. Cambridge, MA: Harvard University Press. 2019.]

Caruso, Gregg D. (2021a) *Rejecting Retributivism: Free Will, Punishment, and Criminal Justice*. New York: Cambridge University Press.

Caruso, Gregg D. (2021b) The public health–quarantine model. *Oxford Handbook of Moral Responsibility*, eds. Dana Nelkin and Derk Pereboom. New York: Oxford University Press.

Caruso, Gregg D. and Stephen G. Morris (2017) Compatibilism and retributive desert moral responsibility: On what is of central philosophical and practical importance. *Erkenntnis* 82: 837–855.

Caruso, Gregg D. and Derk Pereboom (2020) A non-punitive alternative to punishment. In *Routledge Handbook of the Philosophy and Science of Punishment*, eds. Farah Focquaert, Bruce Waller, and Elizabeth Shaw. New York: Routledge.

I Celello, Peter (2014) Desert. *Internet Encyclopedia of Philosophy*. https://www.iep.utm.edu/desert/

Chisholm, Roderick (1982) Human freedom and the self. In *Free Will*, ed. Gary Watson. New York: Oxford University Press.

Clark, C. J., J. B. Luguri, P. H. Ditto, J. Knobe, A. F. Shariff, and R. F. Baumeister (2014) Free to punish: A motivated account of free will. *Journal of Personal and Social Psychology* 106: 501–513.

Clark, C. J., A. Shniderman, J. B. Luguri, R. F. Baumeister, and P. H. Ditto (2018) Are morally good actions ever free? *Consciousness and Cognition* 63: 161–182.

Clark, C. J., B. M. Winegard, and R. F. Baumeister (2019) Forget the folk: Moral responsibility preservation motives and other conditions for compatibilism. *Frontiers in Psychology*, February 7: https://doi.org/10.3389/fpsyg.2019.00215

Clark, C. J., B. M. Winegard, and A. F. Shariff (2019) Motivated free will beliefs: The theory, new (preregistered) studies, and three meta-analyses. Online.

I Clarke, Randolph and Justin Capes (2017) Incompatibilist (nondeterministic) theories of free will. *Stanford Encyclopedia of Philosophy*. https://plato.stanford.edu/entries/incompatibilism-theories/

C Clarke, Randolph, Michael McKenna, and Angela M. Smith (eds.) (2015) *The Nature of Moral Responsibility*. New York: Oxford University Press.

Clegg, Liam F. (2012) *Protean Free Will*. California Institute of Technology, Pasadena. https://authors.library.caltech.edu/29887/

Deery, O., M. Bedke, and S. Nichols (2013) Phenomenal abilities: Incompatibilism and the experience of agency. In *Oxford Studies in Agency and Responsibility*, ed. David Shoemaker, pp. 126–150. New York: Oxford University Press.

Dennett, Daniel C. (1972) Review of J. R. Lucas, *The Freedom of the Will*. *Journal of Philosophy* 69: 527–531.

Dennett, Daniel C. (1973) Mechanism and responsibility. In *Essays on Freedom of Action*, ed. Ted Honderich. London: Routledge and Kegan Paul. [Reprinted in *Free Will*, ed. Gary Watson. New York: Oxford University Press.]

Dennett, Daniel C. (1978) On giving libertarians what they say they want. In Dennett's *Brainstorm: Philosophical Essays on Mind and Psychology*. Montgomery, VT: Bradford Books.

Dennett, Daniel C. (1983) Intentional systems in cognitive ethology: The "Panglossian Paradigm" defended (with commentaries), *Behavioral and Brain Sciences* 6: 343–90.

I Dennett, Daniel C. (1984a) *Elbow Room: Varieties of Free Will Worth Wanting*. Cambridge: MIT Press.

Dennett, Daniel C. (1984b) I could not have done otherwise: So what? *Journal of Philosophy* 81: 553–565.

Dennett, Daniel C. (1988a) The moral first aid manual. In *The Tanner Lectures on Human Values*, ed. S. McMurrin, pp. 121–147. University of Utah Press and Cambridge University Press.

Dennett, Daniel C. (1988b) Coming to terms with the determined. Review of Ted Honderich's *A Theory of Determinism: The Mind, Neuroscience, and Life-Hopes*. *The Times Literary Supplement*, November 4–10: 1219–1220.

Dennett, Daniel C. (1991) *Consciousness Explained*. New York: Little Brown and Company.

Dennett, Daniel C. (2001a) Consciousness: How much is that in *real* money? In *Oxford Companion to the Mind*, ed. R. Gregory. New York: Oxford University Press.

Dennett, Daniel C. (2001b) Implantable brain chips: Will they change who we are? *Lahey Clinic Medical Ethics Newsletter*, Spring: 6–7.

Dennett, Daniel C. (2001c) Review of George Ainslie's *Breakdown of Will*. *The Times Literary Supplement*, December 7: 8.

Dennett, Daniel C. (w/Christopher Taylor) (2002) Who's afraid of determinism? Rethinking causes and possibilities. *Oxford Handbook of Free Will*, ed. Robert Kane, pp. 257–277. New York: Oxford University Press.

I Dennett, Daniel C. (2003a) *Freedom Evolves*. New York: Viking.

Dennett, Daniel C. (2003b) Review of Daniel Wegner's *The Illusion of Conscious Will* (Making ourselves at home in our machines). *Journal of Mathematical Psychology* 47: 101–104.

Dennett, Daniel C. (2003c) On failures of freedom and the fear of science. *Daedalus: Journal of the American Academy of the Arts and Sciences*, Winter: 126–130.

Dennett, Daniel C. (2003d) The self as responding – and responsible – artifact. *Annals New York Academy of Science* 1001: 39–50.

Dennett, Daniel C. (2004) The mythical threat of genetic

determinism. *The Chronical of Higher Education*, January 31: B7–B9. [Reprinted in *The Best American Science and Nature Writing*, ed. Steven Pinker, pp. 45–50. New York: Houghton Mifflin Company.]

Dennett, Daniel C. (2005) Natural Freedom. *Metaphilosophy* 36(4): 449–459.

Dennett, Daniel C. (2008) Some observations on the psychology of thinking about free will. In *Are We Free? Psychology and Free Will*, eds. Baer, Baumeister, and Kaufmann, pp. 248–259. New York: Oxford University Press.

Dennett, Daniel C. (w/Christopher Taylor) (2010) Who's still afraid of determinism? Rethinking causes and possibilities. *Oxford Handbook of Free Will*, ed. Robert Kane, 2nd edn. New York: Oxford University Press.

Dennett, Daniel C. (2011a) My brain made me do it (When neuroscientists think they can do philosophy), *Max Weber Lecture Series*. European University Institute, Florence, Lecture N. 2011/01: 1–14.

Dennett, Daniel C. (2011b) Review of Bruce Waller's *Against Moral Responsibility*. *Naturalism.org*. http://handle.net/10427/000494 [Also includes Tom Clark's response to the review and Dennett's rejoinder to Clark and Waller.]

Dennett, Daniel C. (2012) Erasmus: Sometimes a spin doctor is right. *Praemium Erasmianum Essay 2012*, Essay written for the Praemium Erasmianum Foundation on the occasion of the award of the Erasmus Prize, Amsterdam, November 2012.

Dennett, Daniel C. (2013a) *Intuitions Pumps and Other Tools for Thinking*. New York: W. W. Norton and Company.

Dennett, Daniel C. (2013b) Review of Adrian Raine's *The Anatomy of Violence: The Biological Roots of Crime*. *Prospect*, May 3: 64–68.

Dennett, Daniel C. (2014a) Reflections on free will. Review of Sam Harris's *Free Will*. Online at: https://samharris.org/reflections-on-free-will/

Dennett, Daniel C. (2014b) Seduced by tradition. In *Moral Psychology: Free Will and Moral Responsibility*, ed. Walter Sinnott-Armstrong, pp. 75–80. Cambridge, MA: MIT Press.

Dennett, Daniel C. (2014c) Daniel Dennett on free will worth wanting. In *Philosophy Bites Again*, eds. D. Edmonds and N. Warburton, pp. 125–133. New York: Oxford University Press.

Dennett, Daniel C. (2014d) Are we free? Neuroscience gives the wrong answer. *Prospect*, October.

Dennett, Daniel C. (2017) *From Bacteria to Bach and Back: The Evolution of Minds*. New York: W. W. Norton and Company.

Duff, R. A. (2001) *Punishment, Communication, and Community*. New York: Cambridge University Press.

Duff, Antony (2017) Legal punishment. *Stanford Encyclopedia of Philosophy*.

Einstein, Albert (1929) What life means to Einstein: An interview by George Sylvester Viereck. *Saturday Evening Post*. October 26, 1929: 17, 110–117.

Enns, Peter (2006) *Incarceration Nation: How the United States Became the Most Punitive Democracy in the World*. New York: Cambridge University Press.

I Eshleman, Andrew (2014) Moral responsibility. *Stanford Encyclopedia of Philosophy*. http://plato.stanford.edu/entries/moral-responsibility/

Feinberg, Joel (1970) The expressive function of punishment. In *Doing and Deserving*, by J. Feinberg, pp. 95–118. Princeton: Princeton University Press.

Feinberg, Joel (1988) *Harmless Wrongdoing*. New York: Oxford University Press.

Feltz, A. and E. Cokely (2009) Do judgments about freedom and responsibility depend on who you are? Personality differences in intuitions about compatibilism and incompatibilism. *Consciousness and Cognition* 18(1): 342–350.

Feltz, A., A. Perez, and M. Harris (2012) Free will, causes, and decisions: Individual differences in written reports. *Journal of Consciousness Studies* 19(9–10): 166–189.

C Fisher, John Martin (ed.) (1986) *Moral Responsibility*. Ithaca, NY: Cornell University Press.

I Fischer, John Martin (1994) *The Metaphysics of Free Will*. New York: Blackwell Publishers.

Fischer, John Martin and Mark Ravizza (1998) *Responsibility and Control: A Theory of Moral Responsibility*. New York: Cambridge University Press.

I Fischer, John Martin, Robert Kane, Derk Pereboom, and

Manuel Vargas (2007) *Four Views on Free Will.* New York: Blackwell Publishing.

Flanagan, Owen (2017) *Geography of Morals: Varieties of Moral Possibility.* New York: Oxford University Press.

Floud, Jean E. and Warren Young (1981) *Dangerousness and Criminal Justice.* London: Heinemann.

Focquaert, Farah, Gregg Caruso, Elizabeth Shaw, and Derk Pereboom (2020) Justice without retribution: Interdisciplinary perspectives, stakeholder views, and practical implications. *Neuroethics* 13: 1–3.

Forber, Patrick and Rory Smead (2018) Punishment isn't about the common good: It's about spite. *Aeon.* https://aeon.co/ideas/punishment-isnt-about-the-common-good-its-about-spite

Frankfurt, Harry (1969) Alternative possibilities and moral responsibility. *Journal of Philosophy* 66: 829–839.

Frankfurt, Harry (1971) Freedom of the will and the concept of a person. *Journal of Philosophy* 68: 5–20.

[I] Frede, Michael (2011) *A Free Will: Origins of the Notion in Ancient Thought.* Berkeley, CA: University of California Press.

Gibbard, Allan (1990) *Wise Choices, Apt Feelings: A Theory of Normative Judgment.* Cambridge, MA: Harvard University Press.

Gladwell, Malcolm (2008) *Outliers: The Story of Success.* New York: Little Brown and Company.

[I] Haji, Ishtiyaque (2009) *Incompatibilism's Allure.* Peterborough, Ontario: Broadview Press.

Hampton, Jean (1991) A new theory of retribution. In *Liability and Responsibility: Essays in Law and Morals*, eds. R. G. Frey and Christopher W. Morris, pp. 377–414. New York: Cambridge University Press.

Hampton, Jean (1992) An expressive theory of retribution. In *Retributivism and Its Critics*, ed. Wesley Cragg, pp. 1–25. Stuttgart: Franz Steiner Verlag.

Hampton, Jean (1994) Liberalism, retribution and criminality. In *In Harm's Way: Essays in Honor of Joel Feinberg*, eds. Jules Coleman and Allen Buchanan, pp. 159–182. New York: Cambridge University Press.

[I] Harris, Sam (2012) *Free Will.* New York: Free Press.

Harris, Sam (2014) The marionette's lament: Response to Daniel Dennett. https://samharris.org/the-marionettes-lament/

Hart, H. L. A. (1968/2008) *The Concept of Law*, 3rd edn. New York: Oxford University Press.

Hart, H. L. A. (2008) *Punishment and Responsibility: Essays in the Philosophy of Law*, 2nd edn. Oxford: Oxford University Press.

Henrich, Joseph and Michael Muthukrishna (2020) The origins and psychology of human cooperation. *Annual Review of Psychology* 71.

I Hoefer, Carl (2016) Causal determinism. *Stanford Encyclopedia of Philosophy*. https://plato.stanford.edu/entries/determinism-causal/

C Honderich, Ted (ed.) (1973) *Essays on Freedom and Action*. London: Routledge and Kegan Paul.

I Honderich, Ted (2002) *How Free Are You? The Determinism Problem*. 2nd edn. New York: Oxford University Press.

C Hook, Sidney (ed.) (1958) *Determinism and Freedom in the Age of Modern Science*. London: Collier Books.

Hume, David (1739/1978) *A Treatise of Human Nature*. New York: Oxford University Press.

Hume, David (1748/2000) *An Enquiry Concerning Human Understanding*. New York: Oxford University Press.

I Kane, Robert (2005) *A Contemporary Introduction to Free Will*. New York: Oxford University Press.

C Kane, Robert (2011) *Oxford Handbook of Free Will*, 2nd edn. New York: Oxford University Press.

Kant, Immanuel (1785/1981) *Grounding for the Metaphysics of Morals*, trans. J. Ellington. Indianapolis: Hackett.

Kaufman, W. (2008) The rise and fall of the mixed theory of punishment. *International Journal of Applied Philosophy* 22: 37–57.

Kelly, Erin (2018) *The Limits of Blame: Rethinking Punishment and Responsibility*. Cambridge, MA: Harvard University Press.

Knobe, J. (2014) Free will and the scientific vision. In *Current Controversies in Experimental Philosophy*, eds. E. Machery and E. O'Neill, pp. 69–85. New York: Routledge.

C Lehrer, Keith (ed.) (1966) *Freedom and Determinism*. New York: Random House.

Levy, Neil (2009) Luck and history-sensitive compatibilism. *Philosophical Quarterly* 59(235): 237–251.

Levy, Neil (2011) *Hard Luck: How Luck Undermines Free Will and Moral Responsibility*. New York: Oxford University Press.

Levy, Neil (2016) Does the desire to punish have any place in modern justice? *Aeon*, February 19. https://aeon.co/ideas/does-the-desire-to-punish-have-any-place-in-modern-justice

McCarthy, J. (2002) Free will – even for robots. Unpublished memo, Feb. 14, 2000. Simple deterministic free will, unpublished memo, May 16, 2002. Published online at: www-formal. stanford.edu/jmc/freewill.html

MacKay, Donald M. (1960) On the logical indeterminacy of a free choice. *Mind*, 69: 31–40.

I McKenna, Michael and D. Justin Coates (2019) Compatibilism. *Stanford Encyclopedia of Philosophy*. https://plato.stanford.edu/entries/compatibilism/

I McKenna, Michael and Derk Pereboom (2016) *Free Will: A Contemporary Introduction*. New York: Routledge.

Matravers, M. (2000) *Justice and Punishment: The Rationale of Coercion*. New York: Oxford University Press.

Mele, Alfred (1995) *Autonomous Agents: From Self-Control to Autonomy*. New York: Oxford University Press.

Mele, Alfred (2006) *Free Will and Luck*. New York: Oxford University Press.

Nadelhoffer, Thomas (ed.) (2013) *The Future of Punishment*. New York: Oxford University Press.

Nadelhoffer, Thomas and Daniela Goya Tocchetto (2013) The potential dark side of believing in free will (and related concepts): Some preliminary findings. In *Exploring the Illusion of Free Will and Moral Responsibility*, ed. Gregg D. Caruso, pp. 121–140. Lanham, MD: Lexington Books.

Nadelhoffer, T., D. Rose, W. Buckwalter, and S. Nichols (2019) Natural compatibilism, indeterminism, and intrusive metaphysics. https://doi.org/10.3129/osf.io/rzbqh

Nagel, Thomas (1979) *Mortal Questions*. New York: Cambridge University Press.

I Nelkin, Dana (2019) Moral luck. *Stanford Encyclopedia of Philosophy*. https://plato.stanford.edu/entries/moral-luck/

Nichols, S. (2004) The folk psychology of free will: Fits and starts. *Mind and Language* 19(5): 473–502.

Nichols, S. (2007) After compatibilism: A naturalistic defense of the reactive attitudes. *Philosophical Perspectives* 21: 405–428.

Nichols, S. (2012) The indeterminist intuition: Source and status. *The Monist* 95(2): 290–307.

Nichols, S. and J. Knobe (2007) Moral responsibility and determinism: The cognitive science of folk intuitions. *Nous* 41(4): 663–685.

Nietzsche, Friedrich (1886/1992) *Beyond Good and Evil*, trans. Walter Kaufmann. New York: Random House.

Nussbaum, Martha (1988) Nature, function, and capability: Aristotle on political distribution. In *Oxford Studies in Ancient Philosophy*, ed. J. Annas and R. Grimm. Oxford: Clarendon Press.

Nussbaum, Martha (1992) Human functioning and social justice: In defense of Aristotelian Essentialism. *Political Theory* 20(2): 202–146.

Nussbaum, Martha (1997) Capabilities and human rights. *Fordham Law Review* 66: 273.

Nussbaum, Martha (2000) *Women and Human Development*. Cambridge: Cambridge University Press.

Nussbaum, Martha (2003) Capabilities as fundamental entitlements: Sen and social justice. *Feminist Economics* 9 (2–3): 33–59.

Nussbaum, Martha (2006) *Frontiers of Justice*. Cambridge, MA: The Belknap Press.

Nussbaum, Martha (2011) *Creating Capabilities: The Human Development Approach*. Cambridge, MA: The Belknap Press of Harvard University Press. https://plato.stanford.edu/entries/legal-punishment/

[I] O'Connor, Timothy (2018) Free will. *Stanford Encyclopedia of Philosophy*. https://plato.stanford.edu/entries/freewill/

Pereboom, Derk (1995) Determinism al dente. *Nous* 29(1): 21–45.

[C] Pereboom, Derk (ed.) (1997) *Free Will*. New York: Hackett Publishing Company.

[I] Pereboom, Derk (2001) *Living Without Free Will*. New York: Cambridge University Press.

Pereboom, Derk (2008) A hard-line reply to the multiple-case manipulation argument. *Philosophical and Phenomenological Research* 77(1): 160–170.

[I] Pereboom, Derk (2014) *Free Will, Agency, and Meaning in Life*. New York: Oxford University Press.

Pereboom, Derk (2019) Free will skepticism and prevention of crime. In *Free Will Skepticism in Law and Society: Challenging Retributive Justice*, eds. Elizabeth Shaw, Derk Pereboom, and Gregg D. Caruso, pp. 99–115. New York: Cambridge University Press.

Pereboom, Derk and Gregg D. Caruso (2018) Hard-incompatibilist existentialism: Neuroscience, punishment, and meaning in life. In *Neuroexistentialism: Meaning, Morals, and Purpose in the Age of Neuroscience*, eds. Gregg D. Caruso and Owen Flanagan, pp. 1–22. New York: Oxford University Press.

ᴵ Pink, Thomas (2004) *Free Will: A Very Short Introduction*. New York: Oxford University Press.

Popper, Karl (1951) Indeterminism in quantum physics and classical physics. *British Journal for the Philosophy of Science* 1: 179–188.

Pynchon, Thomas (1973) *Gravity's Rainbow*. New York: Viking.

Rawls, John (1971) *A Theory of Justice*. Cambridge, MA: Harvard University Press. Revised edition, 1999.

Rawls, John (1985) Justice as fairness: Political not metaphysical. *Philosophy and Public Affairs* 14 (Summer): 223–51.

Rawls, John (2001) *Justice as Fairness: A Restatement*, ed. Erin Kelly. Cambridge, MA: Harvard University Press.

Rose, D. and S. Nichols (2013) The lesson of bypassing. *Review of Philosophy and Psychology* 4(4): 599–619.

Rosen, Gideon (2002) The case for incompatibilism. *Philosophical and Phenomenological Research* 64(3): 699–796.

Rosling, Hans (2018) *Factfulness: Ten Reasons We're Wrong About the World – and Why Things Are Better Than You Think*. New York: Flatiron Books.

Sarkissian, Hagop, Amita Chatterjee, Felipe De Brigard, Joshua Knobe, et al. (2010) Is belief in free will a cultural universal? *Mind and Language* 25(3): 346–358.

Scanlon, Thomas (1998) *What We Owe Each Other*. Cambridge, MA: Harvard University Press.

Scanlon, Thomas (2013) Giving desert its due. *Philosophical Explorations* 16: 101–116.

Sen, Amartya (1980) *The Tanner Lectures on Human Values*, ed. S. McMurrin. Salt Lake City: University of Utah Press.

Sen, Amartya (1984) *Resources, Values, and Development*. Oxford: Basil Blackwell.

Sen, Amartya (1985) *Commodities and Capabilities*. Oxford: Oxford University Press.

Sen, Amartya (2009) *The Idea of Justice*. New York: Penguin Books.

Shariff, A. F., J. D. Greene, J. C. Karremans, J. Luguri, C. J. Clark, J. W. Schooler, R. F. Baumeister, and K. D. Vohs (2014) Free will and punishment: A mechanistic view of human nature reduces retribution. *Psychological Science* published online June 10: 1–8.

Shaw, Elizabeth (2019) Justice without more responsibility? *Journal of Information Ethics* 28(1).

C Shoemaker, David (ed.) (2013–2019) *Oxford Studies in Agency and Responsibility, Volumes 1–6*. New York: Oxford University Press. [Vol. 2 co-ed. with Neil Tognazzini; Vol. 5 co-ed. with Justin Coates and Neal Tognazzini]

Sommers, Tamler (2007) The objective attitude. *The Philosophical Quarterly* 57(28): 321–342.

Sommers, Tamler (2012) *Relative Justice: Cultural Diversity, Free Will, and Moral Responsibility*. Princeton NJ: Princeton University Press.

Sommers, Tamler (2018) *Why Honor Cultures Matter*. New York: Basic Books.

Strawson, Galen (2010) Your move: The maze of free will. *New York Times*, July 22.

Strawson, Galen (2018) *Things That Bother Me: Death, Freedom, The Self, etc.* New York: New York Review of Books. [See chapter 4, "Luck swallows everything."]

Strawson, P. F. (1962) Freedom and resentment. *Proceedings of the British Academy* 18: 1–25.

Tadros, Victor (2011) *The Ends of Harm: The Moral Foundations of Criminal Law*. New York: Oxford University Press.

I Talbert, Matthew (2016) *Moral Responsibility: An Introduction*. Malden, MA: Polity Press.

I Talbert, Matthew (2019) Moral Responsibility. *Stanford Encyclopedia of Philosophy*. https://plato.stanford.edu/entries/moral-responsibility/

Tasioulas, John (2006) Punishment and repentance. *Philosophy* 81: 279–322.

Taylor, Richard (1963/1992) *Metaphysics*, 4th edn. Englewood Cliffs, NJ: Prentice-Hall.

I Timpe, Kevin (2008) *Free Will: Sourcehood and Its Alternatives*. New York: Continuum Press.

Todd, Patrick (2011) A new approach to manipulation arguments. *Philosophical Studies* 152(1): 127–133.

Todd, Patrick (2013) Defending (a modified version of) the zygote argument. *Philosophical Studies* 164(1): 189–203.

van Inwagen, Peter (1983) *Essay on Free Will*. New York: Oxford University Press.

Vargas, Manuel (2007) Revisionism. In *Four Views on Free Will*, John Martin Fischer, Robert Kane, Derk Pereboom, and Manuel Vargas, pp. 126–165. New York: Blackwell Publishers.

Vargas, Manuel (2013) *Building Better Beings: A Theory of Moral Responsibility*. New York: Oxford University Press.

Walen, Alec (2014) Retributive justice. *Stanford Encyclopedia of Philosophy*. https://plato.stanford.edu/entries/justice-retributive/

Walker, N. (1991) *Why Punish?* New York: Oxford University Press.

Wallace, R. Jay (1994) *Responsibility and the Moral Sentiments*. Cambridge, MA: Harvard University Press.

Waller, Bruce (2011) *Against Moral Responsibility*. Cambridge, MA: MIT Press.

Waller, Bruce (2015) *The Stubborn System of Moral Responsibility*. Cambridge, MA: MIT Press.

Waller, Bruce (2016) *Restorative Free Will: Back to the Biological Base*. Lanham, MD: Lexington Books.

Waller, Bruce (2018) *The Injustice of Punishment*. New York: Routledge.

c Watson, Gary (ed.) (1982) *Free Will*. New York: Oxford University Press.

Weigel, C. (2011) Distance, anger, and freedom: An account of the role of abstraction in compatibilist and incompatibilist intuitions. *Philosophical Psychology* 24(6): 803–823.

Wittgenstein, Ludwig (1961) *Notebooks 1914–1916*, ed. and trans. G. H. von Wright and G. E. M. Anscombe. New York: Harper/Blackwell.

Zaibert, Leo (2018) *Rethinking Punishment*. New York: Cambridge University Press.

Zimmerman, Michael J. (2011) *The Immorality of Punishment*. Broadview Press.

Index